ROGUE
AGENT

ROGUE AGENT

FROM SECRET PLOTS TO PSYCHOLOGICAL WARFARE, THE UNTOLD STORY OF ROBERT BRUCE LOCKHART

JAMES CROSSLAND

PEGASUS BOOKS

NEW YORK LONDON

ROGUE AGENT

Pegasus Books, Ltd.
148 West 37th Street, 13th Floor
New York, NY 10018

First Pegasus Books cloth edition May 2025

Plate section picture credits:
Page 1: World Archive / Alamy Stock Photo (top); Lilly Library, Robert Bruce
Lockhart Collection (bottom); page 2: Album / Alamy Stock Photo (top);
Chronicle / Alamy Stock Photo (bottom); page 3: Lilly Library, Robert Bruce
Lockhart Collection (top); page 4: Newspaper from Telegraph historical archive, Gale
Primary Sources (top left); National Portrait Gallery, London (top right); Movie
poster from Hoover Institution, Lockhart Collection (bottom); page 6: Lilly Library,
Robert Bruce Lockhart Collection; page 7: Hoover Institution, Lockhart collection;
page 8: Kurt Hutton / Stringer, GettyImages.co.uk (top); Malcolm Dunbar /
Stringer, GettyImages.co.uk.

ISBN: 978-1-63936-895-2

10 9 8 7 6 5 4 3 2 1

Printed in the United States of America
Distributed by Simon & Schuster
www.pegasusbooks.com

For Durey

CONTENTS

PREFACE

Sir Robert Bruce Lockhart was a man of many seemingly irreconcilable parts. He was a diplomat, journalist, intelligence gatherer and propagandist, who charmed his way into the confidences of everyone from Leon Trotsky to Anthony Eden. In the First World War, Prime Minister Lloyd George made Lockhart his personal representative – British Agent – in Bolshevik Russia. Years later, Winston Churchill approved his appointment as director-general of the Political Warfare Executive, a secret department tasked with waging psychological warfare against the Third Reich. Lockhart was also Britain's wartime liaison to the government-in-exile of occupied Czechoslovakia and a deputy under-secretary at the Foreign Office. When not playing the part of Whitehall insider and being tasked with important missions by prime ministers, Lockhart was a best-selling author and right hand of one of the world's most powerful men, the press magnate and occasional cabinet minister Lord Beaverbrook.

Throughout this extraordinary career, Lockhart filled his address book with the details of diplomats, spies, generals, admirals, literary titans, unscrupulous journalists and notorious revolutionaries, many of whom praised him as 'a delightful companion', who was 'circumspect to a fault' and possessed of 'dynamic qualities'. In a rapidly changing age of war, revolution and extremist ideology, Lockhart knew everyone and did everything.[1]

This is one version of the man. The other is of an inveterate womaniser, drinker, plotter and adventurer, who squandered his enormous potential by getting into a state of perpetual debt and succumbing to crippling bouts of self-doubt and depression. This Lockhart made enemies who were immune to his charms – people like the Bolshevik spymaster Felix Dzerzhinsky, the British military attaché Alfred Knox and even some of the ministers and propagandists with whom he worked during the Second World War. These and other detractors wrote him off as a feckless and unreliable 'prima donna' who was 'weak and unable or unwilling to take over effective control' of situations. This Lockhart got involved in a doomed plot to usurp the Bolsheviks from power in 1918 and spent the next decade trying to forget his failure at the bottom of a bottle. By his own admission, this version of Lockhart 'behaved like a cad' towards his wife Jean, who suffered watching him openly philander his way across Europe for years.[2] It is this Lockhart that has captured the imagination of historians, who have focused almost exclusively on his machinations in Russia in 1918 without paying sufficient mind to the other eighty-one years of his eventful, multifaceted life. This biography does not reject the opinions of those who have dubbed Lockhart a 'wild' and 'unbridled' miscreant who was 'adventurous beyond common sense'. Rather, it acknowledges that Lockhart was not so one-dimensional and that the life he led was defined by exceptional peaks and wretched valleys, the contours of which need to be explored fully to understand the man who shaped them.[3]

I have been helped in this task by the fact that whatever turmoil Lockhart faced there remained one constant throughout his life – a compulsion to write. He authored sixteen books and hundreds of radio scripts, newspaper articles and essays. He composed poetry from a young age and, from 1915 until the late 1960s, kept as many as three daily diaries of varying length and detail. He also filled numerous notebooks with observations and character sketches of the many famous people he encountered on his travels from Malaysia to Russia, across Europe and North America. These published pieces and private notes have left behind a comprehensive picture of what Lockhart thought, who he met and how he carried out his work.

That said, following and interpreting Lockhart's paper trail has not been without its challenges. His memoirs are rich in anecdotes and often quite beautiful prose, yet they suffer like most self-authored histories from obfuscation and distortion of fact. For this reason, I have mostly used them to convey Lockhart's perception of events and to fill the gaps in his archival record. Although such lacunas exist – primarily in the years before 1914 and in the early 1920s – the documents covering the rest of Lockhart's life are as voluminous as they are scattered. The largest collections of private material are held at the University of Indiana's Lilly Library in Bloomington and at Stanford University's Hoover Institution in Palo Alto. The bulk of his professional correspondence can be found in the Lockhart Collection at the National Archives of the United Kingdom, the basement library of the Bank of England in London and among the Papers of Lord Milner at the Bodleian Library in Oxford. These archival materials, and a report from Bolshevik Russia in the Liddell Hart Centre for Military Archives at King's College London, have proved invaluable in tracing the often-blurred lines between Lockhart's private and professional life.

In addition to these collections, it has been both frustrating and rewarding to make use of Lockhart's diaries, which have a story as winding and confusing as that of their author. After Lockhart's death in 1970, the Beaverbrook Press was bequeathed his journals and notebooks and a political advisor at the press named Kenneth Young was employed to edit them into a publishable form. This task was arduous. Aside from Lockhart's often impenetrably small handwriting, some of the material was missing at the time of delivery to the Beaverbrook offices. Most of these journals were later found in uncleared cupboards and, in one instance, in a safe that had been locked and forgotten for decades. This scavenger hunt disrupted Young's timetable, leaving a gap between the publication of the first volume of diaries in 1973 and the second volume's completion in 1980.

The diary project also came under scrutiny from the Foreign Office. Fearing instances of libel – Lockhart was candid in describing his interactions with and the personal habits of important political figures – and the disclosure of national secrets, the government insisted on vetting Young's transcriptions. Particular attention was paid to diary entries covering Lockhart's propaganda work, which continued beyond the fight against

Nazism and into the Cold War via anti-communist articles penned under pseudonyms and his radio broadcasts into communist Czechoslovakia. Despite these obstacles, Young managed to produce a mostly accurate reflection of the original diaries that currently reside in the Beaverbrook collection at the Parliamentary Archives at Westminster. Where omissions exist in Young's published versions, I have used a combination of these unvarnished originals and private papers.[4]

Though he left behind millions of words describing his life and times, Lockhart is still a man of mystery. The declassification of files has lifted most of the veil from his secret work in 1918, but a question mark still hangs over whether these labours continued into the 1920s. There are traces, albeit fleeting, in the archival record that suggest he was still working with the anti-Bolshevik insurgent Boris Savinkov and the fantastically reckless spy Sidney Reilly up until the point they were executed by the Bolsheviks in 1925. Certainly, he maintained a connection to the intelligence services for the rest of his life, if only through his preferred means of doing business and acquiring information – lunches at the Carlton Club or the St James's. Most of the files pertaining to Lockhart's government work were declassified in 1993; however, a few documents in this series remain under lock and key. Lockhart's son Robin, who worked for Naval Intelligence and had an awareness of his father's secret activities, claimed that these documents will never see the light of day. If this is true, I can't help but reflect on the decade I have spent researching Sir Robert Bruce Lockhart, raise a glass of Scotch in toast to his enduring mystery and smile at a remark he made to his dear friend Harold Nicolson in 1932 – 'my whole life is a lie. In fact, it is the best definition of it.'[5]

INTRODUCTION

A PLOT UNDONE

Moscow was a city on edge. It was 30 August 1918 – the day, it seemed, that Vladimir Ilyich Lenin would die. That afternoon, the father of the Bolshevik revolution had delivered a rousing speech at a weapons factory outside the Russian capital, lauding the vital role its workers were playing in arming the revolutionary motherland against its reactionary enemies. Cheers and applause followed, to which Lenin doffed his hat and gave an appreciative wave, before walking towards a waiting car at the factory's gates. At that moment, a furious jeer stabbed out at Lenin from the crowd's friendly hum. Irritated, he turned to address the unseen critic. He barely had the chance to open his mouth before three pistol shots tore through his body, leaving a wound in his neck and punctures in his lungs. Commotion consumed the scene as Lenin's guards grabbed the shooter, batting away the hands of the workers who called for bloody vengeance. This swift apprehension of Lenin's assailant did little, however, to calm the nerves of the other Bolshevik leaders. As news of the attack spread through Russia's corridors of power, fears arose that a counter-revolutionary coup was imminent. The angst was compounded by Lenin's dire state. Not trusting the security at Moscow's hospitals, he had insisted on being taken to the Kremlin for treatment. Behind the gilded doors of one of the palace's master bedrooms, Lenin writhed and screamed through the night as doctors struggled to extract the bullets from his broken body. By the time the clock struck midnight, an eerie pall had fallen over Moscow, where many a mind was consumed by a single thought: the 'Bolshevik leader was not dead, but his chances of living were at a discount'.[1]

These words were scrawled into Robert Bruce Lockhart's notebook shortly before he collapsed into slumber at 1 a.m. on 31 August, exhausted from pondering the day's events. Not that he minded being in Moscow at this moment of terror and uncertainty. Lockhart lived for such drama. Two days shy of his thirty-first birthday, he was the coming man of Britain's diplomatic corps, possessed of a head for foreign languages, a keen intellect and a way with words. These talents, combined with his limitless reserves of self-confidence, made Lockhart just the man to serve as Britain's Agent in Bolshevik Russia. This ambiguous title had been bestowed on Lockhart by no less a figure than Prime Minister Lloyd George who, shortly after the Bolshevik revolution of October 1917, tried to forge a diplomatic link with Russia's new masters. Lockhart had the youth, the creativity and, having previously served as a consul-general in Moscow, the experience of Russia's mysteries to meet Lloyd George's requirements. He had been selected, as he later put it, 'from among God knows what weird choice of candidates for a difficult and exciting mission'.[2]

This mission's primary objective was to liaise with Lenin's regime on behalf of the British government. Simple enough, except that while shaking hands with the Bolsheviks, Lockhart was also plotting their downfall. In the summer of 1918, he became the linchpin of a network of spies, journalists, diplomats and adventurers from Britain, France and the USA, which had taken root across Russia and formed alliances with local counter-revolutionary groups. The network's aim was to get Russia back into the First World War, from which it had been extracted by the Bolsheviks, and, if possible, bring Lenin's great ideological experiment to a permanent end. It was a dangerously ambitious plan that by August 1918 had evolved into a conspiracy that has become known to history as the 'Lockhart Plot'.[3]

Curled up on an ottoman in his apartment in Moscow, this plot's namesake drifted off to sleep in the early hours of 31 August, his mind racing with questions over what Lenin's death would mean for him and his network. Lockhart enjoyed barely an hour's rest before receiving an emphatic answer. His lover, Moura Budberg, was the first to hear the crack of boots on polished wood rattling up the hall. The sound cut so sharply through the building's dead silence that Lockhart's deputy, Captain William Hicks, was roused from his bed, joining Moura at the apartment door just as the approaching footsteps ceased. Then came an urgent knock and a barked demand that the door be opened. Moura and Hicks begrudgingly obeyed, flooding the apartment with armed officers from Lenin's secret police, the Cheka. Having instantly identified his quarry, the leader of the Chekist raiders made a beeline for Lockhart. Pointing his pistol at the British Agent's head, the Chekist demanded that he wake up and get dressed. As he complied in wearied indignation, Lockhart made a show of confused outrage. Beneath the façade, his stomach turned in fear. Somehow the Cheka knew of his plot and, in the paranoid spasm that followed the attack on Lenin, had decided to bring it to an end. Now dressed, Lockhart, Hicks and Moura were herded into a corner of the apartment, where they watched on helplessly as the Chekists tore up cushions and wrenched drawers from sideboards and desks, confiscating letters and notes, along with pistols, ammunition and stacks of roubles. Having seized these compromising items, the raiders then took their prisoners down the stairs to waiting police cars, which ferried them to the Cheka's headquarters, the Lubyanka.

Lockhart and his companions were not the Cheka's only midnight targets. Hours before arriving at the Moscow apartment, Lenin's men fanned out across Petrograd arresting other members of the network. One team of raiders stormed the residence of Henri de Verthamon, France's chief saboteur in Russia. Thinking quickly as the Chekists bounded up his stairs, Verthamon opened a top floor window and leapt onto the adjoining rooftop, over which he scrambled to escape while leaving behind explosives, money and maps. This contraband, combined with the money found in Lockhart's apartment, was used to justify the proclamation made in the Bolsheviks' official newspaper, *Izvestia*, that 'a conspiracy organised by Anglo-French diplomats' was trying to 'organise the capture of the Council of People's Commissars and the proclamation of a military dictatorship in Moscow. This was to be done by bribing Soviet troops.'[4]

The 'liquidation', as *Izvestia* ominously put it, of this conspiracy continued apace the next day. At eight o'clock on the morning of 31 August, a team of heavily armed Chekists arrived at the British embassy in Petrograd. The military attaché, Captain Francis Cromie, was not as willing as Moura or Hicks to open the door to surrender. After ordering the staff to barricade the first-floor offices and take cover, Cromie drew his pistol and stalked out onto the balcony overhanging the embassy's foyer, which was filling up with Chekists who had broken down the front door. This incursion was both a breach of international law and, to Cromie's enraged mind, a mortal threat to all within the embassy. He unloaded his pistol while cursing the invaders for swine, killing two of them before return fire ended his one-man stand. As the gun-smoke cleared into eerie silence, the Chekists advanced up the stairs, stepping over Cromie's dying body and into the first-floor offices he had tried in vain to defend. There they seized documents, pistols and the embassy's terrified staff, who were promptly hauled off to prison. As reports in an outraged British press revealed, these clerks and secretaries were crammed into cells so small they had to take turns lying down to sleep, while being deprived of food and fresh air.[5]

As many as twenty British and French diplomats and their staff were detained in these dire conditions as Verthamon went to ground and Cromie's bullet-ridden body grew cold. Sitting on a bench under the brutal white lights of a Lubyanka interrogation room, the author of this fiasco – the cocksure *wunderkind* hand-picked by a prime minister to alter the course of Russia's history – was now in a state of shipwreck. Lockhart exhaled for what felt like the first time since the raid. His head fell defeated into trembling hands. Wincing at his thoughts, he reached deep into his considerable brain for answers. How had the Cheka known? Who else would they arrest? What would become of him, Hicks and Moura, the woman who had captured his heart and was carrying his child? Amid this pall of unanswerable questions, a single thought above all others cut through Lockhart's mind to taunt him – 'how did you get yourself into this mess?'

CHAPTER 1

NO DROP OF ENGLISH BLOOD

'I must be rising, and I must be going,
On the roads of magic that stretch afar,
By the random rivers so finely flowing,
And under the restless star'

— Neil Munro

Robert Bruce Lockhart was born in 1887 in Anstruther at the mouth of the Firth of Forth – Scotland's gateway to the seas. Though this birthplace portended his globetrotting career, Lockhart carried no memories through his life of this small fishing village. Instead, his first impressions of the world were formed in Beith, a town south-west of Glasgow to which his family relocated in 1888 so that his father, Robert senior, could fill the vacant post of headmaster at the newly founded Spier's School. The position suited the elder Lockhart, whom his son characterised as an archetypal Victorian patriarch and educator. 'Frugal in his wants and Spartan in his self-denial', Lockhart's father was hard-working, religiously devout, taciturn, intellectually curious and a sports enthusiast. He believed that physical pursuits were vital for the health of one's body and soul. Lockhart's mother, Florence Stewart Macgregor, was a less traditional creature. Eschewing the reserve expected of a headmaster's wife, Florence was impulsive and outgoing. Beyond making sure Lockhart and his siblings – John, Norman, Freda, Rupert and Rob (yet another of the many Roberts in the family) – were cared for, she took little interest in mundane matters of the home.

1

With reason, Lockhart believed that his father instilled in him studiousness and the capacity for hard work, while his mother gifted him restless energy and a proclivity for self-indulgence – a dichotomy of character that shaped the tumultuous course of Lockhart's professional and personal life.

Not yet torn by this tension between the hedonistic Macgregor and the disciplined Lockhart within, young 'Bertie' – as he was known to the family – enjoyed a carefree and privileged upbringing. Florence was descended from the founders of Balmenach distillery, one of the oldest whisky producers in Scotland. Robert senior commanded respect from Beith's community and, having been head-hunted by its wealthy benefactor to get Spier's School off the ground, took home a good salary. Aside from money and his family's standing, Lockhart's upbringing was cushioned by love. Florence doted on her children and eight-year-old Bertie reciprocated, penning a letter signed with seventy-four cross-kisses to his mother, expressing his love and despair at her absence during one of her many forays to the Highlands. Lockhart and his siblings also received affection from their activity-mad father, who organised wholesome fishing holidays and supported his sons in whatever sport they chose. This led to Lockhart's youngest brother, John, becoming a renowned sportsman who represented Scotland internationally in both cricket and rugby.

Lockhart was similarly keen on rugby, for which the squat and well-muscled adolescent seemed built. At Seafield House – a school south of Dundee to which the family moved when a new headmaster's position opened in 1895 – Lockhart was given the nickname 'letterbox' on account of being a 'small boy with a wide, half-open mouth and a head too large for his body'. This unpolished exterior was further abraded by his habit of scrapping with schoolyard bullies, probably because they called him a letterbox. As punishment for one such fight at Seafield, Lockhart was made to stand with his back to a teacher as the latter repeatedly kicked a rugby ball into the young man's head. Whatever bruising came of this violent reprimand was nothing, however, compared to the scarring he received when during a family game of cricket he fumbled a catch that led to the ball cracking the bridge of his nose. This break was exacerbated on the rugby field and in the boxing ring, leaving him with a permanently out-of-joint nose.[1]

For all his physicality, the adolescent Bertie was no thoughtless bruiser. In his teens he came to love poetry, particularly the Scottish Romantics who evoked the bleakly beautiful Highlands and the timeless steel shimmer of the lochs. These panegyrics to Scotland's majesty, combined with his mother's tales of Rob Roy, the Jacobite Rising of 1745 and the mist-hewn family history of the Highland Macgregors instilled in Lockhart a sense of pride at being the product of two great Scottish families. He liked to boast that there was 'no drop of English blood in my veins'. This claim referred as much to spirit as to biology. A repeated motif in Lockhart's writings was his belief that Scots are inherently bold and curious, unafraid to embrace the unknown and tame its mysteries through hard work and perseverance. Conversely, 'the Englishman', he concluded after years working alongside Whitehall policymakers and Eton boys turned journalists, 'who rules the greatest empire the world has ever known, is amazingly ignorant of geography'. Stilted by hubris, to be English was to seek easy comfort at the expense of gaining wisdom through adversity. True Scots like Lockhart were 'experimentalists in adventure' and could never tolerate a closeted existence. This self-conceptualisation was fed both by a copy of James Mackenzie's *History of Scotland* his father gave him as a child and Peter Parley's *Universal History on the Basis of Geography*, which drove young Bertie's yearning to blossom into a windswept and well-travelled adult. Turning the latter book's pages on many a rain-grey afternoon at Seafield, Lockhart was entranced by stories of Alexander the Great's military adventures, the Samurai warriors of Japan and the Prophet Muhammed's conquest of Arabia. Rugby, fishing and schoolyard scraps were well and good but, fundamentally, they were easy. They were safe. They were the sorts of things that an Englishman might content himself with.[2]

By the time he reached the cusp of adulthood, Lockhart's discomfort with comfort had grown into a fear that he was destined for the proverbial Englishman's existence. This fear became acute in 1905, when the seventeen-year-old commenced his final year at the prestigious Fettes College in Edinburgh. As this first chapter of his life ended Lockhart stewed on the story to come, believing its narrative would involve him getting an honest job, a steady wage and a family he would take on fishing holidays and bracing Highland hikes. The push and pull within between the Macgregor dreamer and the Lockhart pragmatist left him at an impasse. He could not abide the thought of gliding out of Fettes into a normal life yet had no idea what alternative path he could take. It was left to Lockhart's father to square this circle for his son by sending him on an adventure abroad, albeit to continue his education with the aim of securing gainful employment. The destination chosen was the Tilley Institute in Berlin, where Lockhart was to undertake an intensive course in German, enrich his mind at museums and art galleries, consume a diet free from alcohol and meat and, most perversely of all to his rugby-mad mind, complete this education without once taking to a playing field. Despite deep reservations, Lockhart took heart that he was at least getting the chance to travel and so begrudgingly accepted his father's proposal.

If the elder Robert's aim was to transform his son's listlessness into motivation, then the Berlin plan worked perfectly. The challenge of studying in a foreign land and in a foreign tongue lit a fire under Lockhart, stirring an intellectual curiosity he had let wither amid the rugby scrums at Fettes. He threw himself into his studies, earning plaudits from his professors and discovering his passion for working hard on difficult problems. Lockhart's time at the Tilley Institute also revealed a God-given gift that would serve him well in his career to come – the ability to quickly comprehend and converse in foreign tongues. Within weeks of arriving in Berlin, his teachers concluded that he could transcribe German accurately and speak the language with fluidity. Continuing his studies in Paris in July 1906, Lockhart picked up French in short order, which he came to speak with a near-flawless accent. These experiences of talking, eating and thinking differently on the continent affirmed Lockhart's belief in a connection between his outgoing inner Highlander and the wider world he yearned to embrace. Arriving back in Scotland in 1908, he was buoyed to the point of smugness at the fact that he had been to Europe before venturing south of the border into dull, inward-looking England.[3]

It was at this point that Robert senior's plan to channel his son's adventurous spirit into a conventional existence came undone. Lockhart's wanderlust had been unleashed. He was now certain that his future lay beyond the horizon of Britain's leaden skies. As fate would have it, so did his uncle, Ian Macgregor, the owner of a rubber plantation in the Malaysian state of Negeri Sembilan. Ian paid a visit to the Lockhart family home in the summer of 1908, just as his twenty-one-year-old nephew was preparing for a government entrance exam, success in which would land him a job in the civil service. Mired in tedious preparation for a career he didn't want, it took only a few tales from Ian of swaying palm trees, foreign peoples and easily amassed fortunes to push the pendulum in Bertie's soul. His parents were irritated but Lockhart was determined. He abruptly ceased preparing for his exam and accepted his uncle's offer to travel with him to the distant paradise of Negeri Sembilan.

Like many a colonial adventurer before him, Lockhart believed that 'going native' was essential to his Asian odyssey. As he boarded the ship bound for Singapore at Southampton in October 1908, he did so with a determination to ignore fellow British passengers and spend the journey studying the Malays' language and customs. By imposing this unbending intellectual schedule on himself, Lockhart would arrive at Negeri Sembilan with all the knowledge required to conquer a land of jungle and mystery. This pretension did not last long. After a week at sea, Lockhart took a shine to the daughters of a London shipping magnate and embarked on a romance that scuttled his abstentious plans. His thoughts of exotic adventure were also stamped out when after arriving in Singapore on 1 December 1908 he was ordered by his uncle to head for Port Dickson, a coastal settlement established by the British in the early 1800s as a base from which to trade out of Negeri Sembilan. The port was everything Lockhart hoped to avoid on his great adventure. Existing solely for the purposes of filling white men's pockets, Port Dickson was an underwhelming and distinctly non-paradisical place of warehouses and jetties, whose small population of shopkeepers, fishermen, clerks and porters left Lockhart feeling disenchanted. He was similarly dissatisfied with his position as the Macgregor company accountant, through which he learned a sobering lesson about his new life in Malaysia – the rubber trade was serious business and his uncle expected him to work rather than play.[4]

Ian Macgregor had suffered difficult days at the turn of the century, when Negeri Sembilan's rubber industry was in its infancy and its plantations produced only a fraction of the world's rubber, most of which was still being drawn from the jungles of Brazil. It was not until the rubber boom of 1908 that his plantations started to prosper and Lockhart's wealthy Macgregor grandmother – a key shareholder in the venture – transcended the whisky business on which she had built her fortune and earned the epithet of 'Rubber Queen of Edinburgh'. The amount of family money tied up in Negeri Sembilan meant that Bertie had little time for larks. Instead, having been shoved behind a desk at Port Dickson, he spent long days mired in paperwork that kept him away from the tantalising jungle that lay beyond his sweltering office. Worse still, this unremarkable existence led Lockhart to assume the guise of the comfortable Englishman he claimed to abhor. Like most of the rubber men in Port Dickson, he spent his evenings drinking whisky and sodas and talking export taxes in the clubs that dotted the Strait of Malacca. Even his interactions with the locals were made through well-trodden avenues. On weekends, the sports-loving Fettes graduate schooled Port Dickson's Malay and Chinese dock workers in the art of rugby, captaining a team that managed to defeat the neighbouring state of Selangor's side, despite the latter's profusion of European players.

For all that he slipped into familiar behaviours, Lockhart's linguistic competence set him apart from other European planters, many of whom had set up shop in Negeri Sembilan in the 1890s but had yet to learn the native language. His knowledge of Malay was timely and necessary. In July

1909, Ian gave Lockhart a plantation to run in the inland region of Pantai, where few white settlers lived. In penetrating the jungle, Lockhart felt he could finally claim success in his quest for adventure. The unglamorous and repetitive practice of running a plantation, however, soon brought him down to earth. He had trees and vines cleared, he organised shipments to Port Dickson, he managed the occasional malaria outbreak and he refined his skill with a revolver on the many rats and snakes that plagued his bungalow. In the evenings, Lockhart sat on his porch and read French literature while sipping a gin and tonic. The most excitement he eked out of his time at Pantai was the occasional midnight bicycle ride along jungle paths that bandits were known to roam – not that he ever encountered any. His odyssey into the unknown had become a typical European's colonial existence.[5] This was why when offered the chance to turn his life upside down, Lockhart grasped it with both hands.

With the aim of impressing the locals and keeping things friendly between him and his neighbour, a former sultan who had been deposed by the British, Lockhart convened a *rong geng* at Pantai. This was a traditional Malay dance recital which, though engaging to his workers, left Lockhart feeling rather bored. That was until he caught sight of a young woman who appeared through the whirling colours and heat-haze as a 'radiant vision of brown loveliness in a batek skirt and a red silk coat'. In addition to his dalliance on the ship to Singapore, Lockhart had engaged in romances while in France and Germany. These encounters, however, had been fleeting and meaningless. Now, at the age of twenty-three, he was ready for the full assault on his senses that only love at first sight could bring. Ignoring the former sultan, the dance and all else besides at the event he was hosting, Lockhart spent the remainder of the *rong geng* gawking 'at the frail beauty of this Malayan girl who had disturbed the monotony of my life'.

When he asked his workers about the mysterious woman, the besotted planter was informed that her name was Amai and that she was a princess who was in the process of divorcing her husband. As a member of the former sultan's household, she would soon be betrothed to her benefactor's cousin. She was completely off limits to Lockhart. This only made her more alluring. The advice of his Malay workers and British officials from Port Dickson to let his passions subside went unheeded. Within days of first laying his eyes on Amai, Lockhart arranged a midnight liaison, the essence of which he captured in a poem – 'in the deep silence of an Eastern Night, bathed in the mountain's misty dew, feeling my way with bated breath, where the crack of a broken twig brings death, dear heart, I come to you'. Who knows if it was these pithy lines of devotion that won Amai's heart but, at the conclusion of this daring moonlit meeting, she abandoned the ex-sultan's palace for Lockhart's humble, rat-infested bungalow.[6]

This courtship of Amai was the product of Lockhart's romanticised thoughts of Malaysia meeting the crushing normality of life there. That night at the *rong geng*, the uninterested planter saw in Amai's diminutive beauty a chance to offend local conventions and outrage the sensibilities of the Europeans with whom he had spent too many balmy evenings downing cocktails and discussing rubber prices. Amai was the adventure Lockhart had yearned for since leaving Britain. She was an adventure he embraced wholeheartedly. To keep his lover by his side in the face of local outrage, Lockhart pledged to both Pantai's elders and the colonial officials who feared unrest over the affair that he would convert to Islam. Further evidence of how hard he fell for Amai can be gleaned from the poems he penned during their time together, featuring lines like 'we drink of life and scorn dull care' and 'life without love is death'.

For all that this reads as schoolboy fantasy, Lockhart's romance with Amai was more than a fling. When he returned to Malaysia in 1935, he refused to believe the rumours that his first love was dead and sought her out for a reunion, albeit not for the purpose of rekindling a long-extinguished flame. Reflecting through the seasoned prism of middle age, Lockhart concluded that 'the focus point of my sentimental attachment to Malaya was Amai'. She may have entered his life as a novelty, but the Malaysian princess became the first of many women to leave a profound and lasting impact on Lockhart.[7]

This impact went beyond the emotional. News of the scandalous romance ran through Negeri Sembilan's clubs. Lockhart's beloved rugby team disbanded – his half-back Akbar simply walked into the jungle, never to be seen again, and his plantation's Chinese cook abandoned his post for fear of getting caught up in the retaliation that all assumed would be unleashed on Pantai by the enraged ex-sultan. Such was Lockhart's belief in this threat that he started carrying a pistol on his person at all hours of day and night. And then, in the summer of 1910, this exciting idyll of danger and forbidden love was ended by a fresh drama when Lockhart suddenly and violently fell ill. The couple suspected that the ex-sultan's men had paid off the servants to poison the food, in response to which Amai insisted on preparing all his meals herself from then onwards. As Lockhart shivered and sweated his way into autumn without improvement, it became clear that he had succumbed to a malady less acute though no less danger- ous than that inflicted by arsenic or strychnine – malaria. In vain, Amai deployed a swathe of home treatments while a doctor summoned from Port Dickson administered quinine. When neither approach bore fruit, the doctor returned to the port and sought out Ian, to whom he gave a stark prognosis. Lockhart had to be invalided away from Pantai immediately or else face a slow and painful death far from home.

Ian feared for his nephew's life, but he also saw this medical emer- gency as an opportunity to end Bertie's troublesome romance and bring profitability back to the Pantai rubber operation, which had been suffering from its owner's lack of financial prudence even before Amai consumed his attentions. To save his nephew and restore his business, a day after being informed of Lockhart's dire state Ian arrived at Pantai to take him away. This evacuation was executed at such speed that Amai had no chance to say goodbye to the man she had forsaken her old life to be with. Lockhart, for his part, was too insensible with fever to fully comprehend the abrupt- ness of his parting from the woman who had given meaning to his time in Malaysia. As Ian's driver spun the car around in the clearing outside the bungalow and accelerated in the direction of Port Dickson, Lockhart caught a fleeting glimpse of 'her little silver slippers, which were lying neatly on the bottom step of my bungalow entrance. They were the last I saw of her.' For over two decades, they were.[8]

As Ian intended, his nephew's journey from the drama and disease of Pantai was absolute. Instead of simply being invalided to Singapore, Lockhart was placed on a ship to Japan on the premise that distance would defeat both the infection and the infatuation that afflicted him. A friend of Ian's took this plan a step further, insisting that Lockhart accompany him across the Pacific to where he had business in Canada. Even while fighting off malaria, the travel-mad Lockhart was excited by this unexpected journey, making favourable notes and observations about Japan's alien culture and Canada's breathtaking wilderness.

When hot springs and clear Canadian air did little to improve Lockhart's condition, it was decided that he had to return to Britain for specialist treatment. During this odyssey of convalescence, Lockhart tried to reconcile himself to the situation and find a silver lining, noting in his diary that 'I have seen so much now that I am almost surfeited with beautiful things'. These rich experiences could not, however, obscure the reality that Ian had effectively banished Lockhart from both Malaysia and its rubber trade as penance for his personal and professional missteps. True to the mindset that had guided him to Negeri Sembilan in the first place, Lockhart processed this parlous situation with romantic lament. Writing from his sickbed on board the *Empress of Yokohama* in July 1910, he bid a bitter 'farewell to the land of the soft-scented valley', 'where the dreams of my youth lie broken and shattered'. In Canada, he wrote a poem for Amai, in which he dubbed himself a 'coward' for leaving his 'poor eastern maid', who 'knew no other sin, save that you gave me your heart to break'.

Lockhart's self-pity deepened after he arrived in Liverpool in March 1911 and journeyed north to Tomintoul, a village in the Highlands where his Macgregor ancestors had first distilled whisky and which was now all but ruled over by his domineering grandmother. There, the family gathered to receive him in a flood of mixed emotions. His visible weight loss and alarming lethargy evoked sympathy from Florence and Robert senior, who were relieved that their Bertie was safely back on Scottish soil. What should have been a homecoming of thanks, however, was complicated by the fact that stories of Lockhart's scandalous behaviour had preceded his arrival. The Rubber Queen upbraided her grandson for the damage he had done to the family's reputation, lecturing him on his lack of maturity and decency, and dragging him to church to seek penance. More so than the Amai affair, what irked the Macgregor matriarch most was that Lockhart had somehow managed in the midst of the rubber boom to return home without riches. This forced her to conclude that despite his father's pains to educate him and his uncle setting him up at Pantai, her once-promising grandson had grown into an unreliable, self-indulgent fool.

Showered with criticism, devoid of prospects and beset by fragile health, Lockhart was forced – for the first but by no means the last time in his life – to take stock of who he was and where he was going. In May 1911 he escaped the Rubber Queen's wrath and travelled south to visit his father at Sandhurst in Berkshire, where he had taken on yet another headmaster role. There, Lockhart pledged to the elder Robert that he would get his life in order and cast off the shameful pall of Amai and Pantai. He would stow his wanderlust. He would sit his civil service entrance exam. He would become the man his father had always wanted him to be.[9]

CHAPTER 2

OUR MAN IN MOSCOW

'From the wisdom of your reports, I expected to see an elderly gentleman with a grey beard'

– David Lloyd George

On his twenty-fourth birthday, Lockhart – now recovered from his year-long struggle with malaria – was playing golf when a hollering from across the green stopped him in mid-swing. The source of the noise was his younger brother Norman, who was waving a piece of paper and excitedly calling out to his sibling, 'You're in!'

Norman was referring to the Foreign Office, the entrance exam for which Lockhart had sat a few months earlier in July 1911. Rediscovering the capacity for hard work he had found in Berlin but lost in Pantai, Lockhart had prepared thoroughly for the exam, brushing up on his German and French and employing a law and politics tutor. He also masked his despondency at taking a mundane career path by drawing on his deep reserves of charm and whimsy to sway the selection panel at the interview. This effort to impress was furthered by Lockhart's brother John reaching the height of his fame as a fast bowler at the time, which delighted the cricket-loving panel of mandarins whose job was to decide if the young man before them was fit to serve in Britain's diplomatic corps.

The panel said nothing of Lockhart's dalliance with Amai, noting on his file only that he had been a rubber planter who had quit the business because of poor health. This half-version of events was backed by

personal referees who didn't mention his romantic escapades, asserted that
the malaria was no indictment of Lockhart's overall health and claimed
that he left Malaysia voluntarily despite his success as a planter. This burying
of Lockhart's past and the sporting achievements of his brother alone didn't
get him the job. As the exam results Norman waved in his face revealed,
Lockhart had scored higher than the other candidates in French and law and
narrowly missed out on topping German. It was mostly in arithmetic
and, oddly for someone possessed of an interest in far-off places, geography
that he had stumbled. Lockhart's total score was enough, however, to top
the list of would-be consular officials. With his letter of acceptance in hand,
Lockhart went before his disapproving grandmother, who recognised that
he had now 'passed from the ranks of the ne'er-do-wells into the Valhalla
of heroes'. The Rubber Queen forgave her grandson's past indiscretions
and embraced him, pushing a £100 cheque into his hand and despatching
him to London to begin the next chapter of his life.[1]

Wanting to make the most of this fresh start, Lockhart arrived at the
Foreign Office building in September 1911, clad in the regulation pin-
striped trousers and eager to attack his new vocation of minuting letters
and responding to queries from British subjects across the globe. As in
Port Dickson, however, Lockhart's enthusiasm was soon consumed by the
drudgery of office life. The highlight of his working day was catching a
glimpse of diplomatic heavyweights like Sir Edward Grey and Sir Eyre
Crowe, who would occasionally walk by his desk without acknowledging
his existence. Aside from the tedium, Lockhart felt that something was
amiss about Whitehall and his place in its creaking bureaucratic machine.
Reforms aimed at modernising the Foreign Office's practices, increasing
pay and recruiting young bucks with fresh ideas had been rolled out in
the decade prior to Lockhart's arrival. The installation of telephones and the
introduction of a registry system for keeping track of important documents
had done little, however, to inject modern efficiency into the culture of
the Foreign Office, where 'the long weekend was still normal, and vaca-
tions were of a length which suited gentlemen'. This was one of the many

practices that led to public accusations that the institution was elitist, aloof and its staff ill-equipped to solve the complex international problems of the new century.

Lockhart was frustrated by this institutional inertia. It seemed mad to him that the diplomatic nerve centre of the world's largest empire was presided over by old men whose chief preoccupations were the quality of their quill pens and the straightness of their subordinates' ties. Such rigidity was anathema to the seducer of forbidden Malay princesses, who felt with each passing week that he was treading water in a stagnant pond. He fell into a malaise of self-reflection over whether the respectability he was gaining in Whitehall was worth the sacrifice of his true desires.

Thankfully for Lockhart, these bouts of troubled introspection were as common throughout his life as the opportunities that arose to end them. In this instance, he was thrown a lifeline a few days before Christmas 1911 when he received his first overseas posting – vice-consul in Moscow. Beyond a cursory knowledge of the histories of Ivan the Terrible and Catherine the Great, Lockhart knew nothing of Russia. The spirit of adventure within and the restlessness he felt without ensured, however, that he gleefully accepted the assignment. Thereafter, Lockhart counted the days until he could put the stifling oak and marble of the Foreign Office building behind him.

To remedy his ignorance of the land of the tsars, Lockhart spent his final weeks in London bending the ears of Foreign Office colleagues and Russian émigrés, from whom he prised knowledge of their homeland's politics, culture and history. Owing to the class of Russian he quizzed – petty nobility and cashed-up businessmen – Lockhart concluded that Russia was a country unfettered by stuffy British norms, in which marathons of excess were commonplace. It sounded tailor-made for his indulgent Macgregor sensibilities. Wisely, Lockhart kept this revelation to himself and instead basked in the pride his parents felt in their now seemingly reformed son's career finally taking off. He further pleased Florence and Robert senior when, during a going-away party they threw for him just before Christmas, he took another significant step towards responsible adulthood by getting his private life on the straight and narrow.

With Amai confined to a past best forgotten, Lockhart's attentions were grabbed at the party by a young Australian woman named Jean Haslewood Turner, who was the daughter of a prosperous businessman from Brisbane. Neither Lockhart's memoirs nor his diaries give much away as to why he felt so infatuated with Jean as to propose marriage a mere ten days after first asking her to dance. What is clear is that this impulsive act created porous foundations for a fractious relationship which, blighted by acrimony and affairs, ended in a bitter divorce in 1937. That bleak future, however, seemed inconceivable in the heady final days of 1911 when Lockhart composed yet another of his romantic odes. Simply titled 'Jean', the poem pledged that its author's 'life is yours. You hold it in your hand, to make or mar or bend it at your will, yours, yours all alone, for all time good or ill . . . I live for you, dear heart, and you for me'.

The poem reads as heartfelt, yet it is telling that 'Jean' is one of the few examples within Lockhart's voluminous writings where he fondly spilled ink in his wife's name. Moreover, the other poem of note, which was penned after they parted in January 1912 (Jean returned to Australia to get her affairs in order while Lockhart headed to Moscow to set up their new life together), strikes a sobering and reflective tone. In it, Lockhart refers to him and Jean 'standing on the brink of life's abyss' when they met, drawn together by the need to 'tear from life what pleasure we could'. Dismissing any notion of agency on their part, he wonders whether their pairing happened simply 'because His boundless mercy knew that you had need of me and I of you?' As he put it ruefully on the brink of divorce decades later, his abrupt marriage proposal was part of 'a serious effort to conform to the conventionalities of my new state'. Jean may have been his spouse but to judge by Lockhart's poems, letters and memoirs, it was the other women in his life who stirred his passions.[2]

Lockhart's relationship with Jean was not helped by the fact that shortly after she accepted his proposal he fell in love once more – this time with

Russia. Much like his marriage, the fraught nature of the union was not apparent to Lockhart when he first arrived in Moscow just after New Year's Day 1912. Instead, as he glided through snow-misted streets on a horse-drawn sleigh he felt the joy of life that Whitehall had drained from him return. When the driver reached his destination, Lockhart gleefully tossed him a few roubles and strode out of the ice-clear night air into the fug of the Hotel Metropole's packed foyer. There, he relished the assault on his senses from the gleaming chandeliers of gold and diamond, and the cacophony of unknown words erupting from the human sea of 'steaming furs, fat women and big sleek men', all of whom exuded 'great wealth and crude coarseness'. These were the Russians the well-heeled émigrés in London had promised Lockhart and, before his first week in Moscow was over, he would meet plenty more of them.

Moscow's new vice-consul had arrived at an opportune moment. With the aim of strengthening diplomatic relations following the Anglo-Russian Convention of 1907 – an agreement that settled long-standing grievances over the two empires' shared borders in Central Asia – a delegation of British politicians, clergy and military men had arrived in Moscow just after Christmas on a goodwill tour of the city. In joining this delegation, Lockhart ensured that his supposedly respectable career in Moscow commenced with a three-day binge of orchestras, ballets and multi-course banquets, all washed down with copious amounts of vodka and champagne. During this prolonged party, Lockhart peeled off from the main group of Britons to explore a late-night bar of ill-repute. As he downed glass after glass of vodka in the smoke-wreathed basement room, he watched a troupe of musicians use the sound of deep violas to guide tortured fiddles and haunting vocals, creating the unmistakable cacophony of gypsy folk. So began an infatuation with this evocative genre of music that would last the rest of Lockhart's life.

Fully intoxicated by the wonders of Moscow, the wide-eyed vice-consul continued exploring the city alone after the British delegation returned home head-sore and exhausted. In the coffee shops and art galleries, the gregarious Scot befriended scores of writers, artists and actors. These were

Lockhart's types of contrarians – culturally sophisticated and politically cynical, yet bookishly middle-class enough to not be dangerous. Through winding discussions that ran into the dawn, Lockhart's new comrades espoused to him their distaste for the worship of tsar, God and country, and their concerns for the arrested development of Russia's political and societal progress.

These exchanges prompted Lockhart to reflect on his own politics. Though his background was conservative and embedded in the Presbyterian tradition, from the moment he countenanced becoming a Muslim to pursue a romance that offended all norms of polite society Lockhart realised he was a political and spiritual agnostic. Although he had little time for ideologues, Lockhart's relentless curiosity drove him to tolerate their sermons. In the politically fissile Russia of the early 1900s, this made him a social chameleon. Lockhart was as capable of clinking champagne glasses with beribboned generals and tsarist courtiers as he was of absorbing the ire of those who despised such pomp and privilege. As a witness to the vice-consul's carousing in Moscow attested, his 'cheerful' manner when dealing with Russians of whatever conviction, combined with his 'taste for gypsies, wine and dancing' made him 'a very good mixer'. This skill helped Lockhart achieve much in his renewed quest to 'go native', this time in the log-fired clubs of Russia rather than in the sweating jungles of South-East Asia. In addition to quickly making friends in places high and low, during an evening out in the spring of 1912 Lockhart was bestowed with a Russian epithet by the gypsy singer Maria Nikolaevna Lebedev. As her mother tongue had no equivalent to 'Robert', Maria dubbed him 'Roman Romanovich'. The pride Lockhart felt at being made an honorary Russian was one of the many reasons why, six decades later, he maintained that 'my first two years in Russia were the happiest of my life'.[3]

Lockhart's cultural immersion intensified after he became a lodger in the home of one of his artistic friends, Madame Ertel, the widow of the novelist Alexander Ertel. At Lockhart's insistence, his new landlady gave him lessons in Russian (which he perfected within a year) and deeper insight into an aspect of his new home that was easy to overlook amid the obscene banquets and tantalising musical entertainment – the revolutionary grievances of the country's oppressed. Though the autocracy of the tsars had been challenged in the early 1800s by dissident army officers, it was not until the 1860s that a sustained campaign to change Russia by whatever means necessary began. This was in response to Tsar Alexander II's introduction of reforms in 1861, which were designed to emancipate the peasants and liberalise education. When neither objective was met, groups of nihilists and revolutionary socialists took drastic measures to force the pace of history. This involved attempts to radicalise peasants with propaganda and the shooting and stabbing of police chiefs and court officials. Even the Holy Tsar wasn't safe. In March 1881, a nihilist suicide bomber rushed at Alexander II on the streets of St Petersburg, detonating a dynamite device that ended both men's lives in a storm of fire and smoke.

In February 1905, Russia's new autocrat Nicholas II faced a threat more existential than a terrorist desiring martyrdom when thousands of his subjects took to the streets to demand a revolutionary shake-up of Russia's politics and society. As his predecessor had done in the 1860s, Nicholas responded with proposals for democratic reforms that fell short of his people's demands. This engendered a fresh wave of violence in which thousands of government officials, nobles and ordinary Russians were shot, stabbed and blown apart by bombs. Only a few months before Lockhart arrived in Moscow, the Russian prime minister Peter Stolypin was shot dead at a theatre in Kiev. At firelit evenings spent with Madame Ertel and friends in the rug-smothered front room of her apartment, Lockhart was regaled with these stories of violence amid lamentations on the need for political change. Britain's vice-consul was dossing with dissidents. Lockhart, however, saw no problem with this. Although revolutionary sentiment in Russia had long been simmering, in 1912 it seemed far from the point of boiling over. This was exemplified by the fact that on a day supposedly earmarked for an anti-tsarist uprising, Madame Ertel and her friends chose to stay in bed rather than take to the streets.[4]

Lockhart's subversive dinner companions may have been talkers rather than doers, but Moscow's consul-general was not impressed. A veteran diplomat with a measured temperament, Montgomery Grove wanted a quiet and trouble-free life. In his consulate, beyond issuing passports and handling the petty complaints of Moscow's British diaspora, there would be no time for 'poking one's nose into other matters'. Grove warned Lockhart to be mindful of the company he kept, not just because it was unbecoming of a vice-consul but also because he might attract the unwelcome attention of the tsar's secret police, the Okhrana. Grove's concerns were not unjustified. As one of Lockhart's contemporaries at the St Petersburg embassy noted of this time, 'the Tsarist predecessors of the Bolshevik OGPU [secret police] were exceedingly ingenious' in their monitoring of British diplomats, who were suspected of providing money and support to the kind of subversives with whom Lockhart was supping. In St Petersburg, this paranoia over the Okhrana led to the implementation of new security measures by the British embassy's staff, including an excess of locks being fitted to office doors and nightly inspections of the premises which, in one instance, led to shots being fired at the ambassador by his own staff, who mistook him for an Okhrana snooper.[5]

Far from giving him pause for thought, these warnings were welcomed by the adventure-starved Lockhart, who was once more succumbing to the dispiriting reality of his job. When the hangover from his first days in Moscow cleared and Lockhart first clapped eyes on his workplace, memories of Whitehall's stilted inefficiency and his tauntingly bland accounts book at Port Dickson must have come flooding back. Britain's diplomatic outpost in Moscow was a single room attached to Grove's personal flat, which was located in a faceless apartment building off a side street. There was no messenger to run telegrams and the office was habitually cash-strapped, to the point that Grove relied on a typewriter of Victorian vintage to compose missives. This destitution was reflected in Lockhart's wages, which amounted to £300 a year plus an initial £100 one-off payment to purchase attire becoming of a British official. This was far from the £1,000 per year most senior consular officials in St Petersburg took home. It was the need to eke the most out of this meagre wage that led Lockhart to abandon the swanky Hotel Metropole for Madame Ertel's spare room.[6]

To improve his financial situation and provide an outlet for his stifled creative energies, Lockhart wrote stories inspired by his time in Malaysia and sketches on Russian life for British magazines. With no shortage of guile, he got around the Foreign Office's prohibition on earning independently by writing under the pseudonym of Jean D'Auvergne. Unconstrained by this anonymity, Lockhart let loose on other Britons who refused to embrace Russian life as he had. This mockery was best exemplified in 'The Way of the English', in which Lockhart profiled an Englishman who dines out in Moscow on 24 December to celebrate Christmas Eve, arrogantly indifferent to the fact that the Russian Christmas falls in January. Informed by his late-night experiences, Jean D'Auvergne also titillated readers with stories of the hedonistic delights of vodka and song that could be enjoyed in Moscow. Lockhart balanced this inclination to the louche with cultural observations of Russian writers and their morbid, nihilistic views of their country's rotten political system. Aloof Britons, appalling excess and stewing discontent – these were Lockhart's candid observations of tsarist Russia in its denouement. Though pithy and lacking a political purpose, these early works from behind the veil of an alias show Lockhart's eye for the sensational and his understanding of how to use provocation to engage a reader. They reveal the mind of a man who understood the art of propaganda long before the British government employed him as a propagandist.[7]

The use of the name 'Jean' was owing to Lockhart no longer being alone in Moscow. In January 1913 he travelled back to Britain to marry Jean, who then accompanied him back to Russia. Madame Ertel's no longer being fit for purpose, Lockhart acquired an apartment on Khlebnyi Pereulok (Bread Lane) and pledged to curtail his nightlife in favour of devoting attention to his new bride. To this end, he gave Jean lessons in Russian and tours of the city he had grown so enamoured of. Unfortunately, she was neither as adept at picking up languages nor as instantly besotted by all things Russian as her husband. Regardless, Jean tried to immerse herself in Lockhart's world. Together, the couple dined and drank with the director of the Moscow Arts Theatre, Michael 'Lyki' Lykiardopolus, and played host to visiting British figures of note including H. G. Wells, Lytton Strachey and even the notorious occultist Aleister Crowley. Given Lockhart's pledge to cut out his partying, his interactions with Crowley – known by the unsubtle moniker of the 'Great Beast' – are of note. An unrepentant sexual adventurer who spurned all norms of Christian morality, Crowley's mantra of 'Do as Thou Wilt' reads like it was penned for Lockhart's ears. The fact that Crowley was in Moscow in March 1913 with a burlesque troupe called the Ragged Ragtime Girls, whose members the 'Great Beast' characterised as alcoholics, hysterics and nymphomaniacs, suggests that Lockhart wasn't as compelled to conformity by Jean's arrival as he later claimed.

In addition to revelry, Lockhart was still 'poking his nose' into business that Grove preferred him to ignore. Between using Lancastrian factory owners from the city's British community to keep apprised of industrial unrest, his interactions with Madame Ertel's circle and even the debauched Crowley – who informed Grove and Lockhart about public discontent at tsarist corruption – Lockhart became increasingly interested in Russia's subversives. He also got a taste of how seriously the Okhrana took these threats to tsar and country when, in the summer of 1913, Nicholas II visited Moscow. Given the city's reputation as 'a liberal and therefore disaffected centre', a visit from Russia's God-ordained ruler was a rarity. For this reason, ahead of the tsar's arrival Lockhart was questioned by the Okhrana about the political opinions of the city's British population. It was the first of many times that Lockhart would encounter Russia's secret police, and by all accounts he handled it coolly. Moreover, as he did with all matters of interest and intrigue, Lockhart took note of the police's paranoia and what it indicated about the state of relations between the tsar and his subjects.[8]

Grove might have disapproved of his deputy's interest in Moscow's underground, but Lockhart's willingness to rub shoulders with bohemian revolutionaries, chin-stroking intellectuals and suspicious factory owners made him an invaluable asset to Britain's diplomatic corps. Even after the 1905 revolution, British officials in Moscow and St Petersburg tended to be uninterested in social conditions. Instead, they confined themselves to interacting with courtiers whose loyalties lay with the tsar and the maintenance of Russia's autocratic status quo. This attention to the ruling class was because the British were concerned with attitudes that shaped Russia's foreign policy. The notion that forces from below might one day make these elites and their attitudes irrelevant was unthinkable. His time with Madame Ertel and her big-talking friends led Lockhart to a similar conclusion about the unlikelihood of another revolution breaking out. This impression was reinforced when, days after the outbreak of the First World War in August 1914, Lockhart perched himself on the consulate's windowsill and watched the endless stream of Russian soldiers parading down the street below, their patriotism stirred and their resolve to fight for tsar and motherland seemingly unshakeable.[9]

When news arrived weeks later that these men had been slaughtered in their thousands at the Battle of Tannenberg, Lockhart reassessed his assumptions. On the heels of frontline defeats came home-front food shortages, and with them a swelling hum of discontent across Moscow over incapable generals and the army's lack of shells. Sensing something worth recording for posterity, in January 1915 Lockhart began keeping a diary. The first few months read as the work of someone struggling to marshal their thoughts. Scattered entries remarking on the arrival of a new suit from London, his joy at reading *War and Peace* in its original Russian, long walks taken with Jean, news from Europe's battlefields and the arrogance of Lockhart's friend Hugh Walpole – the novelist turned wartime propagandist – dominate the pages. By the summer of 1915, however, Lockhart's diary entries became more focused on the rising tide of anti-tsarist and anti-war sentiment in Moscow. The informants Lockhart had cultivated within the city's radical community, as well as his political contacts such as the liberal-leaning mayor Michael Chelnokov, all remarked on the 'great deal of [political] unrest against the government'. He noted 'serious disturbances in Tverskaya, whereby some five people were shot and some ten wounded', 'rumours of a strike at Ivanovo Voznesensk', and 'talk of agitation within the army itself'. Even victories couldn't rouse the kind of pro-tsarist sentiment Lockhart had seen a year prior. At a horse race outside Moscow, news of a Russian naval triumph was broadcast over the loudspeakers to the well-to-do crowd, who 'did not seem in the least excited about it'.[10]

Importantly for his career, Lockhart didn't keep these observations to himself. Following a diplomatic reshuffle in the spring of 1915, Lockhart – still not into his thirties – replaced Grove as acting consul-general in Moscow. He immediately changed the way the consulate did business. Recognising the need to firm up the Anglo-Russian alliance, Lockhart established a small propaganda bureau for disseminating anti-German leaflets and articles, funded on a shoestring budget and staffed by his theatre friend Lyki. Owing to the latter's Greek passport and willingness to travel in wartime, Lockhart also dipped his toes into the spy game by sending Lyki to Germany to gather intelligence on the state of the enemy's home front. This was one of the many ventures through which Lockhart practised his opinion that a diplomat's job was 'to observe, collect information, weigh evidence and report' it as intelligence. In this instance, the intelligence was forwarded to Sir George Buchanan, Britain's ambassador in Petrograd (renamed from St Petersburg during the war to sound less German). Within these reports, Lockhart detailed the scale of worker agitation in munitions factories, analysed food prices, assessed the danger of anarchist mutterings in Moscow's clubs – which, naturally, he visited first hand – presented abridged histories of the city's socialist movement and gave his opinion on how military defeats were affecting Anglo-Russian relations. He also provided translations of concerned correspondence over the war's progress between Russian officials, leaked to him by his friend Mayor Chelnokov. Lockhart emphasised to Buchanan that this intelligence came not from 'mere gossip or wild rumours' but from a wide range of sources possessed of 'all shades of political opinion'. So informed, Lockhart's overriding narrative was one of crisis, peppered with remarks to the effect that 'in Moscow, practically every class is more or less strongly opposed to the government'. With the likes of Madame Ertel and Lyki in mind, he conceded that the 'Russian intelligentsia does not seem to be the stuff of which revolutions are made'. He did, however, warn that the anti-tsarist propaganda being spread by socialists was having a noticeable impact on the average Muscovite.[11]

For the most part, intelligence from consulates was ignored by the Petrograd embassy, which relied on its own limited networks for information. Lockhart's keen insights and engaging prose, however, caught Buchanan's eye. Though he didn't always agree with Lockhart's assertions that revolutionary elements in Russia were a cause for concern, Buchanan did share his view that the patriotism of 1914 was dissolving into a maelstrom of civil discontent. Satisfied with the young consul-general's 'excellent work', Buchanan forwarded his reports to the Foreign Office. There, the name Lockhart soon became known. By the autumn of 1915, the diplomats who had paid him no mind three years prior were remarking on Lockhart's 'masterful despatches', and the 'interesting accounts' he produced on Russia's growing political strife. Lockhart's command of Russian was also recognised as a boon to his work, particularly as Buchanan – despite being appointed ambassador in 1910 – had never bothered to learn the language, relying instead on tsarist officials' knowledge of French to communicate. Lockhart's eclectic range of sources demanded fluency in the native tongue, which gave him access to insights beyond those of Moscow's increasingly out-of-touch elites. Foreign Office officials took the well-informed consul-general's advice to heart, deducing from 'Mr Lockhart's despatches' that the tsar's idea of placing Moscow under martial law would 'do infinitely more harm to the prosecution of the war by Russia than any peace propaganda'. By October 1916, Lockhart was even being taken into the confidence of Secret Intelligence Service (MI6) counter-espionage officers in Petrograd, with whom he exchanged intelligence on a suspected pro-German Russian spy.[12]

Lockhart had taken an unorthodox path via evenings with would-be revolutionaries in defiance of his boss's wishes but by the end of 1916 the failed rubber planter's professional potential was starting to be realised. Successful but still money-hungry, Lockhart tried to get a raise for his efforts, only to be told that the Foreign Office had no money to spare even for its more talented employees. This refusal came with a warning that Lockhart should refrain from issuing such demands formally, as it was unbecoming of his station. The brash young diplomat, however, brushed off this reprimand and did little to alter the tone of his subsequent despatches, safe in the knowledge that he was now regarded as 'the most capable of all the consuls' in Russia. It was a well-deserved reputation. Buchanan's wife used to mockingly refer to him as 'the pessimistic Mr Lockhart', but in the late winter of 1917 events were unfolding across Russia that proved Whitehall's man in Moscow was more prophet than doomsayer.[13]

CHAPTER 3

IMPLOSION

'You are a little clever, but not clever enough
A little strong but not strong enough
A little weak but not weak enough'

– Moura Budberg

'Rioting in Petrograd . . . revolution begins. Workmen come out.' These were some of the few words Lockhart found time to scrawl into his diary during the frenzied first days of March 1917, when thousands of people poured onto Petrograd's streets demanding that Nicholas II abdicate his throne. The tsar was in Belorussia at the time, trying and failing to lead his troops in the fight against Germany. Since assuming command of Russia's army in 1915, Nicholas had achieved few victories but gained much ire. His ineptitude as a military leader, the suspicion felt by many of his subjects towards his Hesse-born wife Alexandra and the deterioration of conditions on the home front had undermined confidence in him and his regime. The dire straits of Russia's war effort had also sapped the will to fight from the peasants who comprised the bulk of the army. Nicholas never fully grasped the significance of this. In November 1916, Buchanan had warned the tsar that 'the peasantry, who always regarded the emperor as infallible, were beginning to lose faith in him'. The autocrat's response was to look 'somewhat embarrassed' and pass no comment. Months later, when Petrograd's streets filled with thousands of furious protestors, the head of the Duma – the Russian parliament – sent an urgent telegram to the tsar's headquarters warning that 'the situation is serious. The capital is in a state of anarchy.' Nicholas responded by ordering the army to disperse the mob with bullets. Instead of heeding these words, many soldiers joined the ranks of the disenchanted while others mutinied against their brothers in arms who tried to honour the tsar's brutal decree.

The British ambassador's daughter, Meriel Buchanan, observed the breakdown of tsarist control that followed. The streets around the embassy were at first quiet, but for the odd crack of distant rifle fire and the occasional passing of 'motor lorries, bristling with soldiers and red flags, like enormous hedgehogs'. As the day wore on, however, 'workmen and soldiers' emerged from the freezing winter fog in droves wearing bullet belts and brandishing rifles. Meriel recalled a child 'of no more than sixteen' who passed by the embassy gleefully firing a pistol 'into the air in an aimless, light-hearted way'.

The tsar's orders having fallen on deaf ears and armed citizens now controlling Petrograd's streets, the Duma dissolved itself, albeit not before advising the sovereign that his time was up. Abandoned by his ministers and his army, Nicholas succumbed to the inevitable and abdicated on 15 March. In the space of a few days, tsardom's centuries-long grip on Russia had melted away.[1]

In its place, confusion and cross purposes reigned. After the Duma's dissolution and the sensible refusal of the tsar's brother to claim the throne, two groups jostled to fill the power vacuum, each with their own vision for what Russia's future should look like. An assortment of liberals, centrists and moderate socialists formed the Provisional Government. This was a weak name for a weak assembly. Hurriedly self-constituted, the Provisional Government lacked public support beyond the intelligentsia and the elites, some of whom were far from revolutionaries and secretly yearned for the tsar's restoration. The body's provisional status was owed to its leader, Prince Georgii Lvov, deciding that tricky questions over the tsar's future and the final form of Russia's new government would have to be answered at a later date – ideally once the war with Germany had been fought to a successful conclusion. This policy of continuing the bloodshed despite the revolution was hard to sell to the war-weary Russian people.

As the Provisional Government coalesced around platforms of caution and moderation, a more ambitious assembly known as the Petrograd Soviet took physical control of the Tauride Palace, from which the tsar's former ministers had once governed. Comprised of Socialist Revolutionaries (Russia's preeminent radical group) and Social Democrats (a party that had split in 1903 into moderate Mensheviks and radical Bolsheviks), the Petrograd Soviet enjoyed the support the Provisional Government lacked from the kind of ordinary Russians who had forced Nicholas from his throne. The Petrograd Soviet's calls to give workers a say in Russia's governance and to abolish hierarchy in the army spoke more to the revolutionary moment than Lvov's pledge to prolong meaningful political change in favour of continuing the miserable struggle against Germany. This narrative was backed by the Petrograd Soviet's propaganda newspaper, *Izvestia*, which compared the bourgeois Provisional Government to the weak-willed tsarist ministers they had replaced and mockingly asserted that Lvov's people only held 'offices in government with the consent of the Petrograd workers and soldiers'. Even Russia's minister for war had to concede to the army's chiefs that 'the Provisional Government does not possess any real power, and its directives are carried out only to the extent that it is permitted by the Soviet of Workers and Soldiers' Deputies'.[2]

When the revolution arrived in Moscow five days after it had shaken Petrograd, Lockhart got a first-hand experience of this tussle between the forces of radicalism and moderation for control of Russia. Donning his fur coat and *ushanka* hat, Lockhart secured the consulate's door with an extra padlock and took to the city's streets, marching at a brisk pace to ward off both the cold and the rowdy soldiers who seemed to be overrunning Moscow. His destination was the City Hall, a red-bricked monstrosity that had housed the municipal Duma before its disintegration in the face of the gathering mob. Lockhart assumed correctly that the hall would be a locus for the revolutionary leaders, among whom he hoped to find his friends from the intelligentsia. Instead, the building's steps were scattered with wild-eyed socialists and bloody-minded anarchists, who were urging the soldiers to turn their guns away from the German lines and train their sights on traitors to the revolution. As he picked his way through this bay-ing assembly, Lockhart concluded that the transition of power in Russia was going to favour the furious over the temperate.

This was not entirely true. At least, not yet. There were some liberal members of the former Duma among the crowd who, upon recognising Britain's consul-general, urged the sea of boisterous humanity to part so he could pass. Ignoring the more aggressive members of the crowd who demanded to know Lockhart's business, he marched up the steps into the City Hall. There he found Chelnokov frantically signing decrees and barking orders at nervous subordinates. Lockhart smiled at this sight. The mayor was more a progressive democrat than a radical socialist and he strongly supported Russia remaining as Britain's ally in the fight against Germany. In a brief meeting amid the sweating commotion of the hall's main foyer, Chelnokov admitted to Lockhart that the Bolsheviks and the Socialist Revolutionaries opposed his leadership. Nevertheless, pat-ting the consul-general on his fur-clad shoulder, Chelnokov reassured his friend that he would whip the Moscow mob into shape and convince the Petrograd Soviet that it was in Russia's interests to keep the war going, lest the Germans overrun the country and shatter their fragile revolution.[3]

Heartened by Chelnokov's pledge, Lockhart took his leave and made his way back through the fissile streets of disorder to the calm of his one-room consulate. Staring out the window with a glass of scotch in hand, he tutted under his breath at the sight of a band of youths casually looting a shop across the road. He lamented that a modicum of sense from the tsar might have averted all that was unfolding. As early as the autumn of 1915, Lockhart had noted how Nicholas was losing popularity among Muscovites through his mishandling of the war and his tendency to 'dismiss the good ministers and retain the worst'. Though he felt some personal sympathy for the hapless emperor, from his contemporary notes through to his later

memoirs, Lockhart maintained a consistent view that Russia's unbending
system of autocracy, and Nicholas's inability to enact genuine reforms, was
to blame for the revolution. His distaste for tsardom ensured that Lockhart,
like many Britons, saw the revolution as a chance to wipe Russia's slate
clean of dysfunctional autocracy. This faith in the revolution's potential
did not mean, however, that Lockhart entertained starry-eyed visions for
the country's immediate future. As he reflected on his visit to the City Hall
and compiled a report for the Foreign Office, Lockhart concluded that the
'dual power' arrangement by which the worker-backed Petrograd Soviet
and the middle-class Provisional Government controlled the country wasn't
working and that 'Russia is now on the verge of a great struggle between
the bourgeois and the proletariat'.[4]

Accepting that this infighting between the tsar's revolutionary heirs
would rage beyond his or anyone else's control, Lockhart resolved to spend
his time amid the throes of revolution focusing on the question that pertained most to British interests – would Russia keep fighting the war?
According to Chelnokov and Lvov, the answer was an emphatic 'yes'.
Lockhart's heart wanted to believe this, but his brain knew better. Aside
from the war being unpopular with many Russians, the removal of the tsar
had done nothing to improve the state of the army, which was still plagued
by low morale, desertions and deficits in everything from bullets to boot
leather. Its fighting capabilities were further undermined by the struggle
between the Provisional Government and the Petrograd Soviet.

In mid-March, the latter jammed the first of many spanners into the
works of Lvov's war machine by issuing its Order Number 1. This called
for Russia's soldiers to cease saluting their officers and elect 'representatives
from the lower ranks' to go over their superior's heads and report directly
to the Duma. These representatives would be responsible for keeping 'all
rifles, machine guns, armoured vehicles and others' in the hands of the
rank and file. 'In no instance', the order decreed, were these weapons to 'be
turned over to officers, even at their demand'. Anathema to the smooth running of an army, Order Number 1 was designed to either end Russia's war

or reduce its capacity to fight, so that the struggle would have to become
a purely defensive one against German incursions into the revolutionary
motherland. The Provisional Government's riposte was to shelve reality
and insist to its British and French allies that Russia's soldiers were ready
to launch a massive summer offensive against Germany. Lockhart knew
this was hubris posing as confidence. By May 1917, he had come around
to the view of the war espoused by a fellow diplomat in Moscow – 'Russia
has gone out and America has come in'.[5]

He reported as much to Buchanan, noting that despite Lvov's call to
arms, 'voices in favour of peace are making themselves heard everyday'.
Some of the more extreme peace advocates had even assaulted British citizens in Moscow on the premise that they embodied a reprehensible alliance
with an imperial power. In one instance, a British foreman at a munitions
factory was tied to a pillar with coarse rope by socialist vigilantes and put
on 'trial' for supporting both the war and the tsar's restoration.

As always, these sobering insights into what was really going on in
Russia served Lockhart well professionally. When political dignitaries
arrived in Petrograd from Britain in the spring to assess the state of the
Anglo-Russian alliance, Lockhart was tasked by Buchanan with being
their liaison to the Provisional Government. This assignment was owed to
Lockhart's contacts. In addition to his friendship with Chelnokov he was
also close with Lvov, with whom he often drank tea at private meetings in
the latter's apartment. Lockhart's ability to speak Russian with a fluency
that eluded Buchanan was also important, as the country's new rulers
were not about to converse in French or English. Times had changed
and Lockhart was equipped to move with them in a way the ageing,
monocled Buchanan was not. By interpreting for both Buchanan and a
visiting representative of Prime Minister Lloyd George, Lord Milner, in
meetings with the Provisional Government's war minister, Alexander
Kerensky, Lockhart became crucial to Anglo-Russian relations at a time
when the British were courting 'Kerensky as rich and aged plutocrats pay
court to a ballerina' to keep Russia in the war. In the process, Lockhart

befriended Kerensky, whose quick intellect and slavish work ethic he greatly admired.[6]

Lockhart's work as a liaison between Russia's revolutionaries and visiting foreigners gave him insights into how the revolution was being understood internationally. Although he found Milner to be reasonably well informed, Lockhart was taken aback by the cluelessness of socialists from Britain and France. Visiting Labour politicians and members of the Fabian Society were unable to grasp the complexities of Russia's revolutionary movement and, handicapped by their ignorance of the language, failed to make an impression on their comrades from the Petrograd Soviet, who tended to write them off as bourgeois pretenders.

Arthur Henderson, a Labour politician despatched by Whitehall to become Britain's new ambassador in the summer of 1917, exemplified this type. As a Labour man, Henderson was supposed to provide a smoother conduit for relations between Britain and revolutionary Russia than the conservative-minded Buchanan. However, Henderson soon realised that he didn't understand the language, the country or the radicals trying to run it. The intensity of the Petrograd Soviet was of an order far above anything he had experienced in Britain's union movement. The feeling was reciprocal, with the Petrograd Soviet's press denouncing Henderson and the Labour Party as 'paid slaves of capital'. Accepting that he wasn't cut out for the job, after barely a month in his new post Henderson wrote to Lloyd George advising that Buchanan should stay where he was.[7]

Henderson was wise to bow out when he did. As the would-be ambassador floundered, Kerensky toured the front lines trying to stir up patriotic fervour among the soldiers ahead of the planned summer offensive. Ostensibly, he was an odd choice for his role. A 'short, slim man with dark hair' and a 'deathly pallor', Kerensky had an unassuming, almost ethereal mien. He was also underwhelming in one-on-one conversation, displaying a 'nervous manner' and a tendency to 'speak in quick, jerky sentences'. He was, as a British intelligence officer bluntly put it, a 'nonentity'. This image belied the war minister's quirky charisma and gift of oratory, which came to the fore when he stood before a crowd. On the eve of the offensive, Lockhart heard Kerensky speak at the Bolshoi Theatre, where women were so moved by his words of war that they sobbed and threw jewellery onto the stage when he finished.[8]

No amount of charisma or emphatically stated points, however, could undo the damage done to the army's morale by three years of grinding conflict. This meant that when it began in July, what came to be known as the Kerensky Offensive collapsed swiftly at the cost of tens of thousands of Russian lives. Disaster at the front bred dissolution in the cities. Petrograd's Second Machine Gun Regiment turned on its officers once news arrived that Kerensky's gambit had failed. They were joined by sailors from Krondstadt who brought thousands of already striking workers with them on a march to the Tauride Palace. There, they demanded that the Provisional Government cede all power to the Petrograd Soviet. Far from stirring soldiers and the workers who supplied them to embrace the war effort, Kerensky's offensive had validated the belief that the Provisional Government needed to quit the carnage and focus on revolution. The fiasco also confirmed Buchanan's observation that in trying to govern post-tsarist Russia against the will of its people, Kerensky and his ministers had 'undertaken a task beyond their strength'.[9]

The Provisional Government were not the only ones buckling under the strain of an unmanageable revolution and an unwinnable war. By the summer of 1917, Lockhart had reached the zenith of his influence among Britain's officials in Russia, who recognised and appreciated that he knew 'every grade of Russian society inside out'. The head of Petrograd's MI6 station, Samuel Hoare, thought Lockhart 'the most active and intelligent' British asset in the country. Whether Hoare wanted meetings with Chelnokov and Lvov or details on the army's supplies, he always went to Lockhart, who 'would immediately put me in touch' with the right people. Beneath the ambition and ability that earned him this success, however, Lockhart was being driven by personal despair and an obsessive need for distraction.[10]

As Europe was drifting from peace into war in the summer of 1914, Jean had given birth to a baby girl who died the moment she entered the world. Lockhart recalled himself responding 'mechanically' to this devastating moment, shuffling out of the hospital that same afternoon to 'order the tiny coffin' from the nearest carpenters. When accosted by a beggar on this nightmare errand, Lockhart stopped abruptly and unthinkingly shoved money into their outstretched hands. The stunned beneficiary of this numb generosity then turned and ran, seeing in the consul-general's eyes the absent gaze of a madman. To go by Lockhart's recollection of events, he never fully processed his first child's premature death. Nor did he offer support to a similarly traumatised Jean. Instead, while his wife grieved and suffered in the weeks following the tragedy, Lockhart retreated to the consulate with the aim to 'kill my thoughts with a surfeit of work'. He burrowed deeper into this workaholic bunker when his beloved brother Norman was killed at the Battle of Loos in September 1915, by which time Lockhart had become consul-general and could expand his workload to his heart's content. Given the option to take time away to process these personal catastrophes or bury the hurt in distracting labours, the choice was obvious to the ambitious young man.[11]

In the process of numbing his pain, Lockhart also damaged his relationship with Jean. As the war progressed and his anxieties mounted, Lockhart got further into the habit of spending dusk 'til dawn listening to gypsy bands and downing vodka. Sometimes Jean joined him in this and on other occasions of merriment but as early as February 1915 he observed that her 'nerves were all to pieces and she is very disenchanted'. This schism in the pair's wartime experience became a full marital rupture once Lockhart began seeking solace in the arms of another woman.

The timeline is murky, and his recollections are brief, but it seems that in the summer of 1917 – during which his diary lapsed for the first time – Lockhart commenced an affair with a woman he met on a night out at the theatre. She has gone through history with the name Madame Vermelle, but it has been recently argued that the woman was Vera Lutse, a Polish

soprano who later married a man named Vermel. It has also been suggested that Lockhart's lover was Alisa Maksimovna, whose husband was
a doctor with ties to the Bolsheviks. Under the leadership of the firebrand
Vladimir Lenin, this party of hard-line socialists had refused to cooperate with the Provisional Government and was the most anti-war faction
in Russia. They even derided the Socialist Revolutionaries and the more
moderate Mensheviks when they tried reaching across the aisle to Lvov and
Kerensky. Given Lockhart's free-wheeling attitude to fraternising across
ideological lines and enjoyment of subverting norms, the idea of his lover
being associated with Russia's most radical party is not beyond the realms
of possibility.

Bereft of solid evidence for this connection, however, we are left with
the conventional story of Madame Vermelle and her impact on Lockhart's
life. Within weeks of the affair commencing, news of the consul-general's
behaviour reached Buchanan either via Jean, her outraged friends or
the Okhrana, whom a Soviet journalist later claimed had been monitoring Lockhart's dalliance with the supposedly Bolshevik-connected
Vermelle. Regardless of how the information reached him, the elder diplomat responded sympathetically. He summoned Lockhart for a heart to
heart, during which the latter pledged to end the budding relationship.
As Lockhart admitted 'frankly and without excuses' in his memoirs, his
promise lasted all of three weeks. Left with no choice, Buchanan had
his consul-general recalled to Britain in September 1917 on the grounds
that manning Moscow's diplomatic fort had overworked him to the
point that his nerves were shot. Buchanan's excuse was a ruse to protect
Jean's dignity and Lockhart's reputation, but the cover story was not far
from the truth. Failing to reconcile himself to trauma while dealing with
the turmoil of post-revolutionary Russia, Lockhart had reverted to mindless self-indulgence as a coping mechanism. The result had been a personal
and, through it, professional breakdown.[12]

Lockhart's implosion came in tandem with that of his friends in the
Provisional Government. Lvov resigned as prime minister in July, putting

Kerensky in the unenviable position of leading a government that was irreparably damaged by military failures and sluggish revolutionary progress. Kerensky's approach to leading Russia didn't help matters. Dressed in a khaki uniform and, as a French diplomat recalled, 'installed like the emperor in the imperial Rolls Royce', the new prime minister took on the trappings of military dictator 'with an aide de camp covered in shoulder knots on his left, and a soldier sitting next to the chauffeur'. In this guise of Russia's strongman, Kerensky tried to keep both the Provisional Government and the war going. This was a near-impossible task. Over the summer of 1917, his regime was assailed by an attempted coup from a disgruntled general, riots in the cities, mass strikes in munitions and food factories and the empowerment of the anti-war Bolsheviks who, off the back of Lenin's savagely simple insistence on 'peace, bread and land' for the Russian people, became the largest party in the Petrograd Soviet by the end of August.[13]

As the wheels were falling off Kerensky's regime, Lockhart arrived back in London, the terminus of a bleak journey during which he kept no diary, for his 'mental anguish was extreme, and I wanted to forget'. After taking a few weeks' leave to commiserate with his parents over the loss of Norman, Lockhart dragged himself back to the Foreign Office with shoulders slumped and an expectation of being read the riot act by his superiors. Instead, no one much cared for his indiscretions with Madame Vermelle or the cover story that he was burned out. It was the first week of November 1917, and the world was spinning too fast for the follies of a troubled consul-general to matter. The second revolution prophesied by Lockhart had broken out, bringing the anti-war, anti-imperialist Bolsheviks to power. Now arose the spectre of Russia pulling out of the war and giving Germany the chance to unleash the full force of its armies on the British and the French. For the British government this was a disaster of unfathomable proportions. For Lockhart it was a gift. The Bolshevik revolution had erased his sins and his Russian expertise had positioned him to assume a crucial role in the unfolding drama – a role that would define his legacy and forever change his life.[14]

CHAPTER 4

AGENT OF BRITAIN

'Position of Lockhart is . . . unique'
— Oliver Wardrop

Throughout his travails in Malaysia and Russia, nervousness was a sensation that Lockhart seldom experienced. Neither angry sultans nor snooping Okhrana agents did much to dent the confidence of youth, which had always insulated him from care or concern. However, as the door to Number 10 Downing Street opened and he passed over its threshold, Lockhart felt his pulse quicken. It wasn't every day that a thirty-year-old consular washout was invited to brief the prime minister of Great Britain on the revolutionary present and uncertain future of one of the world's great powers.

Lockhart could at least take comfort from the fact that his reputation preceded him. In the weeks following his return from Moscow, he had been hounded by politicians and journalists in search of the truth behind what was really going on in Russia. As Kerensky was still clinging to power by a thread, Lockhart used the opportunity to try to rally support for his friend, penning an article for the *Daily Mail* under the anonymous guise of 'One Who Knows Him'. In the piece, Lockhart discussed 'the Real Kerensky', presenting him as both the 'symbol of Russia's agony' and the only man capable of pulling his beset country through the bedlam. This public show of support for Russia's knight in shining armour was well-meaning spin. In private conversations with government officials, Lockhart

shared a different view to that which he peddled to the British public. This
was that the Provisional Government was all but finished and the power
vacuum created by its collapse could only be filled by the Bolsheviks, whose
influence on the Petrograd Soviet was now greater than both the Socialist
Revolutionaries and the more moderate Mensheviks.[1]

Lockhart's prophecy was fulfilled in short order when, on 7 November,
Kerensky and his ministers were besieged in Petrograd's Winter Palace
by armed bands of Lenin's followers. This was the culmination of a plan
that had begun gestating weeks earlier in the mind of the Bolsheviks' chief
strategist, Leon Trotsky. Originally from the more moderate Menshevik
wing of the Social Democrats, Trotsky crossed over to the Bolsheviks in
the summer of 1917 after sensing that Kerensky's failed offensive and the
attempted coup that followed had raised the level of discontent in Russia
to a revolutionary boiling point. This put the Bolsheviks in the ascendancy,
for they were the only party in the country that had consistently opposed
the war. Having returned to Petrograd in early October after months of
exile in Finland, Lenin declared to Trotsky and his fellow Bolshevik leaders
that the time had come to wrench power from Kerensky's weakened grasp.

Like his embattled nemesis, Lenin was a public speaker of no mean
skill, albeit one whose refusal to countenance the views of others tended to
rub people the wrong way. This was where Trotsky came in. A smoother
operator when it came to arguing his points, Trotsky also possessed a capacity for strategic thought that complemented Lenin's rage-fuelled passion.
With Trotsky laying out the logistics of isolating garrisons loyal to the
Provisional Government, seizing control of Petrograd's train stations and
cutting the city's communications, the Bolsheviks now had a revolutionary
plan to back Lenin's vision.

It was the plan they executed on 7 November. 'All through that day,'
Meriel Buchanan recalled, 'there was a certain amount of firing going on
in the streets, and armoured cars and motor trollies full of soldiers were
going about' at liberty. This was because the Provisional Government was
in such disarray it couldn't summon enough soldiers to meet whatever

threat was brewing on the streets. As these small groups of Bolsheviks set about their task of taking over transport hubs and radio stations across Petrograd, Kerensky and his ministers battened themselves down in the Winter Palace, defended by 'a few Cossacks, a battalion of women and some children'. He held out for as long as he could but, with the building encircled by Bolsheviks and a mutineer-manned warship on the Neva River having put 'a shell hole in the walls of the Palace', Kerensky eventually fled in a car provided by the American embassy. Most of the remaining ministers were detained as bands of Bolsheviks stomped their way through the palace's halls, smashing furnishings and looting with abandon. It was with confidence that Lenin issued a proclamation later that day that 'the Provisional Government has been overthrown. State power has passed into the hands of the organ of the Petrograd Soviet of Workers'.[2]

Two nights after news of the Bolshevik takeover reached London, the War Cabinet's Lord Milner invited himself to a dinner that he knew Lockhart would be attending. He had been impressed by the consul-general during his visit to Russia and was unbothered by the circumstances surrounding his recall to Britain. Taking Lockhart aside before the first course was served, Milner asked for the young man's thoughts on what was transpiring in Russia, and the impact the Bolshevik coup would have on Britain's war effort. After days of reading sensational press coverage and gritting his teeth through the ill-informed opinions of friends who had never left Britain's shores, Lockhart was keen to share his opinions. He rejected the popular idea that Lenin and Trotsky were agents of the German government and that their revolution was a plot cooked up on the Wilhelmstrasse to bring down Russia from within. He also warned Milner that the Bolsheviks were no fly-by-night rabble. Unlike the Provisional Government, they commanded popular support and offered the kind of radical change that many Russians had long yearned for. Lockhart was convinced that the second revolution would stick and that if the British government wanted any kind of relationship with Russia during the war and after, it would have to treat with Lenin and Trotsky.

Intrigued, Milner set up a meeting between Lockhart and Lloyd George. Days later, as Lockhart was ushered into Number 10, he reflected that he was about to suggest to his prime minister that Britain extend a friendly hand to an anti-war government, presided over by a band of left-wing insurgents whose leader had openly called for global revolution. No wonder he was on edge.

Lockhart needn't have worried. He was not alone in appreciating the need to break bread with the 'reds'. Although the idea of recognising the Bolsheviks as Russia's legitimate government was rejected by the War Cabinet, it was nonetheless accepted that Lenin and Trotsky were now in charge of a country that, for all its front-line floundering, was still one of Britain's key wartime allies. Moreover, anxiety over losing this ally had heightened when Trotsky negotiated a ceasefire with Germany in early December. As Britain drifted further from Russia diplomatically so peace on the Eastern Front drew nearer and, with it, the prospect of Britain and France having to battle the kaiser's legions alone. Headed by the increasingly worn-down Buchanan, the diplomatic corps in Russia was not up to the task of bridging the divide between war-making Britain and the peace-hungry Bolsheviks. For this reason, Lloyd George decided days before seeing Lockhart that a fresh Anglo-Russian diplomatic connection – one more suited to unusual times – was needed. The purpose of their meeting was so the prime minister could confirm that the stories told of Moscow's *wunderkind* were true and that he was, as Milner insisted, the right man for this odd job.

Lloyd George made his decision quickly. Having been guided into the prime minister's study with a pat on the back and a remark that his youthful appearance didn't align with the wisdom of his reports, Lockhart was quizzed on Lenin and Trotsky, their base of support and the extent of lawlessness and food shortages in the cities. Satisfied with the answers he received, Lloyd George shook Lockhart's hand and told him not to get too comfortable in London.[3]

There was little chance of that happening. When he returned to Britain without a job in the autumn of 1917, one of Lockhart's backers in Whitehall,

Arthur Steel-Maitland, found him a position with the Department for Overseas Trade. Lockhart was assigned to the Russian desk but when the Bolsheviks seized power and Anglo-Russian relations broke down he was left without trade to handle. In search of something to do, he gave a talk to London's business leaders, warning them that it would be a mistake to 'abandon Russia and lose sympathy with her people, because a few wild demagogues had upset our hopes and calculations in the war'. Aside from this plea for a return to normalcy in Anglo-Russian economic relations, Lockhart spent the final months of 1917 bereft of purpose and in a state of impatient boredom. One of the few moments of excitement he experienced came in November, when an air raid struck London as he was preparing for a dinner party. Starved of drama, Lockhart revelled in the act of donning a tuxedo while German bombers swooped overhead. He took this attitude to Piccadilly tube station, which he found crammed with panicked Londoners seeking cover. Rather than staying underground with the masses, Lockhart proceeded across town on foot, arriving an hour late at his host's home only to find that no other dinner guests had thought it worth braving the bombs for a night of beefsteak and champagne.[4]

Blessed relief from a life so dull that he yearned for air-raids came on New Year's Day 1918, when Lockhart was invited to attend the first of what would become a score of meetings with the War Cabinet. If the transition from listlessness to attendance at the highest table in the land was not exciting enough, Lockhart was further energised when Milner informed him that in two weeks' time he would be sent to Petrograd as Lloyd George's representative, with a mission to establish a diplomatic link between Britain and the Bolsheviks. This brief was issued to Lockhart at about the same time that Buchanan was preparing to return home. No picture of health to begin with, the rail-thin ambassador had succumbed to stress and exhaustion since the Bolshevik takeover, during which he watched on appalled as Petrograd was consumed by 'a perfect orgy of drunkenness' in which 'not a night passes without the constant firing of rifles and machine-guns'. Lockhart, however, was not going to be Buchanan's replacement.

Nor would he reoccupy his old desk at the tiny Moscow consulate. Instead, he was returning to Russia with a status that lay beyond that of a consul-general or even an ambassador – he was to be Britain's Agent.[5]

This role was not created exclusively for Lockhart. Indeed, the idea of an Agent was not a wholly British one. At the time Lockhart met with Lloyd George, a French Agent was already operating in Ukraine and there were even discussions that he might oversee British interests in that country. This appointment by the Quai d'Orsay was not known to Lockhart at the time and so, after the bemusing title of British Agent was presented to him at the War Cabinet meeting, he researched its origins and meaning. The story he uncovered offered little clarity. In the aftermath of the Urabi Revolution of the 1880s in Sudan, Lord Cromer was given the dual status of consul-general and British Agent in Egypt. This bestowed on Cromer what he described as a 'vague but preponderant power', which he was to wield with the aim of ensuring British interests in Egypt were served in a time of revolutionary fallout. It was a testing assignment. Cromer was operating in a hostile environment where 'the British government never had any definite policy which was capable of execution'. In service to masters who didn't know what they wanted, a degree of 'elasticity' was necessarily built into Cromer's remit and activities.[6]

The same was true for Lockhart who, despite devouring Cromer's memoirs and spending the first week of January in meetings with members of the War Cabinet, Foreign Office mandarins and MI6 officers, was never given a clear outline of what an Agent did. Even the question of whom he was working for remained unanswered. Though nominally attached to the Foreign Office, Lockhart was under no obligation to take orders from Buchanan's replacement in Petrograd, Francis Lindley, or from Oliver Wardrop, who had taken over his former role as consul-general in Moscow. He was also operating beyond MI6's jurisdiction, despite some of his first meetings in Russia being with members of its Petrograd station. If lines of command and control were hard to trace in Lockhart's mission, so too were its objectives. He was told by Milner that he needed to 'do as much harm to the Germans as possible, to put a spoke in the wheels of the separate peace negotiations, and to stiffen by whatever means I could the Bolshevik resistance to German demands'. In short, his task was to keep the Bolsheviks in the war.

The phrase 'by whatever means' added a dangerous ambiguity to this ostensibly straightforward objective. One suspects this wording was deliberate on Milner's part. He understood the free-spirited way Lockhart had operated in Moscow and knew that a man of his abilities would only reach his potential under the loosest operational parameters. While this speaks to the faith Milner and Lloyd George had in Lockhart to determine the shape and style of his mission, it also indicates his expendability. As one historian of Britain's covert operations in Bolshevik Russia has put it, 'if any action he took turned out to be successful, or even promising, it could be backed by the West as the fulfilment of his mission. If that action faltered or led to trouble (let alone disaster), it could be repudiated as having no official sanction.' Lockhart was officially unofficial. Indispensable and yet disposable. Everything and nothing. This didn't mean, however, that Lockhart was going back to Russia armed only with his wits, insights and gift of the gab. In addition to being able to go over Lindley and Wardrop's heads and report directly to Milner, Lockhart was issued with his own set of ciphers that were different to those used by regular diplomats. He was also given discretionary funds and carte blanche to assemble a support team for his mission.[7]

The composition of this team indicates Lockhart's understanding of the need to be prepared for anything. For his deputy, the British Agent had initially wanted Reginald 'Rex' Leeper, an Australian-born Russia expert who was working for the Foreign Office's Political Intelligence Department. The two hit it off at their first meeting, but Leeper convinced Lockhart he would be of more use staying in Britain as the team's liaison to the Bolsheviks' ambassador in London, Maxim Litvinov. And so it proved. Leeper convinced Litvinov to draft a letter of introduction to Trotsky for Lockhart, in which the latter was described as 'a thoroughly honest man who understands our position and sympathises with us'.

With Leeper staying put, his spot as Lockhart's second in command was taken by Captain William Hicks, an expert on gas weapons who had served in Russia for most of the war and had contacts across the country. 'Lean and lanky' with 'a narrow face and iron-grey hair', Hicks was a stark visual contrast to the shorter, youthful-looking, auburn-haired Lockhart. He was also an excellent choice to replace Leeper. 'Hickie', as Lockhart affectionally called him, was dutiful, loyal and a tireless problem solver, who slipped effortlessly into the role of being the British Agent's right-hand man. Less reliable was a military orderly forced upon Lockhart by the War Cabinet. The ex-Irish Guardsmen, Lockhart recalled, 'was drunk when he joined me at the station, slept himself sober during the journey to Edinburgh, drank himself drunk again the next morning' and then 'offered to fight me for half a crown in Princes Street'.

The final two members of Lockhart's entourage were from neither the military nor the Foreign Office. Edward Birse, a Moscow-based businessman who had fled the country after the first revolution in 1917, was selected on account of his extensive contacts across Russia's industrial sector. The fourth team member, Edward Phelan, was an official from the Ministry of Labour whose socialist sympathies, it was thought, would help smooth relations with Russia's new masters. Once Lockhart arrived in Russia, he made three further additions to his team. These were Captain Denis Garstin, a machine-gunner whose flair with the pen got him out of the trenches in 1916 and working with Lockhart's friend Hugh Walpole producing propaganda; Captain Francis Cromie, the Petrograd embassy's vehemently anti-Bolshevik naval attaché; and Raymond Robins, an American Red Cross delegate who believed earnestly in the Bolshevik cause. Eclectic, multi-skilled and as ideologically incoherent as the man leading them, Lockhart's crew embodied the opaque nature of his mission.[8]

This mission began on 14 January 1918 when a naval cruiser ferried Lockhart, Hicks, Birse and Phelan across the North Sea from Scotland to Norway – the drunken orderly had 'lost himself on the way to Queensferry'. From Bergen, the remaining members of the team travelled cross-country by train into Sweden, where Lockhart reacquainted himself with his bohemian friend Lyki, who had fled Russia after the revolution for the safety of Stockholm. The once free-spirited theatre man was now a hardened reactionary, who regaled the Britons with terrifying stories of the Bolsheviks' brutality.

The team's next stop was Finland, where they planned to entrain from Kouvola to Petrograd. This was where their journey hit a snag. The revolution had now spread beyond Russia's borders and a conflict was raging between the Finland Socialist Workers' Party and forces loyal to the ousted conservative government. The main rail line into Russia had been damaged in the fighting, forcing Lockhart and his team to head south to Helsinki with the aim of taking a ship across the water to Petrograd. Having left Birse and Phelan at the station to guard their luggage, Lockhart and Hicks set off down the slush-snow-covered Aleksanterinkatu in search of accommodation. Instead, they found soldiers with rifles, whose incessant firing in their general direction warded them off proceeding further across town to the British embassy. The team spent an unpleasant evening trying to sleep in the station, taking turns to guard the luggage, listening to gun shots cut the night air and watching refugee families piling into trains that were not running. In the morning, however, their luck turned. Awakened from unsatisfactory sleep by a score of gunmen from the Socialist Workers' Party, the Britons were questioned as to their purpose in Helsinki. Thinking quickly in this tense moment, Lockhart produced his glowing letter of recommendation to Trotsky from Litvinov. Within an hour, the revolutionaries had arranged a train to ferry Lockhart and his team into Russia. They even carried the Britons' luggage to their cabins.

As dusk fell on 30 January 1918 Lockhart stepped back onto Russian soil, three months after being cast from it by Buchanan. Then, Petrograd had hummed with dissatisfaction at Kerensky and, in some quarters, excitement at the promise of things getting better once his Provisional Government collapsed. The betrayal of that promise was now starkly apparent. Shops had either been looted and abandoned or, if still open, had

near-empty shelves bearing goods that few could afford. Trams and trains
had ceased running and, for want of firewood and pay, no one was lighting braziers to melt the snow. Nor were they sweeping it from the streets,
leaving the impression that Petrograd was being consumed by the beast of
winter. 'The Imperial city', a French diplomat recalled, was 'already dead
and its magnificence will soon be a memory'. Prior to departing Russia
with her father, Meriel Buchanan found herself pondering similarly bleak
thoughts. She had watched the 'shrieking hooligans who slouched about the
streets drinking, shooting and marauding' even as the thick of winter set
in. 'These men,' she rued, 'unkempt, unwashed, unshaved, totally ignorant,
had become the rulers of Petrograd, the city built by Peter the Great as the
capital for his empire.'

Like the ambassador's daughter who hoped that Russia's soul could
yet be reclaimed, Lockhart's romantic notions of the country he had fallen
in love with took a beating once he walked through the desolate anarchy
of Bolshevik Petrograd. It broke his heart to see people shuffling hungry
through snow-clogged streets past the shattered windows of what had once
been fine houses. Under a flickering streetlamp on the Troiski Bridge,
he stopped his team's progress to regard a dead horse frozen solid to the
ground, abandoned by its master to become one with winter. 'Everyone
looks depressed and unhappy' was the bluntest summary he could muster to describe Russia's withering capital. The only silver lining was that
Petrograd's plight had lowered its rents and empowered those with money.
As Lockhart's people fell into the latter category, during their journey from
the station to the British embassy they were assailed by soldiers trying to sell
them white flour and fresh meat – the latter probably cut from the frozen
horse on the bridge. Having purchased these supplies for a song, Lockhart
took further advantage of the Bolsheviks' new disorder in the days that followed, by acquiring a well-appointed flat with a substantial wine cellar for
next to nothing from an aristocrat who had been left impoverished by the
ravages of revolution. This became the team's base of operations, serving as
both a living space and, sitting as it did on the Palace Quay less than a block

from the British embassy, a shadow island of His Majesty's Government amid the sea of revolutionary red.[9]

Lockhart's arrival on the embassy's doorstep and his manner of addressing Britain's diplomats – described by a contemporary as 'assertive and modest. Arrogant and humourlessly depreciative all at the same time' – confused minds and ruffled feathers. During one of their first meetings, the chargé d'affaires Francis Lindley gave the British Agent a dressing-down for daring to suggest that their government would not recognise the Bolsheviks as Russia's legitimate rulers, even though Lockhart had heard this first hand from almost everyone he met with in Whitehall. Lindley also tried to give the younger man advice on how to handle Trotsky and, in general, acted as if Lockhart worked for him. Equally bothered by the mysterious agent's presence, Moscow's consul-general Oliver Wardrop wrote sniffily to the Foreign Office that his experiences of Russia went back 'beyond the date of Lockhart's birth'. It was wholly unacceptable to Wardrop that this upstart, 'variously described' as 'ambassador, envoy, official representative' and more besides was using his own ciphers to send messages that no one at either the Moscow consulate or the Petrograd embassy could read. These complaints resonated with at least one embittered person in Whitehall, who leaked news of Lockhart's supposedly quiet mission to the press. Having been named as the government's 'unofficial agent' in *The Times*, Lockhart's 'precise position and powers' were then openly questioned in parliament. The foreign secretary, Arthur Balfour, responded blandly that Lockhart was simply representing the British government in its 'informal relations with the de facto government of Russia'. Beyond that, there was nothing to say. The mystery of the British Agent would continue.[10]

Lockhart tried to ignore the rumours and barbs and get on with his job, a key task of which involved striking up a rapport with Trotsky. It was 15 February and the Bolshevik Commissar for Foreign Affairs had just returned from a round of frustrating peace discussions with the Germans at Brest-Litovsk, a fortress town that had been abandoned to the invaders during the Russian army's retreat of 1915. Now, with the Germans advancing ever closer to Petrograd, Trotsky had travelled to Brest-Litovsk with a mission to prevent an even greater disaster than that which befell Russia three years prior. It was a humbling experience for the haughty architect of the Bolshevik takeover. Unwilling to accept Germany's peace terms, which demanded vast tracts of western Russia, yet plagued by the knowledge that his shambolic 'Red Army' could not resist an advance on the capital, Trotsky was in a rage when Lockhart first met him at the Bolsheviks' headquarters, the Smolny Institute. For all that the commissar's eyes shot daggers, the British Agent was fully aware that he was in the company of a well-refined and distinctly bourgeois revolutionary. The Bolsheviks whom Lockhart passed in Smolny's halls were scruffy and unbathed, sprawled across floors matted with cigarette butts and muddy boot prints. In contrast, Trotsky was sitting behind his polished desk, neatly dressed in a freshly laundered uniform. 'His nails,' Lockhart noticed, 'were carefully manicured.'

With his knack for reading people, Lockhart concluded from Trotsky's appearance and temperament that what hurt the preening revolutionary most was his disempowerment at Brest-Litovsk. The humiliation. The fact that the Germans were now the masters of *his* destiny. Trotsky quickly confirmed Lockhart's initial impression that a desperate man sat before him. Despite detesting the capitalist Western powers, the parlous state in which the Bolsheviks found themselves led Trotsky to put an interesting proposal to Lockhart – what if Britain and France sent troops to support the revolutionaries? While other diplomats might have scoffed at the idea of Allied soldiers coming to aid the 'reds', Lockhart had a more open-minded view of the situation. The Russo-German armistice of December was still barely holding, but given Trotsky's reluctance to surrender further Russian territory, a comprehensive peace deal seemed unlikely. The Bolsheviks were still at war with Britain and France's enemy. Moreover, that enemy was poised to march on Petrograd.

As Lockhart recorded in his diary, throughout February a sense of 'impending doom' gripped both his team and other Allied missions in the city, where few believed that the Red Army could do much to halt the German advance. Resigned to invasion, Allied ambassadors opted to evacuate. As one diplomat recalled, the final days of February at the French embassy were spent 'burning papers, dragging luggage about, nailing up packing cases or sealing trunks' while their American counterparts, 'having shown more panic than anyone else over this business', entrained eastwards 'taking the Chinese and, I believe, the Siamese ministers as part of their luggage'. The visible flight of the ambassadors further raised anxiety levels across Russia's capital, feeding the already overstuffed rumour mill. Amid whispers of German spies operating in the city, there were fears of a 'pro-Boche counter-revolution' breaking out. 'Our number,' Lockhart confided to his diary, 'seems up.' Unless of course, the Allies fulfilled Trotsky's wish and sent troops to Russia's rescue. Then, not only would the Germans be thrown back, but Britain and France would cement an alliance with the Bolsheviks with blood and gratitude.[11]

The British Agent's belief in this plan hardened during his subsequent meetings with Trotsky, which occurred almost daily as the threat to Petrograd grew. Snarling defiance, Trotsky asserted to Lockhart that if the Westerners abandoned Russia to German occupation, then the Bolsheviks would continue to 'wage partisan warfare to the best of their ability'. Lockhart was impressed by Trotsky's show of backbone and reported as much to Milner, along with a recommendation that Britain cease backing counter-revolutionary forces in Russia – a policy that the Allies had adopted in the autumn of 1917 – and instead send military aid to the Bolsheviks. While Lockhart could 'not pretend that co-operation will be easy', he argued that a unified Anglo-Bolshevik front was in Britain's best interests. 'If handled tactfully,' he argued, 'Trotsky can become a very valuable asset against Germany.' Indeed, he might even help Britain win the war.[12]

This was Lockhart's first test as Britain's Agent and, though his recommendations aligned with his mission's goals, they marked the first time in his career that his knowledge of Russia was questioned and, with it, his capabilities. His suggestion that Britain rally to the defence of Bolshevism

cut little sway with War Cabinet members like Lord Cecil, who was convinced that Trotsky was a German agent. Cecil also feared that a military
marriage of necessity with the 'reds' would 'discourage what remained of
the anti-Bolshevik elements in Russia' and further 'the spread of Bolshevik
propaganda in this country'. The former army attaché in Petrograd,
General Alfred Knox, was blunter in his criticisms. A career soldier who
had served in Russia since 1914 and developed a good relationship with
the tsar, Knox despised the Bolsheviks. Indeed, he loathed all radicals and,
decades later, was accused by Kerensky of backing the counter-coup against
the Provisional Government in the summer of 1917. At the very least, Knox
had a problem with Kerensky's British friend, whom he sneeringly referred
to as 'young Lockhart' when he was serving as Moscow's consul-general.[13]

Knox's derision turned to anger when Lockhart returned to Russia as
Britain's Agent. In response to the proposal for an alliance with Trotsky,
the attaché opined 'that Mr Lockhart's military advice is so bad that I hope
he will be told not to give a military opinion in future or be recalled'.
Knox also complained that Lockhart's friend Raymond Robins, who
despite being a Red Cross volunteer was fulfilling a similar Agent role for
the Americans, was 'a fanatic' for Bolshevism 'with the temperament of a
hero-worshipping schoolgirl'. This was not an unfounded belief. Lockhart
himself recorded Robins' opinion that Trotsky was 'the greatest Jew since
Christ'. With Robins in one ear and Trotsky in the other, it seemed to Knox
that Britain's Agent spoke to 'no one except Bolsheviks' and, as such, 'his
messages reflect only Bolshevik views'. Unmoved, Lloyd George continued
batting for Lockhart, reminding the War Cabinet that it 'should not refuse
the advice tendered to them by the British representatives in Russia' and
that 'the opinion he had formed of Mr Lockhart was such as to cause him
to hesitate before rejecting any advice he offered'. The prime minister,
however, was in an ever-shrinking minority.[14]

As these debates over Lockhart's competency raged, Lenin took the
matter of intervening on the Bolsheviks' behalf out of British hands. At
a tense meeting of the Bolshevik Central Committee, he indicated with

comic bitterness that while he was 'in favour of taking potatoes and weapons from the bandits of Anglo-French imperialism', he had little faith in a Bolshevik–Allied military partnership forming. At least not in time to save the revolution from being snuffed out by the Germans. Headstrong as ever, Lenin got his way. As Trotsky fumed, the Central Committee sent a delegation to Brest-Litovsk to make peace with the Germans before their armies reached Petrograd.

This decision was made just in time. Having commenced their offensive – the unsubtly named Operation Faustschlag (First Punch) – on 18 February, the Germans had steamrollered over what were once Russian lines, taking prisoners with ease and meeting little resistance. By 2 March, they were less than a hundred miles from the Russian capital. A day later, Lenin's representative at Brest-Litovsk signed a treaty to halt the attack – hopefully for good. The peace was punitive. The Bolsheviks were forced to cede Poland, Belarus and the Baltic States to Germany and to recognise the independence of Finland and Ukraine. In total, they lost nearly 40 per cent of their newly acquired country's agriculture and heavy industry. It was painful and humiliating, but for now it didn't matter. Revolutionary Russia was out of the war.[15]

The question for Lockhart was whether he was out of a job. His mission had been to establish contact with the Bolsheviks and keep them fighting the Germans. The successful completion of the first objective was meant to lead to the second's fulfilment, but Brest-Litovsk had wrecked this trajectory. Moreover, Lockhart had damaged his standing in Whitehall with his lauding of Trotsky and advocation of sending British soldiers to assist the Red Army. Wardrop smelled blood. With a Russo-German peace agreed, he asked the Foreign Office if Lockhart's position would now be 'regularised' and, if not, whether it would be 'best if he applied for a leave of absence'. Knox also weighed in, asking what purpose the British Agent now served.

The sage of Russia no more, Lockhart spat frustration into his diary over receiving 'long and stupid' and 'very depressing' telegrams from the

Foreign Office. His support-base in Whitehall collapsed further, with even Lloyd George letting Knox's attacks go unchallenged. Lockhart's great adventure was seemingly at an end. And yet, he refused to go quietly. Instead, as the ink dried on the Brest-Litovsk Treaty, Lockhart wrote to Milner, insisting that he would stay in Russia to explore the 'considerable possibilities of organising resistance to Germany'. It was a bold decision but, to Lockhart's determined mind, a justified one. He had suffered through scandals and returned empowered to Russia from the precipice of a mental and professional collapse, picking fights with doubters along the way. The British Agent had not been raised to be lowered, and he was far from being done. In fact, he was just getting started.[16]

CHAPTER 5

CROSSROADS

'Flirtation with the Bolsheviks is both wrong as a policy and immoral as a practice'

– General Alfred Knox

Acloud of ash was rising from the embassy's chimney, within which danced the odd stubborn scrap of burning paper. The smoke filled Lockhart's nostrils as he sighed deeply and crossed the building's threshold into the bedlam beyond. Luggage was piled haphazardly in the hallways and people were rushing back and forth to the accompaniment of an agitated voice shouting down a telephone receiver. Gliding through the tumult, Lockhart reached his quarry, Francis Lindley. The chargé d'affaires was in no mood to talk.

It was 28 February and German bombers were circling the skies over Petrograd. Lenin's delegation had left the city for Brest-Litovsk, but the Allies' ambassadors trusted neither the Bolsheviks to make peace nor the Germans to cease war. For this reason, they had decided to evacuate their embassies to Vologda, which a contemporary visitor described as a 'little, simple country town' 400 miles north of Petrograd, comprised of snow-capped 'log houses of one or two storeys'. While the Americans and the French favoured this idyll as their refuge, Lindley had devised a more ambitious extraction plan to relocate Britain's diplomats beyond Russia's borders to the safety of Helsinki. Lockhart had not come to request a seat on Lindley's train but to try skimming the cream of his staff with the aim of bolstering his team. It was a hopeless gambit. The chargé d'affaires was unwilling to release anyone into the hands of the dubious British Agent. If Lockhart insisted on continuing his work in Petrograd, he would have to make do with whoever else was foolish enough to remain in the doomed city.

Lockhart was too full of nervous excitement to feel slighted by the rejection. Shaking Lindley's hand, he took his leave from the embassy and strode out into the snow-blown streets of a city torn asunder by the forces of fatalism and hope. Like the Allied ambassadors, Petrograd's citizens believed the Germans' arrival to be imminent. Their attitudes to this threat varied. Many of the city's bourgeois saw the Germans as liberators who would kick out the Bolsheviks and restore Petrograd to its tsarist glory days. In the cabarets and opera houses, such people indulged in champagne-fuelled gaiety, even as German bombs fell on Warsaw train station. Petrograd's less fortunate shivered in fear of unknowns to come, while bandits pillaged whatever wasn't nailed down in the belief that the Germans would take all. The crime rate had spiked so much that Lindley had put extra guards and armoured cars outside his embassy and Lockhart had taken to carrying a pistol when walking the city's streets.

In truth, he relished the peril almost as much as he did the flight of the ambassadors. By removing themselves to either Helsinki or the provincial backwater of Vologda, the Allies' representatives were effectively cutting themselves off from the day-to-day machinations of Lenin and Trotsky. This was a boon for the ambitious British Agent, who was now the most closely connected Allied representative to the Bolshevik leaders and was in effective command of what remained of Britain's diplomatic corps in Petrograd.[1]

Once Lindley's train pulled out of the station Lockhart cabled Whitehall to confirm this welcome freedom. He wanted a guarantee that 'my position will remain independent and that I shall not be placed in any way under consul general at Moscow' – a reference to Wardrop who, like Lockhart, was staying on to keep some semblance of diplomatic connection to the Bolsheviks. The War Cabinet responded with a telegraphic shrug of the shoulders. The British Agent was always meant to operate independently of the regular diplomats. If the worst that could be expected from allowing this status to continue unfettered was the occasional irritatingly pro-Bolshevik communiqué, then it was worth keeping Lockhart in situ to see what benefits, if any, he could derive for Britain from the parlous situation. It was far from a ringing endorsement, but Lockhart would take it.[2]

The British Agent's first order of business was to relocate his mission from Petrograd to Moscow so he could maintain close liaison with the Bolshevik leaders. Both Lenin and Trotsky believed that the Brest-Litovsk Treaty was a stay of execution from the kaiser's armies and, when their advance inevitably resumed, Petrograd would be first in the firing line. For this reason, the Bolsheviks relocated their capital to Russia's second city in the first weeks of March 1918. Security concerns aside, this move symbolised an important break with the tsarist past. By leaving the grand boulevards and European-style architecture of Petrograd behind, the Bolsheviks were starting a new chapter of Russia's history in Moscow – an ancient capital reborn as a red bastion from which the final repulse of the Germans would be planned, and the global revolution unleashed.

The evacuation from Petrograd was carried out swiftly and in secret, with Trotsky leaving on a late-night train guarded by hundreds of Latvian Riflemen who had sworn to give their lives to protect Russia's newly appointed War Commissar. In testament to the success of Lockhart's charm offensive, Trotsky offered him and Hicks a place on his train and invited the Britons to dine with him during the evening journey. Over a hearty meal of cabbage soup, fried potatoes and veal, Trotsky – clad in khaki and talking only of bullets and bayonets – insisted to Lockhart and Hicks that when the fighting resumed his fledgling Red Army would be ready and able to defend the revolution against Germany. The idea seemed fanciful, but Lockhart couldn't help but be impressed by Trotsky's passion and certainty.[3]

The train arrived on the morning of 17 March and Lockhart and Hicks bade farewell to the War Commissar, after which they got to work establishing their new base of operations at the Hotel Elite. While the building itself was well guarded and provisioned, the city beyond its grand foyer bore an ominous resemblance to the one Lockhart had just left. Moscow's rich and prosperous anxiously awaited the Germans' arrival while anarchists and brigands roamed the streets, robbing and murdering at will.

Indifferent to the dysfunction and danger, Lockhart was determined to reacquaint himself with his old stomping grounds. One night, he and Hicks took in an opera at the Okhotny Ryad, which despite the throes of revolution was still packed with Moscow's bourgeoisie, seeking drunken respite from the bleak reality beyond the theatre's doors. Lockhart settled into a plush seat and imagined he was back with his intelligentsia friends in the carefree days before the war, discussing the thoughts of Nikolai Tchaikovsky or the words of Leo Tolstoy. The happy moment was fleeting. No sooner had the audience lights dimmed then the doors of the viewing balcony were violently flung open and armed men in balaclavas surrounded Lockhart and the other patrons. Jewellery and watches were handed over in a panic by those around him as Lockhart dug into his pockets for roubles, gloomily accepting that to survive the night he would have to return to his hotel suite poorer. However, when the brigands reached him and Hicks the robbery abruptly ended. To the pair's shock, the chief of the assailants threw up a salute and declared that 'We do not rob Englishmen. I apologise for the state of my country which forces me to adopt this manner of earning a living.' He and his gun-toting comrades then left the stunned Britons to enjoy their evening.[4]

When not dicing with the dangers of revolutionary Moscow's nightlife, Lockhart embraced his workaholic tendencies. He had chosen to establish his office at the Hotel Elite on Petrovka Street, putting him within walking distance of the Hotel Metropole – the first Russian building Lockhart stepped into in 1912, which had now become the meeting place of the Soviet Congress. In keeping the revolutionaries close, Lockhart's approach to Allied–Bolshevik relations was the antithesis of that practised by the diplomats at Vologda, where the eighty-year-old American ambassador David Francis spent much of his time hosting afternoon teas to which the local Soviet representative was seldom invited. Devoid of the threat of violence and brigandage, the diplomats of Vologda viewed the revolution from afar, playing card games and enjoying good-natured debates over whose countries had the deadliest snakes. In Moscow, meanwhile, Lockhart became a familiar face at the Soviet Congress and met almost daily with Trotsky. He also spent time with Lenin who, unlike his energetically verbose War Commissar, 'rarely wasted a word' and had an understated and unnerving calmness about him. The father of the revolution was altogether too cold a man for the British Agent's comfort.[5]

Regardless, Lockhart resolved to ingratiate himself with both Bolshevik leaders. How else could he accomplish his aim of persuading them to restore the Eastern Front? This, both Lockhart and the Allied war planners believed, was imperative to bring the war to a victorious conclusion. As feared, the Brest-Litovsk Treaty had led to the Germans transferring troops westwards, imperilling the British and the French who were still waiting for the Americans to arrive on European shores in substantial numbers. Berlin's investment in its gains at Russia's expense, however, combined with the lack of threat posed by the shambolic Red Army, also meant that a sizeable German force remained in the east. Enough, it seemed, for the Germans to tear up the Brest-Litovsk Treaty and march their armies unopposed through Russia to seize the northern Arctic ports of Murmansk and Archangel, at which the Allies had stored thousands of tonnes of bullets, shells, rations and vehicles. The British and the French feared that this invasion of Russia, combined with a renewed German offensive in France, would bring the kaiser victory. The cocksure British Agent, however, believed he could prevent this disaster. There was, as he put it to the Foreign Office, still 'a game to be played' in Russia.

The question was how to correctly move the pieces on the board. The Allies conceived of two options to thwart Germany, both of which required the reconstitution of the Eastern Front. The first option was to convince the Bolsheviks to rejoin the war. This was something that Lockhart believed possible. Trotsky had repeatedly told him that Brest-Litovsk was merely a ceasefire, and once it inevitably broke, the Red Army would wage a 'holy war' on reactionary Germany to defend the revolution. The second option was to move Allied troops onto Russian territory to engage the Germans, preferably with the Bolsheviks' blessing, but without it if necessary. Most Allied leaders lacked confidence in the Red Army's fighting ability and, unlike Lockhart, refused to believe Trotsky's claim that the Bolsheviks were eager to recommence a war from which they had just extracted themselves. In the Allies' corridors of power, therefore, the landing of troops seemed the only option.[6]

The plan was of a scale to match its hoped-for objective of ending the Great War. British and French marines would land at Murmansk and Archangel, where they would secure the precious stores of ammunition, food and fuel, creating a foothold from which to reopen the Eastern Front. Meanwhile, the Japanese would disembark at Vladivostok on Russia's Pacific coast. There, they would seize the 600,000 tons of munitions stored in and around the town before entraining westwards along the Trans-Siberian railroad, crossing the vastness of Russia to link up with the Western Allies and enter the fray. Hopes were also high that the Czech Legion would join this renewed campaign. This 40,000-strong force of well trained and well-equipped men had been fighting for the Russians but, after Brest-Litovsk, had refused to lay down their arms. They wanted to relocate to the Western Front and continue the struggle against the Austro-Hungarian Empire, from which they sought to carve out an independent Czechoslovak state after victory was achieved. In the early spring of 1918, however, the Czech Legion was stranded east of Ukraine. This left them far from the Western Front but well placed to form the vanguard of the Allies' fresh assault on the Germans from the east.

The Allied intervention plan was ambitious to the point of being fan-tastical, but there were grounds to believe the Bolsheviks might accept

imperialist boots marching across red Russia's soil. When German-backed
Finnish troops threatened Murmansk in early March, Trotsky approved
the landing of 170 British marines to assist the Bolsheviks in repelling the
invaders. Likewise, the Bolsheviks gave the Czech Legion permission
to take the Trans-Siberian railway east so that they could take ship from
Vladivostok on an odyssey across oceans to get to the fighting in France. In
tandem with the Bolsheviks' seemingly welcome attitude to Allied soldiers
on their territory, the French consul-general Fernand Grenard discussed
the idea of using French military advisors to bring the Red Army up to
scratch, while Trotsky doubled down on his narrative of defiant resistance
to Germany by asking Lockhart for Allied help to resume the fight.

Lockhart was not the only Allied representative who warmed to this
idea. His friend Raymond Robins agreed that an Allied–Bolshevik partnership offered the best chance of defeating Germany and, once the war
was won, an excellent platform on which to build a peaceful world order.
The French government's Agent in Russia, Jacques Sadoul, thought likewise and harangued Paris for an agreement to provide military aid to the
Bolsheviks and recognise the legitimacy of their regime. In the spring of
1918, therefore, Lockhart was one of a small group of insiders in Russia
who saw a window – small yet teeming with possibilities – in which the
communist East and the capitalist West could have laid foundations for a
very different relationship to that which developed in the decades to come.[7]

Not for the first time in his career, Lockhart's ambitions were shattered
by the reality in which his political masters dealt – specifically, the reality of
their contempt for the Bolsheviks and indifference to their wishes. When
rumours of the Japanese plan to land troops at Vladivostok began swirling
around Moscow in early March, Trotsky voiced his concerns to Lockhart.
The Bolsheviks may have been pragmatic enough to accept a minor British
intervention at Murmansk, but they were too suspicious of Tokyo's intentions to countenance thousands of Japanese soldiers marching across Siberia
in the general direction of Moscow. Trotsky's fears were justified. The
Japanese intended to create a buffer state in Siberia that would shield their

home islands from the spread of Bolshevism while expanding Japan's sphere of influence at Russia's expense, strengthening the aspirant nation in anticipation of a realigning of the international order after the war's conclusion. The British foreign secretary, Lord Balfour, assured Lockhart that this was not the case, and that the Japanese were interested only in securing the stores at Vladivostok and taking the fight to the Germans. Apart from feeling affronted at being lied to, Lockhart seems to have taken Balfour's missive as an insult to his intelligence. Why else would the thirty-year-old British Agent reply to the seasoned foreign secretary with impudent mockery, bluntly asking him, 'Can you honestly expect any Russian to believe this? Are there any English who know Japanese who would believe this?'

Perhaps the empowerment proffered by the ambassador's flight to Vologda had gone to his head. Maybe it was the stress of life in semi-lawless Moscow or exasperation at yet another rejection of his viewpoint. Whatever the reasons, Lockhart's exchanges with Whitehall on the issue of Allied intervention became increasingly barbed over the spring of 1918. Having pointed out that, even if Tokyo was in earnest, the Bolsheviks' *perception* of their intervention was what mattered for the future of Allied–Bolshevik relations, Lockhart implored the Foreign Office to realise that Japan's incursion would 'rouse [the] greatest indignation among every class of Russian'. In a move that confirmed Whitehall's suspicions that Lockhart 'proposed to play with the Bolsheviks' and had become hopelessly 'entangled in their webs', the British Agent forwarded a warning from Trotsky to the Foreign Office. In it, the War Commissar declared that if the Western Allies did nothing to either prevent Japan's march across Siberia or condemn it once it happened, then all 'socialist Russians would regard this action as a direct result of a secret understanding between the Allies and Germany and England and America would get the blame'. When the Foreign Office responded by calling Trotsky a hypocrite for opposing the Japanese expedition while asking for Western Allied assistance, Lockhart fired back with a salvo of condescension. It 'must be impossibly difficult', he mused haughtily, 'for anyone in England to follow' events in distant Russia.

However, for those select few like himself who were on the ground and knew the 'facts' of the situation, Japan's intervention was clearly a disastrous idea that would kill any notion of Allied–Bolshevik rapprochement. For this reason, Lockhart requested that the Foreign Office 'empower me to inform Lenin that [the] question of Japanese intervention is shelved'.[8]

Lockhart was torn to shreds for his impudence. On Foreign Office minute sheets, various mandarins scrawled out their views that the British Agent was either a Bolshevik sympathiser or simply 'hysterical', his communiqués 'impertinent in tone and substance'. Knox once again demanded his recall while Lord Cecil quipped that 'Mr Lockhart's advice may be bad, but we cannot be accused of having followed it'. It fell on Balfour to collate this venom into an official response to Lockhart that was professionally polite yet laced with reproach and threat. There was much talk of a 'misunderstanding' between the British Agent and the Foreign Office, amid assurances that 'we wish to know exactly what you think', given that 'you have personal knowledge of the Bolshevik leaders which I do not possess'. This personal knowledge, however, was the problem. It was made clear to Lockhart that his opinions would only be valued if they were unbiased which, coloured by his closeness to Trotsky and the influence of Robins, they clearly were not. To Balfour's mind, facts were facts, however unpleasant Lockhart and his 'red' friends might find them. Acknowledging that Trotsky had asked for Allied help, Balfour explained in a schoolmasterly manner that 'there are only two approaches through which Allied aid can reach Russia. One is on the North, the other on the East. We have received no invitation to use the first and the very suggestion that Japan should use the second, under whatever safeguards for the integrity and security of Russia, is seemingly regarded as an intolerable wrong.' For Russia to survive, Lockhart had to 'induce those who at the present moment control her destiny to see facts as they are' and to welcome Allied intervention from whosoever was willing to offer it.

The phrase 'who at the present moment control' Russia caught Lockhart's attention. In one of his more blistering missives to the Foreign

Office, he had poked the bear by suggesting that the real purpose of the Allied landings was not to fight the Germans but to usurp the Bolsheviks. This inference that regime change was the aim of Allied policy elicited another slap on the wrist from Balfour, who reminded Lockhart that it 'had been repeatedly and clearly explained' to him that 'His Majesty's Government have no desire to interfere in the internal affairs of Russia but are only concerned in the vigorous prosecution of the war'. This dressing-down came with yet another guarantee that Tokyo also had no interest in Russia's internal politics and its Siberian expedition was concerned only with opening a second front against the Germans. No one, Balfour assured the British Agent, was coming to put the Bolsheviks to the sword.[9]

Lockhart didn't buy it. His closeness to the Bolshevik leadership – and with it, his immersion in their suspicions of Western intentions – doubtless played a part in informing his view. However, logic also dictated that people who believed that Trotsky and Lenin were German agents and their revolution was a threat to Western civilisation would use the excuse of war to wipe out Bolshevism. There was, moreover, a force within Russia that could seemingly make this dream a reality. In the aftermath of the 1917 revolution, dissident generals relocated their troops to the Caucasus, Siberia and the Don region south of Moscow, with the aim of waging a counter-revolutionary struggle against the Bolsheviks. These forces – known as the Whites – were disorganised and beset by disagreements over who or what should fill the power vacuum once they retook Russia. Some favoured another attempt at parliamentary democracy. Most wanted tsarist autocracy restored and the godless Bolsheviks destroyed. Despite lacking unity of aims, the Whites' counter-revolutionary intentions were solid enough to both concern the Bolsheviks and intrigue the Allied leaders, who yearned for Russia to quit its revolutionary experiment and get back to fighting Germany.

As Lockhart well knew, the Allies had been supporting the Whites for months. In the autumn of 1917, the US president, Woodrow Wilson, authorised secret payments to the White generals and deployed America's consul-general in Petrograd, DeWitt Poole, to southern Russia to liaise with the Don Cossacks, who were the most loyal and capable of tsarist troops. Poole recommended the release of millions of additional roubles to fund these White forces and, upon returning to Petrograd, persuaded his French and British counterparts to do the same. Poole's chief spy, Xenophon Kalamatiano, also established a network of agents across Russia whose task was to gather intelligence on the Red Army's capabilities and distribute funds to anti-Bolshevik groups. Kalamatiano was one of many Allied agents involved in such subversive work in the spring of 1918. Another revolution wrecker of note was Captain George Hill of the Royal Flying Corps, who had arrived in Petrograd in 1917 to train the Russian air force but, in the wake of the revolution, started working for MI6 under the codename IK8. A cavalier adventurer with a mind fit for mayhem, Hill relished his mission of hindering the encroaching Germans by whatever means necessary, to which end he led 'a splendid band of irregular troops comprised of ex-Russian officers', blowing up fuel depots and sabotaging communications infrastructure in Ukraine. At the same time, Hill ran a secret courier network of over twenty agents who sewed documents into the lining of their coats to move secret information – often from counter-revolutionary groups in Moscow and Petrograd – out of Russia and back to Britain.[10]

Like the money being funnelled to the Whites, Lockhart knew of Hill's activities. Shortly after relocating to Moscow he got in touch with the MI6 man, who revealed that he had full government support to engage in anti-Bolshevik operations. Lockhart also realised that Allied agents who *favoured* a rapprochement with the Bolsheviks were denied such backing. Robins spent much of the spring travelling between Lenin's office at the Kremlin and the makeshift American embassy in Vologda, desperately trying to conjure an agreement from Washington to send aid to the Bolsheviks. His mission was as hopeless as that of the similarly pro-Bolshevik Sadoul, whose dogged insistence that the Allies cooperate with Lenin and Trotsky led the American ambassador, David Francis, to conclude that he was a double agent.[11]

Lockhart liked Robins and, though he found the Frenchman a bit highly strung, he mostly agreed with Sadoul. His heart was with these men who sought to get Washington and Paris to recognise the Bolsheviks as Russia's legitimate rulers, and give tacit endorsement to their revolution's gains. The British Agent's inner Macgregor – adventurous and guided by emotion – informed his sympathy for Robins and Sadoul's out-of-the-box thinking. The colder pragmatist in Lockhart, however, accepted that his mission was not to help the Bolsheviks but to defeat Germany. He had hoped to achieve this by granting the Bolsheviks' wish for Japan to stay out of Siberia while gaining their consent for Western Allied troops to land at the Arctic ports. In the face of refusals from both Whitehall and the Bolshevik leaders to agree to these terms of intervention, Lockhart was left with a Gordian knot that could only be cut with compromise. The decision he faced in May 1918 was what form this compromise would take.

In his memoirs, Lockhart placed the location of his decision at Vologda, which he visited in the first week of May to discuss Allied intervention policy with the émigré diplomats. By the time the British Agent set out from Moscow for this meeting, Robins had folded his cards and was preparing to return to the USA. Having noted defeatedly in his diary that 'the tide was at ebb now and we are alone in all matters', Robins decided on a final gambit to broker an Allied–Bolshevik accord by carrying a personal letter from Lenin to Wilson. Any hopes he nursed of convincing his president to treat with the Bolsheviks were dashed by the fact that, as Britain's intelligence chief in Washington reported, 'Colonel Robins is not taken seriously here and will not be received by President Wilson.' Senators, congressmen and the chiefs of staff also ignored Robins' letter, which further crushed his already fractured spirits. Sadoul, meanwhile, had run afoul of the French ambassador Joseph Noulens. A passionate anti-Bolshevik, Noulens refused to tolerate Sadoul's red streak and so confiscated his ciphers, like a parent taking away a troublesome child's favourite toy. By sticking to their impossible task of uniting the Allies and the Bolsheviks, Robins and Sadoul had played themselves out of the game.[12]

Lockhart feared this fate and accepted that disempowerment lay in his future if he continued to butt heads with Whitehall. In Malaysia, he had failed as a rubber planter and in pre-revolutionary Moscow he had dashed his budding career on the rocks of feckless passion. He had been a loser before. He refused to be a loser again. And so, 'to escape the stigma of having stood out against the united opinion of all the other Allied representatives . . . I capitulated', and agreed with the worthies of Vologda that Allied troops would have to land in Russia whether Trotsky liked it or not. Brandy and port were drunk. Pats on the back were had and Ambassador Francis reported to Washington that 'Lockhart strongly favours Allied intervention with or without Soviet approval'. This, at least, was the story Lockhart told in his memoirs. In truth, weeks before this Road to Damascus moment, the British Agent had already begun his turn against Lenin and Trotsky for reasons that belied his later claims to pragmatic careerism. Rather, it was the two most powerful forces in Lockhart's life – the allure of a woman and the promise of adventure – that sent him on the path to plotting the Bolsheviks' destruction.[13]

CHAPTER 6

DOUBLE GAME

*'I knew nothing about spying and very little about the secret
service except its existence.'*

– Robert Bruce Lockhart

t started with a handshake. Briefly, their eyes met. Pleasantries were
exchanged. A nod, a smile and then a return to mingling with others. It
was an easily forgotten moment, but they would both remember it forever.
Moura Benckendorff was unlike any woman Lockhart had met. 'Slim, with
dark hair and eyes which, in tranquillity looked like wells of melancholy
and danced with merriment when she was amused', she was 'attractive
beyond all Russian women of her generation'. This was the passionate Scot's
superficial first impression. In the weeks after first meeting her at a party in
Petrograd on 2 February 1918, however, Lockhart discovered that Moura
was more than a pretty face. She 'was not merely fascinating' to talk to
but 'remarkably well-read, highly intellectual and wise beyond her years'.
These qualities gave Moura entry into all strata of society. 'Men adored her,'
Lockhart recalled, 'especially authors, composers, painters and poets' but
this was not the limit of her talent for seduction. Moura was also capable
of melting the hardened exteriors of diplomats, generals and other men of
power and influence. At a pre-war ball in Berlin, she was asked by Kaiser
Wilhelm II to dance multiple times. No less than an emperor, Lockhart
succumbed to Moura's allure. His admiration of her mind and yearning
for her body increased with each encounter, either at dinner parties where

Lockhart grew irritated at the presence of other guests, or on rare occasions when they took freezing moonlit strolls together along the Neva River. By the time he relocated to Moscow, barely a month after first meeting her, Lockhart had fallen 'desperately in love' with Moura.[1]

There was much in her background to explain the infatuation. Moura Zakrevsky was born to a noble Ukrainian family in 1892 and raised among servants and society gatherings. Her father was a high-ranking tsarist official and, as a young girl, she was a feature of the lavish dinner parties at the family's estate at Berezova Rudka, where she would sing and dance for the guests. Moura loved the attention. She relished the pomp and, as she grew older, she resolved to continue this life of gaiety and privilege, marrying an Estonian count named Djon Benckendorff in 1911. At Yendel – the couple's manor house outside Tallinn – Moura established herself as a socialite par excellence, drawing esteemed guests from St Petersburg, Paris, Berlin and Kiev. The hostess soon became a mother, giving birth to Pavel in 1913 and Tania in 1915. With a wealthy and handsome husband, two healthy children and a life of indulgence in which, even among emperors and statesmen, she shone as the star attraction; Moura, it seemed, had it all.

Except that, like Lockhart, she was inherently restless and easily bored by her spouse. Djon was a buttoned-down sort, content to while away his days at Yendel chopping wood in the surrounding forest and basking in the solace of country life. When war broke out, however, duty compelled Djon to leave his idyll and become a staff officer in the tsar's army. Moura, for her part, refused to sit placidly at home awaiting his return. Drawn like a moth to the flames of wartime Petrograd, she regularly took the 200-mile train journey to the Russian capital, where she threw herself into the champagne circuit and entertained actors and poets. Like the British Agent with whom she would fall in love, Moura struck a balance in her socialising between feckless pleasures and political intrigue. At her and Djon's apartment in Petrograd, she established a salon to host tsarist officials and foreign diplomats, including many from the British embassy. She had a particular fondness for the latter clients. As a teenager, Moura had lived with her father in London when he worked at the Russian embassy. There, she learned to speak English fluently and developed Anglophile tendencies that stayed with her forever.

Her affection for the British drew Moura into Lockhart's orbit long before their first encounter in February 1918. Yendel being near to the Royal Navy's base at Tallinn, she hosted parties for the British officers stationed there. Through these gatherings, Moura struck up a friendship with Lockhart's future associate Francis Cromie, who was the kind of dashing ladies' man to whom the countess gravitated. Handsome men in uniform were not Moura's only points of contact with the British. In Petrograd she befriended Meriel Buchanan, with whom she volunteered as a nurse at a military hospital. Through Meriel and Cromie, Moura became a familiar sight at the British embassy, where she impressed George Buchanan, who gave his daughter's intelligent and enchanting friend a job translating British propaganda into Russian. This led to Moura working alongside Denis Garstin before he joined Lockhart's team in 1918. If becoming part of the furniture at the British embassy wasn't enough, Moura also made friends with the Royal Air Force officer cum MI6 saboteur George Hill, who attended her salons to eavesdrop on diplomatic conversations. So enmeshed was Moura in Petrograd's British community, she attended the last Christmas party held at the embassy by the Buchanans in 1917 where, Meriel recalled, 'we drank champagne and laughed to hide the sadness in our hearts'. No doubt it was a time for tears. As an instinctive liberal with a penchant for parties, Moura was wary of the fanatically serious Bolsheviks and their plans to upturn the carefree world she adored.[2]

Thankfully, Countess Benckendorff was nothing if not adaptable. Even before the Bolsheviks came to power, Moura found a vocation that equipped her for life in a Russia where revolution and intrigue would supplant banquets and balls. At her salons, she developed a knack for acquiring information through disarming chatter and, through her work with Garstin, she experienced the thrill of being involved in subversion and propaganda. Inevitably, the adventurous socialite dipped her toes into the spy game. As Hill recalled of one of his visits to 'Madame B's' salon in the summer of 1917, his host 'was in the Russian counter-espionage service and made it her business to collect any pro-German Russians at her house'. Hill's suggestion that Moura was working for the Provisional Government to sniff out pro-German traitors seems fanciful, particularly given the direction his story of 'Madame B's' took in his memoirs. As Hill told it, while at Moura's salon he deliberately 'gave tongue' to a group of pro-German aristocrats. This led to him being tailed home by two men, one of whom he ended up 'running through' with a swordstick in an alley-way brawl. Fearing for his life the second attacker fled, leaving the heroic British spy standing tall.

Like a lot in Hill's memoirs, this account of blood on Petrograd's streets and intrigue in Moura's apartment reads as a dubious cloak-and-dagger yarn. And yet, his conclusion that Moura was spying on her clients cannot be dismissed. She had a connection – allegedly, a romantic one – to Kerensky at the time Hill's story took place and, given the Provisional Government's quest to keep Russia in the war, it makes sense that the prime minister would have deployed a well-placed asset to uncover traitors who wanted an accord with Germany. It is also notable that both the French and Russian intelligence services believed that Moura was working either against the Germans or possibly *for* them as a double agent during the war. Some members of Britain's intelligence community shared this view, interpreting her ingratiation into the British embassy as an infiltration operation. It is true that Moura used her time with the Buchanans to acquire information – she admitted as much to Lockhart years later. The question of what she did with this information remains ambiguous, but it is unlikely given that Cromie, Hill, Lockhart, Garstin and Hicks all came to trust her, that Moura was working against British interests. As one MI6 officer concluded when assessing the mysterious socialite, Moura had 'a flair for getting herself into all sorts of compromising situations' and was 'a fund of information on all spheres of society'. She was also, however, a 'staunch upholder of all the British Empire stands for'.[3] These were some of the many reasons why Moura fit perfectly into Lockhart's world of obscure intentions and unclear parameters.

Her immersion into the British Agent's life had intensified in the weeks after the Brest-Litovsk Treaty was signed, during which the pair acted like the war was a million miles away. Lost in a burgeoning courtship of sleigh rides, effortless conversations and drink-fuelled evenings with Cromie, Hicks and Garstin, Moura recalled these as 'the nice, happy times' when Bertie became her 'baby boy'. While their affair had not yet been consummated physically, they were connecting intellectually and emotionally in a manner beyond that of friends. In the process, they were paying little mind to either Djon or Jean. The former had returned to Yendel in fury after the Bolshevik revolution. As a patriotic tsarist, Djon couldn't countenance throwing in his lot with Lenin. This led to a souring of his relations with Moura who, despite her wariness of the Bolsheviks, accepted that tsardom had had its day. In other words, Moura had an open-minded view of the situation that aligned more with Lockhart's opinions than her husband's.

Lockhart was on a similar path to detachment from Jean, who had stayed in Britain when he returned to Russia in January 1918. The first letters he sent home were affectionate and open, discussing his concerns for the mission while offering words of reassurance that all was well and that he loved her deeply. A combination of Jean's responses – in which she warned Lockhart that his 'reports have no sympathy' in Whitehall – his courting of Moura and the intensity of his work, however, changed things. Consumed with all things Russian, Lockhart gradually switched from penning heartfelt missives to passing brief tidings to Jean via Rex Leeper, who became a conduit for the troubled pair. Doubtless Jean sensed that her husband was gleefully leaping down the Russian rabbit hole of intrigue, networking and, even with Germans at the gates and Bolsheviks in charge, socialising. This led Jean to suggest that she join him in Moscow. Her feelings of estrangement heightened further when Lockhart responded via a Whitehall intermediary that revolutionary Russia was too dangerous a place for her request to be accepted.[4]

Lockhart had Moura in mind when composing this response, but he also had more credible reasons to keep Jean away. Aside from the perils of life in Russia's near-lawless cities, he was consumed at this time with adapting his team to its new post Brest-Litovsk mission. When Lindley had evacuated Petrograd in the final week of February, he had refused to give Lockhart any of his staff. This did not mean, however, that the British Agent was left alone. Hicks was loyal to a fault and Garstin was engaged in the most interesting wartime assignment he'd ever had. As such, both agreed to stay on with Lockhart in Moscow. Cromie took his duty of keeping Russia's Baltic Fleet out of German hands seriously and spent the spring making plans to scupper its ships in the event of a German advance. To ensure he was in place when the time came to execute this grand act of sabotage, after Hicks and Lockhart left Petrograd, Cromie took effective control of Britain's abandoned embassy building on the Palace Embankment, and kept in close touch with his compatriots in Moscow. Once he had arrived in the Bolsheviks' new capital and established himself at the Hotel Elite, Lockhart was pleasantly surprised to find that three volunteers had chosen to forsake following Lindley into exile in favour of joining his mission. These new additions to the team were Guy Tamplin and George Lingner, who specialised in ciphering, and Captain Alfred Hill (not to be confused with George Hill), who had been in Russia since 1914 doing intelligence work for the army.

Beyond this core, Robins continued providing information until he left for America in May, and Lockhart also kept in contact with Hill from MI6 who, like the British Agent, had been told by his superiors that he could 'remain in Russia with a fairly free hand'. The *Manchester Guardian*'s correspondent in Russia, Arthur Ransome, was also an important contributor to Lockhart's team. Like Robins, the left-wing journalist was enamoured of the revolutionary moment, to the extent that he became romantically involved with Trotsky's secretary. Having taken a room at the Hotel Elite only a few doors down from Lockhart's suite, Ransome would often swing by to provide the British Agent with intelligence. This paved the way for

Ransome's official recruitment into MI6 in September 1918. Rounding out
Lockhart's new team was Moura, who maintained contact with Cromie in
Petrograd and after relocating to Moscow in April shared whatever useful
pieces of information she acquired with her dashing lover.[5]

As part of his team's reconfiguration, Lockhart let Birse and Phelan go
home and, in March, cabled Whitehall to request that the military careers
of Cromie, Hicks and Garstin 'will not in any way suffer from this decision
to come with me on my mission and that whatever evil effects may result
from my political work will not affect them in any way'. It was a suspect
choice of words that speaks to how Lockhart was changing the parameters
of his mission in the wake of Brest-Litovsk. The striking of trade deals and
the launching of fact-finding excursions to industrial cities were no longer
priorities, making Phelan and Birse surplus to requirements. In their place,
Lockhart relied on a coterie of saboteurs and spies to achieve his aim of
re-establishing the Eastern Front. This is where the story Lockhart told in
his memoirs – that he was merely a quasi-diplomat fighting the good fight
for Allied–Bolshevik relations only to reluctantly convert to the cause of
intervention – starts to unravel.[6]

While Lockhart spent most of March and April clashing with
Whitehall on the question of intervention, he was also putting himself 'in
touch with practically everyone' of note in Russia's counter-revolutionary
underground. So pronounced was Lockhart's dabbling in anti-Bolshevik
intrigue that Robins began to suspect his intentions, confiding to his
diary in mid-April that his friend was 'too gay', given the dreadful state
of Anglo-Bolshevik relations. More so than Robins, Ransome was fully
aware of the British Agent's double game. He knew that even as Lockhart
presented himself to Trotsky with 'a red-cloth bound *History of British
Socialism* under his arm', the scheming Scot was receiving intelligence on
the Whites from Hill and using Trotsky's secretary cum Ransome's mistress
to acquire personal information about her boss. She was not the only well-
placed female Lockhart used as a source. Not long after the commencement
of their courtship, Moura provided her lover with reports on conditions in

Petrograd, not all of which were concerned with anti-Bolshevik plots. On one occasion, Moura asserted that the Germans were planning a seaborne assault on the city for 1 May. Curiously, this report from the socialite was identical to that received by the American ambassador David Francis at Vologda, suggesting that Moura's capabilities as an intelligence asset had grown since her days of eavesdropping on Petrograd's preening elites.

It is also possible that Lockhart and Hill had something to do with Moura commencing work for the Bolshevik secret police – the Cheka – in May 1918. In the middle of this month, Moura travelled to her native Ukraine to gather intelligence for the Bolsheviks on the status of the anti-socialist puppet government that had been established in Kiev by the Germans. Though the evidence is not conclusive, Lockhart and Hill either pushed Moura into this dangerous work to get her embedded into the Cheka as a double agent or, at the very least, obtained information from her on anti-Bolshevik forces in Ukraine. In this respect, it is interesting that Lockhart reported to Whitehall on 25 May that he had been informed by a 'reliable source' about Bolsheviks in Ukraine who were double-crossing Moscow by getting in 'contact with the Germans'. Moura recalled this as a time when 'we talked about "the Mission"', yet when her lover was penning his memoirs in the 1930s she requested that he remove all mention of her 'Mata Hari touch' from the manuscript. Whatever Moura was up to in 1918, the details were sensitive enough that she didn't want them known over a decade later.[7]

Aside from intelligence work, Lockhart also got into the exfiltration business. On 15 May, he was visited at the Hotel Elite by an imposingly tall yet nervous-looking man who, despite being unfamiliar to Lockhart, addressed him as 'Roman Romanovich' – the name by which he was known to his Russian friends and contacts. In the long silence that followed, the confused British Agent's eyes adjusted to the man's countenance. With squinting and imagination, he identified the visitor as a former assistant of Kerensky's who, having cut off his once formidable beard to avoid detection by the Cheka, had sneaked incognito into the hotel to request help evacuating the former head of the Provisional Government to Britain.

Since his hasty retreat from the Winter Palace the previous year Kerensky had been in hiding, trying in vain to rally support for a counter-coup against the Bolsheviks. Owing to divisions within the Whites – many of whom couldn't stand Kerensky – his plans went nowhere. This led Kerensky to conclude that he needed political and financial support from abroad for his anti-Bolshevik crusade. Initially, he had gone to Wardrop to ask for a passport so that he could flee Russia to find allies in Britain. Fearing the political ramifications of assisting an enemy of Lenin's, Wardrop turned the former prime minister down. His decision aligned with Whitehall's thinking. When Lockhart notified the War Cabinet of his mysterious visitor's plea for assistance, he was flatly told 'you should discourage [the] proposal for Kerensky to visit England'.

The brash British Agent ignored this unambiguous order. Days after receiving Kerensky's beardless emissary, Lockhart informed the War Cabinet that he had forged a Serbian passport for the fugitive prime minister and despatched him to Murmansk. Furthermore, Lockhart advised the cabinet that once Kerensky arrived in London it would be wise to keep his identity a secret, as he was still in touch with 'various important people of different parties' in Russia – an opaque reference to the kind of anti-Bolsheviks that Lockhart and his team were working with.[8]

Before his supposed snap turn against the Bolsheviks at Vologda, therefore, Lockhart had made himself the linchpin of a covert network that had links to counter-revolutionaries. The question is why, given this status, did he continue to argue with Whitehall in favour of an Allied accord with the Bolsheviks? The answer was simple. Free of the firm political convictions that drove the likes of Robins and Sadoul to irrelevancy, Lockhart was hedging his bets. While he hoped for an Allied–Bolshevik agreement, the British Agent was not naïve enough to refrain from preparing for an open breach between Whitehall and the Kremlin, which by April 1918 seemed more likely than the fantasy of Trotsky's men linking arms with British and French soldiers. This was because, fearing further German incursions into Russia, Lenin had extended a diplomatic olive branch to Berlin. This led to the appointment of a German ambassador in Moscow, Count Wilhelm von Mirbach, on 23 April. Lockhart was annoyed at having a representative of Britain's enemy on his patch and interpreted Mirbach's smirking arrival as marking the end of any chance of Allied–Bolshevik rapprochement. This impression was furthered by Trotsky's growing unwillingness to meet with Lockhart as regularly as he once had.

As this shift in Bolshevik attentions from Britain's Agent to the German ambassador was happening in Moscow, in distant Vladivostok the Japanese finally landed, albeit in small numbers and on the pretext of responding to an incident in which drunken Red Army soldiers had killed three Japanese shopkeepers in the town. Tokyo's argument that it was only try-ing to protect the lives of Japanese citizens in Vladivostok was irrelevant to the Bolsheviks. What mattered was that 500 sets of Japanese boots had been planted on Russian soil without invitation. Between this development and the tentative re-establishment of Russo-German relations, the gulf between the Allies and the Kremlin was widening and Lockhart was being left in the void between.[9]

As his estrangement from Lenin and Trotsky grew, Lockhart also started questioning his initial assumption that their revolution was unassail-able. After the Japanese landed at Vladivostok, the Czech Legion that had been making its way eastwards towards the port began fighting Red Army garrisons along the Trans-Siberia Railway. The Czechs won these battles convincingly and kicked the Bolsheviks out of several Siberian towns, cast-ing the revolution's future in central Russia into doubt. In the red centres of Moscow and Petrograd, the Bolsheviks' grip on power also seemed to be waning. The food shortages that had blighted both the tsar's regime and the Provisional Government's had persisted into the Bolshevik era, even after Lenin's Decree on Food Procurement laid down new measures for the distribution of grain. Many Russians were still borderline starving, and the lack of bread and sense of despair were fuelling crimes of hate and desperation. In early March a Cheka officer was hauled from his sleigh in the middle of Petrograd and then robbed and stripped naked by bandits.

A worse fate awaited two off-duty Chekists, who were gunned down at a Moscow bar weeks later. Other anarchists reignited the wave of mindless terrorism that had gripped Russia in the early 1900s by marauding through the streets, detonating bombs and chanting 'death to world civilisation'.

Such sweeping threats to all and sundry meant that even Allied officials were not spared the brigandage. One morning, Robins awoke to find a 'group of 10 to 12 anarchists with bayoneted guns' surrounding his Red Cross truck. The gang hauled the driver out of the cab and beat him mercilessly, before making off with both his vehicle and its precious cargo of food and medicine. Wardrop's consulate was also raided multiple times by armed bandits, who needlessly fired shots into the walls and smashed flower vases while demanding the staff's wallets. Lenin and Trotsky had been in power for six months, but to Lockhart's mind they were miles from mastering the basics of feeding and protecting their population.[10]

The Bolsheviks' efforts to halt the lawlessness also troubled the British Agent. On the morning of 12 April, he and Robins were visited at the Hotel Elite by a man named Jacob Peters, who insisted they take a drive with him. A Latvian dockworker turned anti-tsarist insurgent, Peters had been hounded from Russia by the Okhrana in the early 1900s, finding refuge in East London. There he became affiliated with a group of fellow émigré subversives who robbed a jewellery shop in Houndsditch in 1910, engendering the so-called 'Siege of Sidney Street', in which the Home Secretary Winston Churchill oversaw Scots Guards engaging in a firefight on London's streets. Though charged with killing three police officers, Peters was acquitted of involvement in the fracas and returned to Russia, where he became devoted to the Bolshevik cause. He ascended through the party's ranks and in December 1917 was made second in command of the Cheka under its ruthless head, Felix Dzerzhinsky, a zealous yet calculating spymaster whom the contemporary press accurately dubbed the 'black pope of Bolshevism'.

It was on Dzerzhinsky's orders that Peters paid his visit to Lockhart and Robins that crisp April morning and insisted they get into the back of his Rolls-Royce. Unable to refuse this order masquerading as a request, the pair were then driven across Moscow on a tour of its anarchist haunts, most of which were old mansions that had been abandoned by their wealthy owners when the revolution broke out. In a tone of polite menace, Peters explained to his passengers that he and Dzerzhinsky had deduced that the mansions were the font from which the city's lawlessness was emanating. To restore order, they had decided to reduce the once fine abodes to charnel houses. As one of the Chekists involved in this operation at the so-called 'House of Anarchy' on Malaya Dmitrovka street recalled, the 'anarchist blackguards' had brought up 'innumerable arms of all kinds to this house, machine-guns protruded menacingly from the windows and even a mountain gun [mini-howitzer] stood at the entrance'. This necessitated a forced entry by Chekists and soldiers from the Latvian Riflemen Brigade, who blasted open the doors with grenades before butchering their enemies within.

With Peters as their guide, Lockhart and Robins were forced to inspect the aftermath of the Cheka's operation. The mansion's ceilings and walls were scattered with bullet holes and bodies lay strewn on blood-soaked rugs. Some of the dead were still sitting unarmed at tables strewn with shattered bottles and cold ashtrays. The slain were not just bandits. Lockhart's eyes were drawn to the army uniforms some wore. He was also perturbed by the twisted corpses of several young women, whose murders Peters justified by callously shrugging his shoulders and suggesting they were prostitutes. This and all other atrocities against the anarchists, Peters assured his horrified guests, were needed to end Moscow's crime wave and suppress the Bolsheviks' political enemies.[11]

This was a moment when Lockhart should have paused to consider his situation. He had set up a clandestine network, elements of which were in contact with the Whites, at a time when Lenin and Trotsky were getting tough on their enemies. Moreover, two weeks before Peters flaunted the buckets of blood he was willing to spill defending the regime, Lockhart had despatched one of his first communiqués to Whitehall in which he spoke openly of reaching out to the Bolshevik-opposed Socialist Revolutionaries, to 'learn if there was any intention of starting a counter-revolution'. Lockhart was playing with fire. However, between the thrill of commanding his team of subversives, his growing distaste for Bolshevism and his passionate affair with Moura, the same adventurer who had trifled with a sultan in Malaysia and dogged rifle-firing revolutionaries in Finland refused to abandon the dangerous path down which he was creeping.

This was why, two weeks after Peters' ghoulish display of the anarchists' fate, the undeterred Lockhart met with the Socialist Revolutionary leader Boris Savinkov. An insurgent of legendary standing in Russia, Savinkov had made his name before the war leading a paramilitary group that carried out myriad acts of terrorism, including the killing of tsarist officials. In 1917, he had served briefly in Kerensky's cabinet but once the Bolsheviks came to power he went underground and became a leading light of the movement to depose Lenin and Trotsky. Savinkov conveyed this status to Lockhart by bragging about how he had 2,000 followers assembled in cells across Moscow and Petrograd. Some were trained in bomb-making while others were gifted propagandists or deeply imbedded spies. All of them, the terrorist assured the British Agent, were inured to violence of the most heinous kind. Their plan was to launch an uprising against the Bolsheviks that would be triggered by the slaying of Lenin the next time he stepped foot beyond the safety of the Kremlin's high walls.

For all that it was risky and ethically dubious, this scheme made sense to Lockhart. Beset by Japanese landings and Czech uprisings, the Bolsheviks were looking more and more like chancers whose time was running out. Cromie and Moura had reported that anti-Bolshevik sentiment was rising in Petrograd, while Lockhart's own eyes and ears led him to conclude that a counter-revolutionary moment in Moscow was also fast approaching. Poised and prepared to topple a crumbling regime, Savinkov seemed to Lockhart like a man whose time had come.[12]

Some in Whitehall thought likewise. Savinkov insisted to Lockhart that Allied troops had to land at Archangel and Murmansk in tandem with the attacks launched in Moscow and Petrograd by his Socialist Revolutionaries, which would include the 'murder [of] all Bolshevik leaders on [the] night of Allied landing'. Then, backed by Allied bayonets, Savinkov proposed that he would form a 'government which will in reality be a military dictatorship'. These plans were so jarring that even the cavalier British Agent sought official guidance on whether to continue talking to the murderously ambitious Savinkov, to which he received a simple two-word reply from the War Cabinet's Lord Curzon: 'I approve.' This brevity reflected the squeamishness the cabinet felt in dealing with a terrorist. As Curzon confided to the internal minutes, however, 'Savinkoff's [sic] methods are drastic' but 'probably effective'. The French diplomats in Moscow thought the same, providing Savinkov with thousands of roubles to get the people and weapons he needed in place for the big day.[13]

With his connection to Savinkov's coup plan, his network of informers and saboteurs, and the assistance he gave to Kerensky, the British Agent was already committed to working against the Bolsheviks by the time he announced his volte-face on intervention to the diplomats at Vologda. Lockhart was no spymaster but after months of plotting with subversives he was enjoying acting like one. For this reason, as his discussions with Savinkov intensified, the British Agent began talking to another dubious character who was equally determined to obliterate Bolshevism. Lockhart was not to know that this man would engender the destruction of his empire of intrigue, the ending of his mission and a widening of the already substantial rift between Moscow and the West. His name was Sidney Reilly.

CHAPTER 7

ENTER ST1

'I first heard of Sidney Reilly as a cipher, and knew of him only as ST1, his secret service name. He had been sent out to tackle the new situation which had arisen with the advent of the Bolsheviks.'

– Captain George Hill

Lockhart wasn't sure if Sidney Reilly was 'a madman or a crook'. Perhaps he was a naïve English traveller – the sort that had been popping up across Russia since February 1917 in search of revolutionary thrills. No, when he looked into Reilly's darting hooded eyes and heard the conviction in his words, Lockhart realised he was talking to a man on a mission, despatched by no less a figure than the chief of MI6 to gather intelligence on the Bolsheviks and their enemies. His business in Russia was deadly serious. And yet, given the way Reilly had barged onto Lockhart's bailiwick, he couldn't help but laugh.

In the early evening of 7 May, Lockhart had picked up the ringing phone at his Hotel Elite office and been told a curious story. As the sun was sinking behind the Kremlin's ornate domes, a 'dark, well-groomed, very foreign-looking man' in a Royal Flying Corps uniform had arrived at its gates. He told the guards he had been sent to Moscow by Lloyd George to replace Lockhart, whose reports had been deemed unsatisfactory by the War Cabinet. The man insisted that the gate be opened so that he could present his credentials to Lenin personally. Perhaps with a mind to keep the bizarre visitor within arm's reach of detainment, he was allowed to enter

the Kremlin's grounds and briefly talk with one of Lenin's aides. As this
meeting unfolded, a call was placed to Lockhart. The man seemed like a
lunatic, but the intensity of his 'deeply lined, sallow face' and the forthright
nature of his words demanded an explanation from Britain's Agent.

Lockhart didn't have one. When a voice of broken English muttered the
name 'Sidney Reilly' down the phone to him, he drew a blank. Intrigued
by the story of the mystery man's arrival, however, Lockhart put down
the phone and placed a call to Ernest Boyce, the MI6 head of station in
Russia. Boyce was one of the professional intelligence officers who thought
Lockhart was too young and inexperienced for the job Lloyd George had
bestowed on him. Lockhart didn't think much of Boyce and his ilk either.
Apart from the swashbuckling Hill, he found MI6 people in Russia to be
ill-informed on the intricacies of revolutionary politics and overly preoc-
cupied with proving that Lenin and Trotsky were German agents. This
unfavourable impression of MI6 was not altered when Boyce confirmed that
he knew of Reilly's arrival in Russia but had no inkling of his intention to
denounce Lockhart while making a spectacle of himself on Lenin's doorstep. Having acquired more questions than answers from Boyce, when the
British Agent summoned the unwelcome visitor to his office the next day
for an explanation there were two burning questions on his mind – who was
Sidney Reilly and why had he crashed so absurdly into Lockhart's world?[1]

As was its author's intention, the life story of Sidney Reilly – real name
Sigmund Rosenblum – was a mess of contradictory exaggerations and bare-
faced lies. He told people he was the son of an Irish sea captain, but he was
likely born near to or in the Ukrainian Black Sea port of Odessa in 1873.
As a young man, Rosenblum fell in with anti-tsarist revolutionaries and
was forced out of the country, finding sanctuary first in France and then
in Britain in 1895. There, he worked as an informer for Special Branch, a
division of the Metropolitan Police that monitored émigré revolutionaries
and suspected terrorists. This included radicals from the same circles the
fugitive had recently run in. It was the first of many instances throughout
Rosenblum's life in which he embraced perfidy for money. Around this

time, he adopted the name Sidney Reilly to enhance his Irish credentials and hide his Jewish ancestry, of which he was far from proud. The name was likely bestowed on him by his handler at Special Branch, William Melville, whose wife's maiden name was Reilly. It was one of many aliases this man of ambiguous provenance – once described by a superior as looking like a 'Jewish-Jap type' – adopted throughout his life.

His reputation as an unscrupulous infiltrator and 'clever schemer' ensured that the newly christened Reilly found employment as a spy during the Russo-Japanese War of 1905. His record in the First World War was more ambiguous. He claimed to have pulled off several espionage triumphs in Germany, yet in truth spent most of the war in New York selling arms. Not content with this profitable business, in 1917 Reilly approached officers at New York's MI6 station to ask for a job which, he later claimed, involved carrying out acts of sabotage designed to draw the USA into the fighting. Like so much of Reilly's life story, the facts of this tale cannot be verified. What is known is that Reilly had 'great abilities as a linguist', could 'pass equally well as a Russian or a German' and, as a character witness reported to the British Secret Service (MI5), 'his knowledge of Russia always appears to be extensive and accurate'. And so, for the same reason Lockhart was handed the role of British Agent in January 1918, two months later Reilly was summoned to the office of MI6's chief, Mansfield Cumming ('C'), and tasked with travelling to Russia armed with '£500 in notes and £750 in diamonds' on a mission to contact 'all our men in Vologda, Kiev, Moscow etc'.[2]

Cumming had doubts about his new recruit. Aside from Reilly's principal wartime activity being the selling of weapons to both sides – which purportedly involved 'sending bad ammunition to the Russians' – he was a known philanderer with a penchant for extravagance. This was confirmed when Cumming requested that MI5 do a background check on Reilly, which found that his favourite haunts in London were the Ritz and the Savoy. When a similar request for information was made to MI6's New York station, they declared Reilly to be 'without patriotism or principles' and wholly 'untrustworthy and unsuitable' for intelligence work.

Even one of Reilly's closest MI6 comrades believed he had committed murder to make a widow of the woman he wished to marry. As 'C' confided to his diary, Reilly was a 'very doubtful' character and his deployment to Russia a 'great gamble'.

Cumming, however, was desperate. The revolution had up-ended Britain's intelligence networks in Russia and forced some personnel to abandon the country altogether and set up shop in Scandinavia. Aside from Hill's network of couriers, human infrastructure for gathering and forwarding information was also lacking. Owing to his ambiguous status, Lockhart was beyond the reach of Cumming to direct. To remedy this situation and get a clearer picture of what was happening in the Bolsheviks' world, Cumming needed someone who could pass as a native speaker, navigate Russia's labyrinthine politics and operate under MI6 auspices. Bereft of better options, 'C' had to try his luck with Reilly.[3]

The man code-named ST1 started as Cumming feared he might. Rather than heading to Archangel as instructed, Reilly disembarked at Murmansk on 4 April, whereupon he encountered the British marines who had landed there a month earlier to protect the port's munitions. Suspicious of a supposed Irish traveller with a tinge of Eastern Europe to his voice and a passport bearing the misspelled name 'Reilli', the marines detained him. Thankfully for ST1, this inauspicious start to his mission was salvaged when one of Boyce's deputies arrived to interview him. After the prisoner produced an encoded message hidden under the cork of an aspirin bottle, Boyce's man recognised that Reilly was working for MI6 and sent him on his way.

True to his brazen character, this initial blunder did nothing to steer Reilly back onto the path of the agreed plan. Instead of heading to Vologda or Moscow he made for Petrograd, where he spent weeks catching up with old contacts and establishing a network of informers, all while failing to notify Lockhart of his arrival in the British Agent's backyard. Reilly did, however, cable his first report to Cumming at this time, informing him that for the Allies to win the war they had to secure Murmansk and Archangel and prevent the Russian Baltic Fleet from falling into German hands, if needs be by blowing it up.

There was nothing sensational about this assessment. Reilly's observations aligned with Cromie and Hill's missions and, in his reference to securing the ports, he was in accord with Lockhart's changed mind on the need for Allied intervention. Beneath these conventional recommendations, however, Reilly's hatred of Bolshevism shone through in his reports. Having taken in the sights of smashed-up shops and starving citizens, Reilly concluded that the country's 'new masters were exercising a regime of bloodthirstiness and horror hardly equalled in history'. His impressions of Moscow were much the same, leading him to dub the revolutionary capital 'a city of the damned'. Like Lockhart, however, Reilly sensed that Moscow pulsed with a promising 'current of murmuring, of bitterness, of counter-revolution'. Heartened by this, he concluded that the Whites and the Socialist Revolutionaries needed to be courted. With their cooperation, ST1 believed he could orchestrate an insurrection that would stomp Bolshevism out of existence and etch the name 'Sidney Reilly' into the history books.[4]

If Reilly mentioned this grand plan to Lockhart at their initial meeting, the latter didn't let on about it. Recalling this first encounter with the self-proclaimed 'Ace of Spies', Lockhart wrote in his memoirs that he 'dressed him down like a schoolmaster and threatened to have him sent home' while barely controlling the urge to break into hysterics at the brass of the man. After taking this drubbing on the chin, Reilly went underground, moving back and forth between Moscow and Petrograd and liaising with Boyce and Hill, while convening meetings with counter-revolutionaries in the flat of one of his mistresses. Reilly realised 'it was important', Lockhart's son Robin wrote in his biography of the spy, 'not to compromise the leader of the British Mission' and so kept out of the British Agent's way. Like much of the younger Lockhart's tale of Reilly's exploits, this version of events conforms to the argument laid down by his father decades earlier – Reilly was a loose cannon with whom Lockhart had very little contact.

At a surface level, this story sounds credible. Reilly was older than Lockhart and on a special assignment for MI6. Moreover, given that his meandering journey to Moscow ended with a visit to the Kremlin rather than to the Hotel Elite, Reilly clearly didn't recognise the British Agent's authority. Combine this with the fact that in his memoir Reilly reduced Lockhart to a walk-on character while comparing himself to Napoleon, and one gets the impression that the 'Ace of Spies' was a megalomaniac who would have scoffed at Lockhart's attempts to either browbeat or direct him.[5]

The archival evidence tells a different story. Far from keeping his distance, Reilly became connected to Lockhart and his team shortly after arriving in Moscow and recognised the younger man's leadership, going so far as to gift him a cigar case, the engraving on which described the 'Ace of Spies' as the British Agent's 'faithful lieutenant'. This probably overstates the matter. Reilly's operations were linked to Lockhart's mission, but they still had a life of their own. After leaving Lockhart's office ST1 went his own way for a time, assuming the persona of a Greek businessman (Mr Constantine), a Turkish merchant (Mr Massino) and even a Chekist (the farcically named Sigmund Rellinsky). In these guises, he passed money to and shared intelligence with various anti-Bolshevik insurgents. These included Savinkov, whose mutual detestation of Bolshevism formed the basis of a partnership between the notorious terrorist and the MI6 adventurer that would last into the mid-1920s.

Lockhart was aware of this alliance. Indeed, given that he was meeting with Savinkov at this time and becoming an advocate of Reilly's idea that Allied intervention had to occur imminently, it is likely that Lockhart was in the loop of their conversations. He certainly did his bit to forward their agenda. Having travelled a second time to Vologda at the end of May, Lockhart obtained an agreement from the French and American ambassadors to support Allied intervention on a mass scale, such that the forces deployed could offer effective support for Savinkov. So shrill did Lockhart's demands for this invasion become in the weeks that followed that by late June a minute sheet etched with grumblings over the British Agent's preachy tone was being passed around the Foreign Office.[6]

Reilly also struck up a relationship with Cromie and Hill. Like Lockhart, Hill presented Reilly in his memoirs as a shadow on the periphery of his work, stating that we 'had independent jobs', although 'naturally, we kept each other informed of our activities'. This glosses over some key details of the partnership that he, Cromie, Lockhart and Reilly developed in the summer of 1918. As Robin Bruce Lockhart noted when interviewing Hill decades later, the latter and Reilly 'took two hundred thousand pounds in Russian roubles in suitcases *which my father* had given Reilly to give to Archbishop Tikhon in Moscow to strengthen the Church's resistance to the Bolsheviks'. Cromie also met with Reilly several times throughout May and June to discuss their shared interest in destroying the Baltic Fleet. Lockhart was a party to these discussions, ensuring that money was available for Cromie to fund anti-Bolshevik propaganda among Russian sailors, purchase explosives and pay off dockworkers to detonate the ordnance and sink the fleet when necessary. Given Reilly's affiliation with this scheme and his habit of asking for large sums of money – he had requested one million roubles from 'C' the first week he arrived in Russia – it is perhaps no coincidence that Cromie's demands for thousands more roubles to fund 'several schemes of paramount importance to [the] Allies' increased shortly after Reilly established himself in Petrograd.[7]

The clearest indication of Reilly's closeness to Lockhart's mission was the fact that he was by the British Agent's side when a curious incident took place at the All-Russian Congress of Soviets on 6 July. Lockhart had been invited by Trotsky to observe the congress at Moscow's Bolshoi Theatre in the company of other Allied representatives. Part way through the evening, the congress was abruptly halted and soldiers from the Latvian Rifle Brigade flooded the building.

This drama was prompted by an act of terrorism that had occurred streets away at the German embassy, where two well-dressed men had presented themselves claiming to be Cheka officers. The pair demanded to see Ambassador Mirbach on the grounds that they had urgent information about a plot to assassinate him. They were not lying. Seconds after being ushered into Mirbach's study, the infiltrators revealed themselves to be members of the Left Socialist Revolutionaries – the party's radical fringe. To break the Brest-Litovsk Treaty and encourage Germany to reinvade Russia and crush the Bolsheviks, the pair unloaded their pistols into Mirbach and made their escape by blasting open a window, leaving a second live grenade next to the dying ambassador to make sure their assassination was successful.

News of Mirbach's murder was wired to the Bolshevik leadership at the Bolshoi, where they suspended proceedings and ordered the building to be locked down. So anxious was the mood in the theatre that one of the usually sound Latvian Riflemen fumbled a grenade down a stairwell, triggering an explosion that further frayed everyone's nerves. Reilly and a representative from the French mission who was also in Lockhart's viewing box felt this tension acutely. As the Riflemen swept the building on the hunt for explosives and assassins, Lockhart's guests produced documents from their pockets that they tore into tiny pieces, chewed frantically and swallowed. In his recollection of this event, Lockhart made no mention of joining in his companions' feast of paper. However, he did later report to Whitehall that he had destroyed his documents after Count Mirbach's murder. This perhaps suggests that some of the papers Reilly ate were Lockhart's or that he followed ST1's lead in burning his own compromising material once the lockdown of the Bolshoi was lifted and he returned to the Hotel Elite.

The question of what was in Lockhart's documents and those consumed by Reilly and his unnamed French counterpart is open to conjecture. However, it might not be a coincidence that the grenades used by Mirbach's assassins were supplied to them by the French ambassador Joseph Noulens who, like Lockhart and Reilly, had been passing money to the Socialist Revolutionaries for months. Moreover, the man to whom Noulens gave the grenades occupied a room at the Hotel Elite on the same corridor as Lockhart and Hicks' suite. Whether this meant that the British Agent was

tied in some way to the plot to murder Mirbach or not, the fact remains
that he and Reilly were working together on various subversive activities
when the assassination occurred.[8]

These activities continued even after the failure of Savinkov's grand
uprising, which was launched after Mirbach's assassination despite the
much-demanded Allied landings failing to materialise. As Lockhart ruefully reported to Whitehall, without British and French rifles to back him,
Savinkov's counter-revolution was 'completely suppressed and most of the
leaders captured' within a day. Innervated by this failure, Lockhart pledged
to himself that the same mistake would not be made again. Throughout
July he convened more secret meetings with counter-revolutionaries, from
whom he received intelligence on the troop strength and fighting preparedness of both the Red and White armies. It helped that 'many of the
leaders of these organisations were old personal friends' of Lockhart's – yet
another dividend paid from his ability to mix as freely with reactionary
White monarchists as with insurgents from the Socialist Revolutionaries'
Left and Right wings. Some of these meetings took place in the company
of France's consul-general, Fernand Grenard, who, like his ambassador Noulens, detested the Bolsheviks and was prepared to see blood on
Moscow's streets if it meant an end to their rule. Desperate to keep the
flames of counter-revolution flickering in the wake of Savinkov's failure,
Lockhart and Grenard sourced millions of roubles from both of their governments and the wealthy dispossessed of tsarist Russia, which they handed
over to anyone who promised action against Lenin and Trotsky. At the
same time, Lockhart demanded that Whitehall organise a 12,000-strong
invasion force for landings at the Arctic ports and, pondering a coordinated
intervention in Russia's east, talked of how Japanese and Czech troops 'can
successfully overrun Siberia up to the Volga'. By July 1918, Lockhart was
unwaveringly committed to bringing down the Bolshevik regime.[9]

The groupthink proffered by Lenin-hating French diplomats and the
subversion-mad Reilly was not the only reason Lockhart's support for a
counter-revolutionary uprising intensified over the summer. By this time,

he had accepted that the country he fell in love with was dead beyond the
point of resurrection. The debauched evenings and bohemian revelries of
pre-1917 Russia had been eradicated by the Bolsheviks' violent repressions
and increasingly erratic gambits to stay in power. This bleak reality was
made clear to Lockhart on 17 July, when word reached him that the tsar
and his family – who were being held under house arrest by the Bolsheviks
in the Siberian town of Ekaterinburg – had been dragged into a dank
basement and riddled with bullets. As the first Allied representative in
Russia to receive word of the massacre, Lockhart wired Whitehall immediately. He did so with a heart made heavy by the realisation that news of
the royal family's murder was being met with shrugs of indifference by
many in Moscow. Those whom the Scot had found charmingly carefree
years earlier had seemingly been numbed to horror by the extremis of life
under Bolshevism.

Increasingly fearful of enemies within, after deciding to slay the
Romanovs the Bolsheviks turned their attentions to the Allies' ambassadors. Days after the massacre at Ekaterinburg, the vice-commissar for
foreign affairs, Karl Radek, arrived in Vologda with a pistol in his hand
and orders to cajole the diplomats back to Moscow. Francis understood
that Radek intended to use him and his colleagues as hostages in the
event that the Allies or the Czechs made a move on the capital. Frightened
yet defiant, the American ambassador held his ground with Radek, dismissing the unwanted visitor's demands as an affront to diplomatic protocols
and refusing to comply unless made to by force. The gravity of what
he was threatening now apparent to him, Radek backed off. This gave
Francis and the other diplomats time to make ready a train that shuttled
them from Vologda to the relative safety of Archangel, cutting one of the
last threads that bound the Allies and the Bolsheviks together. Lockhart
interpreted Radek's mission to Vologda as a sign that those Allied officials who remained were living on borrowed time in Russia. Backed into
a corner with the world arrayed against them, the Bolsheviks appeared
ready to eject, imprison or shoot any perceived enemy at a moment's notice.

Nothing seemed beyond the men whom Lockhart had hoped to call friends months earlier.[10]

Now more than ever, Lockhart was looking for action to alleviate the danger. When Allied troops finally landed in Russia on 4 August, however, they did so on a scale that was just enough to further spook the Bolsheviks without emboldening the likes of Savinkov or the Whites to rise en masse as Lockhart, Reilly and Grenard wanted. The initial British force comprised fewer than 5,000 men, of whom only a few hundred could be landed in the initial wave owing to bad weather. This was followed by a few thousand more French and American troops, who deployed in small waves in the weeks that followed.

Lockhart was appalled. He had explained at length to Whitehall that the counter-revolutionary groups with whom he had been liaising needed the landings to be 'made in force', so that the Bolsheviks' end would seem certain enough to prompt a general uprising across the country. As the beleaguered British Agent put it to his political masters, 'the support we will receive from Russia will be in direct proportion to [the] numbers of troops we send'. Instead, after endless squabbling with the War Cabinet and his own fraught journey from staunch opponent of intervention to impassioned advocate, Lockhart's advice that Archangel, Murmansk and Vladivostok needed to be invaded simultaneously and in 'the most impos-ing manner possible' had fallen on deaf ears.

The inevitable occurred. When news of the humble Allied invasion broke across Russia the White generals second-guessed their next move and started quarrelling. Still reeling from the failure of their miscalculated uprising in July, Savinkov's people also failed to take action. Indeed, at the time of the Allied landings, Savinkov was on the run from the Cheka and heading east towards Kazan. This no-show by the legendary insurgent likely informed Hill and Lockhart's memoirs, which pivot away from the support they gave Savinkov in the first half of 1918 to depicting him as a blowhard morphine addict who was prone to drinking himself into uncon-sciousness. At the time, however, Savinkov's personal vices were the least of Lockhart's concerns. Between the absence of a counter-revolutionary groundswell in the cities and the paucity of Allied troops in the north, it was clear that after months of build-up the intervention was a flop that would do nothing to dislodge the Bolsheviks from power.[11]

Aside from the political consequences, the intervention shattered Lockhart's team. As he was still enlisted in the army, Garstin had been recalled to Archangel ahead of the invasion, only to die heroically in a firefight with the Red Army 'after capturing one armoured car by his own efforts and exposing himself in an endeavour to secure another'. In Petrograd, the Cheka responded to the landings by swooping on several Socialist Revolutionary cells, which they assumed were about to activate in concert with the invaders. Six of Hill's couriers were collared, along with French intelligence officers who worked for Noulens. Reilly's apartment in Petrograd was also raided, forcing the 'Ace of Spies' to doss with one of his mistresses. Prudently, Hill absented himself from the cities to visit his anti-German saboteurs in Ukraine until the heat died down. Boyce, however, was too high profile a figure to melt into the warren of safehouses Hill and Reilly had set up and so was arrested by the Cheka. Though he was only detained for twenty-four hours, this move against MI6's head of station was an unambiguous signal to all Allied representatives that the Kremlin's gloves were now off.

With the intelligence officers of Petrograd scattered and the Vologda ambassadors evacuated to Archangel, it fell on those remaining in Moscow to bear the brunt of the Bolsheviks' fearful wrath. A day after the landings, the Red Army was 'converting houses in the centre of the city into improved fortresses in the belief that there will soon be a serious rising' and Chekists were prowling the streets checking identity papers. Armed with safe conduct passes he had acquired from the Bolshevik leaders in happier times, Lockhart passed through the checkpoints untouched to Wardrop's consulate. There, he intended to discuss with his one-time detractor how best they could work together to ride out the storm. They had no time to formulate a plan. Lockhart had barely begun complaining to Wardrop about the omnishambles of the Allied landings when he looked out the window and saw that the consulate was being surrounded by armed Chekists. Racing downstairs, Lockhart and Wardrop deployed indignant bluster to the full, stalling the intruders at the door long enough for the clerks in the first-floor offices to burn sensitive papers and destroy ciphers. When the Chekists finally pushed past the obstructing pair they arrested Wardrop's staff and ransacked his consulate for contraband. Once every drawer had been broken into and every seat cushion slashed open, Dzerzhinsky's men then abandoned the building and nailed the doors shut behind them. Having flashed his safe conduct passes, Lockhart received a grunt of acknowledgement and an order from the Chekists' commander that he leave the premises immediately. This spared him from a shakedown but all was far from well. Upon returning to the Hotel Elite, Lockhart found that Lingner, Tamplin and Alfred Hill had been arrested and his room turned over and sealed shut.[12]

Much like Peters' flaunting of the anarchists' fates, Lockhart should have taken the raids on the consulate and his office as a cue to extract himself from Russia. He toyed with the idea, tentatively making plans in the first week of August to head for Sweden. This flirtation with retreat, however, was as brief as it was insincere from the man for whom personal ambition was oxygen and the courting of peril instinct. When the Bolsheviks shut down his operation at the Hotel Elite, Lockhart simply relocated to the Bread Lane apartment he and Jean had shared during his time as consul-general, ahead of establishing a new office on Great Lubyanka street, mere blocks away from the Cheka's headquarters. Far from fleeing the flames, Lockhart was determined to dance in them.

His Macgregor impulsivity and thirst for adventure partly explains this. Lockhart's pragmatism, however, was also key to his decision-making in the first days of August. Months of backing counter-revolutionaries and arguing for a mass Allied invasion meant that he had staked his professional reputation on the anti-Bolshevik struggle. Until his labours in that struggle bore fruit, it would be career suicide to throw in the towel. Lockhart's hopes that the Whites and the Socialist Revolutionaries would deliver him this 'win' had been dashed by the failure of both parties to respond in any meaningful way to the Allies' lacklustre landings. This setback, however, had not altered the situation. The Bolsheviks were still a threat to Russia and the Allies' war effort, even as their regime seemed to be tottering on the edge of a precipice. While other Allied officials had fallen to raids and repression, Lockhart was still at liberty and free to operate within his mission's loose parameters. He alone remained with the power to push the Bolsheviks into the pit of oblivion and as such could not walk away.

Moura was also a factor in Lockhart's decision to continue his mission. In June, she had capped off their brief but intense affair by informing him that she was pregnant. After recovering from the shock of this news, Lockhart was convinced by Moura that the best course of action was for her to return to Yendel and entice Djon to sleep with her, providing cause to believe that the child was her husband's. The plan was foolish on many levels. For one thing, the countess had fallen irrevocably out of love with Djon, who had thrown his full support behind the Germans, welcoming their occupation of Estonia as liberation from Lenin. The journey to Yendel was also dangerous. In transit during the Socialist Revolutionary uprising of July, Moura stopped over in Petrograd for two days, during which she witnessed the brutal public execution of scores of suspected spies and insurgents by the Cheka. When she finally arrived at Yendel exhausted and on edge, Moura found herself physically repulsed by Djon and unable to carry out the plan. Now carrying Lockhart's child, she could not deny the intensity of her love for him any more than she could walk away from their thrilling life of machination.

Having dispensed with the idea of seducing Djon, on 15 July Moura set off on a perilous journey back to Moscow, using train, horse-cart and foot to return to the waiting arms of her beloved 'baby boy'. This act of devotion, coupled with the prospect of a child – a gift made greater by the premature death of his and Jean's daughter – meant that Lockhart 'was unwilling to leave Russia because of Moura'. The latter affirmed her commitment to

Lockhart by moving in with him and Hicks at the Bread Lane apartment, giving her lover a sense of comfort even as Chekists raided Allied buildings and his personal relations with the Bolsheviks plummeted to a nadir. With his muse by his side, however, Lockhart was convinced he could outrun any enemy and weather any storm. This feeling of being bulletproof, combined with the need to find triumph in the tangle of his fraught mission was the reason why, when Reilly resurfaced in August with a pair of mysterious Latvian soldiers and a plan to achieve the victory he craved, the British Agent was all ears.[13]

CHAPTER 8

THE GREAT GAMBLE

'Whoever controlled the Letts, controlled the capital.'
— Sidney Reilly

The Latvian Riflemen had been a constant presence throughout Lockhart's time in Russia. They had been cheek by jowl with him on Trotsky's train to Moscow; he had witnessed them lock down the Bolshoi; and at the body-strewn House of Anarchy he had seen the bloody fruits of their work. Their willingness to kill in defence of the revolution had also been evident in the executions they carried out during Savinkov's uprising, and in their battles with the Czech Legion. The Latvian Riflemen were, quite simply, the Bolsheviks' praetorian guard. And yet, like the Czechs with whom they clashed in Siberia, the Latvians had nationalist ambitions that complicated their apparent embrace of Lenin's new order. The terms of the Brest-Litovsk Treaty had placed Latvia under German occupation. This bred both a hatred of the kaiser among the Riflemen and, to some within their ranks, a disdain for the Bolsheviks who had gifted their homeland like a trinket to a foreign conqueror.[1]

Lockhart and his team were aware of the Riflemen's anti-Bolshevik feelings. Hill worked with the Latvians as part of his anti-German guerrilla operations in Ukraine, through which he came to believe that discontent with Lenin and Trotsky was palpable across several battalions. So convinced was Hill of their anti-Bolshevik credentials that after Savinkov's failure he concluded that the Riflemen were the most promising counter-revolutionary force remaining in Russia. Their extensive training and ability to fight insurrectionary battles was also appreciated by Lockhart who, having received 'reports from other sources of unrest among the Letts [Latvians]', advised the War Cabinet of the need for 'say five million roubles' to 'organise a rising against [the] Germans' in Latvia. While the dissident Riflemen in this instance were not targeting the Bolsheviks, their willingness to go against Brest-Litovsk and threaten the Russo-German peace in the name of liberating Latvia was something the British Agent took note of.

Cromie was also interested in the Latvians, specifically their sailors from the Baltic Fleet, whom he wanted to co-opt into his scheme to scupper Russia's warships. To cultivate these saboteurs, Cromie frequented a Latvian club in Petrograd where, imbibing one evening in June, he met two Riflemen who introduced themselves as Jan Schmidkhen and Jan Bredis. The attaché struck up an instant rapport with the pair, who bent his ear with remonstrations over how the Bolsheviks had sold Latvia down the river to preserve a revolution that had given the Riflemen nothing but bloody hands in service to cruel masters. With Lockhart's enthusiasm for counter-revolutionaries in mind, Cromie saw potential in Schmidkhen and Bredis, who claimed to have connections to similarly disgruntled officers within the Riflemen's ranks. The question was, could the disaffected duo incite enough of their comrades to act on their misgivings about the Bolsheviks and give Lockhart the uprising he needed?

Reilly thought so. Having been summoned by Cromie to a meeting with Schmidkhen and Bredis, the spy determined that they were earnest in their hatred of Bolshevism and, like all Latvians in supposed thrall to the revolution, were little more than 'foreign hirelings' who 'serve for money'. Projecting the worst of his cynical self into this assessment, Reilly decided that the Riflemen 'were at the disposal of the highest bidder' – they were the kind of people with whom the unscrupulous 'Ace of Spies' could do business. If he and Cromie 'could buy the Letts', Reilly argued, then their 'task would be easy'. The task to which he referred was the launching of an anti-Bolshevik coup. Like Lockhart, Reilly was undeterred by Savinkov's failures, the half-hearted Allied landings and the Cheka's repressions. His 'conviction that someday he was destined to bring Russia out of the slough and chaos of Communism' was too great for his counter-revolutionary dreams to die. Schmidkhen and Bredis offered the best available chance of achieving this grand design. And so, Reilly told Cromie to write a letter of introduction for them to take to Lockhart in Moscow where, he hoped, the next stage of planning the Latvian Riflemen's betrayal of the Bolsheviks could begin.[2]

As he opened the envelope and read Cromie's letter, Lockhart paused to cast a critical eye over the two men who had appeared unannounced at his door. The Allied landings at Archangel had just taken place and Moscow was riven with paranoia. Despite assurances from the invasion force's leader, Major General Frederick Poole, that his sole aim was to restore the Eastern Front, the Bolsheviks were certain the Allies had come to crush their revolution. Misinformation and hearsay fuelled this fear. The Kremlin had yet to confirm the intervention force's unimpressive size, yet rumours swirled that a horde of Allied troops was cutting a swathe from Archangel down to Moscow, assisted by Socialist Revolutionaries blowing up railway lines and seizing telegraph stations. So convinced of collapse were some Bolsheviks, they ordered their papers to be burned in the Kremlin's gardens. One official told Lockhart that measures were being taken to dynamite Petrograd ahead of the Allies' advance. Conflicting with this intent to raze Russia's former capital to the ground, Cromie was informed that Lenin would soon arrive in Petrograd, where a motorboat would ferry him up the Neva and across the Baltic to refuge in Sweden. This story was untrue, but Lenin was desperate enough in the first weeks of August to have his commissar for foreign affairs, Georgi Chicherin, request a German intervention to push back the Allies. Berlin's refusal to answer this plea only heightened anxieties in Moscow.[3]

In this climate of animosity towards all things Allied, Lockhart had his guard up against Schmidkhen and Bredis, who stood silent and unreadable before his desk as he methodically scanned Cromie's letter for signs of

forgery. Lockhart knew the Cheka were onto him. He had rightly interpreted his forced visit to the House of Anarchy as Peters baring his teeth
in threat. Weeks later, irregularities in his correspondence with Whitehall
led Lockhart to conclude that his communications had been tapped, though
to what extent he could not determine. Given the scale of his subversive
activities, the ability to read only a fraction of the cables emanating from
the Hotel Elite office would have been enough to raise Cheka eyebrows.
This was why Lockhart initially assumed the Latvians were *agents provocateurs* sent by Dzerzhinsky to entrap him. It was with relief, therefore, that
Lockhart noticed basic misspellings in Cromie's letter – a quirk of his writing that only intimates were aware of. This assuaged the British Agent's
concerns over the missive's authenticity and confirmed to him that the attaché must have vetted Schmidkhen and Bredis before entrusting them with
his message. Lockhart's mind was further put at ease by the pair's discussion
of Latvia's future, which they showed more interest in than any wild plans
to assassinate Lenin, as Savinkov once suggested, or march on Moscow in
the manner dreamed of by the Whites. Instead, Schmidkhen and Bredis
proposed a mass surrender of the Riflemen to General Poole's forces, which
would ease the Allied advance across Russia, restore the Eastern Front and
lay a foundation for an offensive that could push the Germans from their
homeland. Surely if the Latvian duo were working for Dzerzhinsky they
would have suggested something more sinister to Lockhart than simply
refusing to fight the Allies on the Bolsheviks' behalf?

Intrigued by their ideas, Lockhart requested further meetings with
both Schmidkhen and Bredis and someone high enough up the Riflemen's
chain of command to make their planned surrender happen. In response,
Schmidkhen brought an additional conspirator to Lockhart's office on
Great Lubyanka street, which served as the location for these meetings
on 14 and 15 August after the raid on the Hotel Elite. This third man was
Colonel Eduard Berzin, who commanded the Riflemen unit charged with
protecting Lenin himself. The British Agent was as impressed by the colonel's soldierly pragmatism as by his passion when speaking of Latvia's need

to be free of foreign yoke, and the weariness he felt at the bloody role the Riflemen had played in perpetuating the revolution's misery. Tired of the Bolshevik experiment himself, Lockhart empathised, and agreed to provide Berzin with funds to bribe those Riflemen still loyal to the Bolsheviks. He also gave Schmidkhen and Bredis safe conduct passes that would allow them to cross the Allies' lines and negotiate a surrender with General Poole. Berzin's further suggestion that the Riflemen could 'organise a revolt in Latvia similar to the revolt in the Ukraine' also appealed to Lockhart, who judged it to be an 'interesting and plausible proposal' for hastening the war's end. So taken was Lockhart with Berzin that he conveyed the substance of their meetings to the American consul DeWitt Poole (no relation to the general at Archangel), the French consul Grenard and his military attaché, General Jean Lavergne. All were excited by Berzin's proposals and pledged to contribute to the cause, bringing the total amount available to the Latvians up to 1.4 million roubles.[4]

The question of whether this war chest was intended to fund a direct attack on the Bolsheviks is where Lockhart's narrative gets murky. Having supervised Schmidkhen's and Bredis' despatch from Petrograd with Cromie's letter, Reilly followed in their wake to Moscow, where he attended the Berzin meetings in his 'Mr Constantine' guise and came away thrilled by what he heard. Such was Reilly's enthusiasm that Lockhart claimed that after the 15 August meeting he handed stewardship of all future negotiations with the Latvians over to the MI6 man. This seems a strange decision. In contrast to almost everyone else who encountered the 'Ace of Spies', Lockhart appears to have considered Reilly 'an extremely able man and, in my opinion, the cleverest of our agents in Russia' – the sort who could be trusted to funnel millions of roubles to Berzin, 'keep an eye on their [the Riflemen's] movements and help to stimulate their reluctance to oppose our troops'. Aside from this dubious depiction of Reilly as trustworthy and professional, Lockhart's decision to remove himself from the burgeoning plot with Berzin also appears peculiar. He had been passing money to and discussing subversive schemes with White generals and Socialist Revolutionaries for months. So why now did Lockhart need Reilly to do the job that he had been doing since April?

The answer Lockhart offered to posterity seems plausible. After the Cheka's raids in early August, the Bolsheviks were poised to kick him out of the country. Since Lockhart was packing his bags in anticipation of departure when Schmidkhen and Bredis entered his life, it made little sense for him to get involved in another grand plot. Following this logic, having transferred the Latvian burden onto Reilly on 15 August, Lockhart abstained from all work and spent his intended last days in Russia packing up the apartment, playing football with Hicks and Tamplin, and visiting his favourite gypsy singer, Maria Nikolaevna Lebedev, at her home outside Moscow. 'She sang a few of our favourite songs to us in a low voice, which was scarcely louder than a whisper,' he recalled, and 'kissing me on both cheeks, begged us to remain with her.' It was a forlorn request, for the British Agent had finally decided to end his great adventure.[5]

This version of events is peppered with untruths. Although preparations were afoot in August for the remaining Allied diplomats to leave Russia, there is little reason to believe that Lockhart intended to join them. For one thing, in the moving tale of his final parting from Nikolaevna, the 'us' to which he referred was himself and Moura. Her presence, and that of the baby inside her, are reason enough to take Lockhart's claim to have spent August preparing to abandon Russia, the woman he loved and his unborn child with a grain of salt. The idea that Lockhart washed his hands of the Riflemen is also questionable. It is true that after first meeting Schmidkhen and Bredis, Lockhart received intelligence from Hill suggesting that he 'would be asked to leave' Russia and 'possibly even be arrested before leaving'. This danger, however, was far from novel for the British Agent. For months he had suffered the unwanted attentions of the Cheka, felt the cold shoulders of Lenin and Trotsky and accepted that he was living on borrowed time in their world. This hadn't stopped Lockhart from passing ever-increasing sums of money to Savinkov and the Whites, nor had it compelled him to cast Schmidkhen and Bredis from his door when they first arrived with Cromie's letter in hand. His over-egging of Reilly as the capable mastermind of the Latvian plot, therefore, was likely a front to conceal the reality – Lockhart was as involved in this counter-revolutionary scheme as he had been in those that preceded it.[6]

The secret report Lockhart subsequently compiled for Foreign Secretary Lord Balfour, detailing his work in Russia, backs this assertion. Crossed-out sections in the draft version reveal that, far from doing 'no work' after 15 August, Lockhart had 'one or two meetings' with White leaders and with Reilly himself, who assured him that the talks with Berzin were going 'smoothly'. Lockhart also omitted from the final typed version of the report his awareness of Cromie's plans to recruit another group of disaffected Latvians for the purposes of sabotaging transport infrastructure in Petrograd. Despite later claiming that the destruction of ciphers after the raid on his hotel suite meant he could no longer send secret messages, Lockhart cabled details of these August machinations to General Poole at Archangel via consulates in Scandinavia and Switzerland. In one of these cables, reference was made to how 20,000 Latvian Riflemen were 'desirous of throwing in their lot with the Allies'. Likewise, at some point after 15 August, Lockhart told a secretary at the American consulate that he had an 'opportunity to buy-off Lettish troops'.[7]

In both his contemporary correspondence with Whitehall and, to a lesser extent, in his memoirs, Lockhart was forthcoming when discussing his dealings throughout 1918 with Savinkov and the Whites. Why then, in both the public and the archival record, did he obscure what he was up to in the final weeks of August 1918? The answer is simple. To protect his career and legacy and, one suspects, to deprive his detractors of the satisfaction of being proved right, Lockhart tried to minimise his role in one of the most notorious fiascos in British covert history – the failed attempt to destroy Bolshevism by way of a counter-revolutionary coup. Though it came to be known as the 'Lockhart Plot', the folly was a collaborative effort. Its principal co-authors were the volatile 'Ace of Spies' and the cocky yet desperate British Agent, who laid the plot's groundwork by providing money and safe conduct passes and establishing the parameters of the Allied–Riflemen alliance. In keeping with Lockhart's character and mission, those parameters were fluid, allowing the initial discussions of mass surrender to the Allies to mutate into talk of uprisings in Latvia and a full-blown coup against the Bolsheviks, in which blood would be shed and buildings blown up.[8]

The development of the plot along this dangerous trajectory was somewhat inevitable. The Riflemen's surrender to General Poole was meant to further the Allies' advance into Russia but both Lockhart and Reilly must have been aware that this colossal betrayal by the Red Army's finest would destabilise the Bolshevik regime. As Hill put it in his official report to the War Office, 'the proposed turning of the Lettish troops to our cause ... could not be achieved without very seriously affecting the Moscow and Petrograd centres'. As this outcome aligned with the counter-revolutionary fantasy Reilly conceived of after meeting Schmidkhen and Bredis, it made sense to suggest that Berzin's paid-off Riflemen could lead 'a movement in Moscow' to destroy the Bolshevik regime. According to Hill – who was brought into the plot by his excitable MI6 comrade – Reilly intended to have Lenin and Trotsky arrested at gunpoint by their erstwhile praetorian guards at the upcoming Bolshevik Executive Council Congress. Reilly's further plans have become the subject of speculation. Hill suggested that 'although Reilly hated Bolshevism, he knew it would be a mistake to make martyrs of the men who formed the first Communist Government'. He therefore intended only to parade the revolutionary major-domos 'through Moscow with the nether garments missing', humiliating them such that their followers would abandon the Bolshevik cause.[9]

Hill's assertion that 'no one was to be killed' in this scenario was perhaps an instance of protesting too much. Latvian and Chekist accounts of the plot – and indeed, any common-sense assessment of what was bound to happen during a coup d'état – suggest that Reilly intended for Lenin and Trotsky to be executed. There is circumstantial evidence for this. In mid-August Boyce asked one of his Russian assets if they were willing to 'do away with one of two prominent members of the Soviet government'.

Reilly also talked with Hill about imposing a military dictatorship in the wake of the Bolsheviks' toppling and although supposedly the idea was rejected, he did discuss the matter of murdering Lenin with Berzin. Given his visceral hatred of Bolshevism and obsessive plans to dismantle Lenin and Trotsky's regime, it seems unlikely that the 'Ace of Spies' would have been satisfied to 'kill them with ridicule' rather than with bullets.[10]

Whether Lenin and Trotsky's fate was to be shot dead or stripped half-naked, Lockhart claimed in his memoirs to have 'categorically turned down' Reilly's idea to use the Riflemen as foot-soldiers for a coup. His report to Balfour, however, contained a different version of his response to ST1's audacious plan. Conceding that he 'was not a military expert', Lockhart told Reilly that he 'saw no point in a movement in Moscow as we [General Poole's invasion force] were too far away and there was no one to replace the Bolsheviks but the Germans'. This suggests that the *idea* of using the Riflemen to topple the regime wasn't as much a problem for Lockhart as the logistics of how to bring them into play. Given the frustration Lockhart felt following Savinkov's poorly planned uprising in July, his concern to do things properly this time around makes sense. Moreover, he took these concerns to Poole and Grenard, to whom he outlined Reilly's proposal. Lockhart's version of the consuls' response to this overture in both his report to Balfour and in his memoirs painted Reilly as an eccentric out of step with the more sober Allied officials. Poole and Grenard 'demurred and pointed out that there was nothing to gain' from ST1's dangerous scheme. Better, they thought, to stick with the less bloody idea of turning the Riflemen's minds to surrender. That, according to Lockhart, was as far as he and his American and French counterparts were prepared to go.[11]

In admitting to Balfour that he was aware enough of Reilly's plot to shoot it down, Lockhart was practising a classic method of obfuscation – hiding a damaging lie within a comparatively innocuous truth. The lie in question pertained to what happened on 25 August, when several parties to the Allied–Riflemen conspiracy gathered at the American consulate in Moscow. The decision to convene under the protection of the Stars and

Stripes is telling. As the Bolsheviks held less animus towards the Americans than they did towards the British and the French, the consulate had been left un-raided following the Allied landings. It was the best location to discuss something clandestine that one could find in Moscow's maelstrom of Cheka snoopers. The guest list reveals the need for this secrecy. Poole had with him his top spy, Xenophon Kalamatiano. The Lenin-detesting Grenard was also in attendance, accompanied by his military advisor General Lavergne and his explosives expert, Henri de Verthamon. The similarly sabotage-happy Hill was there too, along with his partner and driving force of proceedings, Reilly. In some accounts of the meeting one of the Latvians, possibly Schmidkhen, was also present. All told, this was a secret international gathering of diplomats, spies and saboteurs that would not have needed to take place if the only matter on the agenda was the bribing of Riflemen to lay down arms.

Lockhart denied he was present at this meeting. However, as with many aspects of the British Agent's version of events, there is cause to doubt his word. Cheka sources allege that he accompanied Reilly to the consulate. Poole later alluded to Lockhart's knowledge of what had been discussed there and, in his report to Balfour, Lockhart used the term 'we' when referring to the Allied diplomats at the meeting. He also sent a telling cable after 25 August, in which he referred to having discussed an unidentified matter with Grenard and Lavergne, which left him unable to 'close my eyes to the serious magnitude of the task that lies before us'. Lockhart claimed to 'foresee political dangers which may result from a military expedition commanded by military men who, by apparent facility of their initial military success, may be led to minimise the extreme complexity of [the] political problem which confronts us'.

Something violent was about to happen in Russia. Lockhart knew about it and he feared the challenge of narrating events to the Russian public in a way that made the Allies look good. The depth of Lockhart's concern over this can be gleaned from his ominous warning that, 'by the time this telegram reaches you [the] whole situation may have changed'.

Whether he was at the meeting or briefed by Reilly afterwards, whatever was discussed at the American consulate on 25 August convinced Lockhart that the climax of his mission was approaching, and that all involved would be in great danger.[12]

All but one. Amid the coterie of Bolshevik-haters and habitual plotters, there was someone at the American consulate who did not belong. René Marchand was a French journalist whom Grenard believed worked for his country's intelligence service. This was as incorrect an assessment of Marchand as one could have. Like Robins, Sadoul and Ransome, Marchand was a 'fellow traveller' on the road to revolution and was appalled to hear talk 'of secret activity of the most dangerous character' at the meeting. This included Reilly's plans to blow up a bridge across the River Volkhov with the aim of severing Petrograd's supply lines and driving the already starving population into a general uprising. Marchand also heard Verthamon speak of explosives and detonators stashed at his lodgings for use in the bridge-blasting operation, which would be followed by a coup from the Riflemen and the most heinous counter-revolutionary act of all. In contrast to Hill's delightfully absurd version of Reilly's plans, Marchand reported the latter's intention to 'leap onto the stage' at the Bolshevik Congress, 'seize Lenin, Trotsky and the other leaders' and have the Riflemen shoot them. Based on Poole and Grenard's unbothered reactions to this talk of explosions, coups and executions, Marchand concluded that these plans were approved by the Allied diplomats and the governments they represented.

After the meeting ended, the disgusted journalist marched over to the Cheka's headquarters – the Lubyanka – and reported what he had heard to Dzerzhinsky. A week later, Poole was smuggling himself into Finland while Grenard and Lavergne were barricading themselves in the American consulate. Pursued by Chekists, Verthamon was sneaking into the Swedish embassy in search of refuge, while Reilly and Hill were darting from safe-house to safehouse trying to stay one step ahead of their pursuers. Lockhart, Boyce and Hicks were in prison and Cromie was lying dead on the floor of the British embassy. Seemingly, with one visit to the Lubyanka, Marchand had unleashed the storm that Lockhart had warned Whitehall was coming. Reilly thought as much. Reflecting on the plot's unravelling years later, he claimed to have had an 'uneasy feeling' about Marchand. At the consulate meeting, Reilly tried to shield his and Verthamon's violent talk from the suspicious journalist but, as 'the room we were in was long and badly lighted', Marchand was still able to eavesdrop on their talk of destroying bridges and starving Russians. This assertion that he was onto Marchand was Reilly trying to bury his own amateurish blunder. By blaming Grenard's guest, the 'Ace of Spies' sidestepped the true reason why the plan to destroy Bolshevism failed so spectacularly – he, Lockhart, Cromie and anyone else charmed by Schmidkhen, Bredis and Berzin had been duped.[13]

The men whom Cromie befriended over many a glass of vodka were not Latvian dissidents. Schmidkhen and Bredis' real names were Sprogis and Buikis and they were – as Lockhart had initially suspected – *agents provocateurs* in the pay of the Cheka. Despatched to Petrograd in June to sniff out anti-Bolshevik conspiracies, the Latvians soon crossed paths with Cromie and 'Mr Massino', the supposed Turkish businessman whom Dzerzhinsky rightly suspected was also Moscow's mysterious 'Mr Constantine'. Though the precise nature of Reilly's mission under these aliases was unknown to him, Dzerzhinsky was aware of his courier networks, his connections to Savinkov and his affiliation with Lockhart, whom the unsmiling spymaster had never trusted. As one of the Cheka chief's deputies, Pavel Malkov recalled, the silver-tongued Scot with the flawless Russian accent was too smooth and his purpose in Moscow too ambiguous not to raise Dzerzhinsky's suspicions. His 'unconcerned attitude' amid the revolution's drama and his gift of the gab might have charmed others, but the Cheka leaders knew that beneath the British Agent's genial façade lay an 'intriguer' who was 'skilful at stealthy craftiness' and 'at inciting other people'.

Dzerzhinsky realised that it would take only a smattering of insurrectionary chatter from Sprogis and Buikis to hook the British Agent. The inclusion of a third Cheka asset, Berzin, was the masterstroke. The supposedly 'sound' Riflemen commander convinced Lockhart that masses of Latvian troops could be won over to the Allied cause. A scheme of such scale necessitated Lockhart bringing in the French and the Americans, widening the Cheka's net in the process. As to the purpose of Dzerzhinsky's plan, it has been suggested that he intended to use the Riflemen's surrender to lure General Poole's troops into a massive Red Army ambush in northern Russia. Quite possibly, Reilly's development of the plot into a coup, complete with mutterings of murdering Lenin and Trotsky, forced Dzerzhinsky to turn his focus away from the Allied invasion force – which the Bolsheviks had realised by late August was small and unthreatening – towards their nearer enemies in Petrograd and Moscow. Either way, within days of Sprogis' and Buikis' first meeting with Lockhart the Cheka had their man and his secret network right where they wanted them.[14]

Two acts of terrorism forced Dzerzhinsky to reel in his ever-growing catch. On the morning of 30 August, the head of the Petrograd Cheka, Moisei Uritsky, was gunned down by a former Kerensky supporter with ties to the Whites. Later that day, a Socialist Revolutionary named Dora Kaplan fired three shots at Lenin outside a factory in Moscow, leaving the Bolshevik leader fighting for his life. In the space of twenty-four hours, assassins affiliated with groups the Cheka knew to be funded by Lockhart and his associates had tried to kill two of the Bolshevik regime's key figures. Moreover, these attacks occurred mere days after Marchand had come knocking at the Lubyanka's doors with his concerning story of what went on in the American consulate. A spymaster of Dzerzhinsky's calibre didn't deal in coincidence. Instead, deciding that the attacks on Uritsky and Lenin heralded the activation of the anti-Bolshevik plot of which Marchand spoke, on the evening of 30 August Dzerzhinsky ordered his men to shut down Lockhart and his friends.

The speed with which the dominoes fell reveals the conspirators' lack of basic security measures. When Verthamon escaped the Chekists by jumping out of the window of his lodgings in Petrograd he left behind eighteen pounds of nitrocellulose, detonators, a cipher sheet, 30,000 roubles and the names and addresses of other network members. The seriousness of this contraband was enough to justify the summary execution of Verthamon's people when they were duly apprehended. Hill's couriers were rounded up next, their mission to warn Reilly of the dragnet cut short by the long arm of the Chekists, who had been watching them for weeks. Reilly's network of note-passers was also broken up by a series of raids, which were made possible by the foolish 'Ace of Spies' leaving out a card in his Petrograd flat with a safehouse address on it, which Berzin jotted down during one of their meetings.

Kalamatiano aped Reilly's ineptitude. With the Cheka closing in, he refused to join Poole on the next train to Finland and instead returned to the American consulate. A solid structure with a high outer wall and a cellar crammed with weeks' worth of food, the site of the conspirators' plotting became their refuge from Dzerzhinsky's wrath, particularly after the neutral Norwegians agreed to add another layer of diplomatic protection to the building by flying their flag over it. The Bolsheviks were unwilling to storm this sanctuary, but they had no problem surrounding it with rifle-toting Chekists and armoured vehicles. Grenard and Lavergne made it through the doors before the ring of iron closed but Kalamatiano wasn't so lucky. His cover story to the besiegers that he was an American citizen trying to get his passport renewed fooled no one. Worse yet, the Chekists inspected Kalamatiano's walking cane, within which were stored rolled-up notes on the Red Army's strength and positions. This sufficed to seal his fate. The spy was interrogated, held in appalling prison conditions for months and finally executed by firing squad in December 1918.

Kalamatiano was not the only prominent member of the conspiracy to die as a consequence of its unravelling. On the afternoon of 31 August, Cromie was gunned down at the British embassy which, unlike the American consulate, was not regarded as sacrosanct by the Bolsheviks. Believing that the embassy's staff were sheltering counter-revolutionaries, Dzerzhinsky ordered an armed incursion in disregard of diplomatic protocol and international law. This set terrifying parameters for the Bolsheviks' 'red terror' – a brutal suppression of enemies real and imagined that led to the deaths of hundreds across Moscow and Petrograd in the days that followed.[15]

Lockhart and Reilly had rolled their dice on the Riflemen and come up catastrophically short. Why and how did they make this grievous miscalculation? The plot's brazenness was in keeping with Reilly's style but even by Lockhart's cavalier standards moments of sloppiness abounded in its conception. In addition to relying on Cromie's bad handwriting as an assurance he wasn't dealing with *agents provocateurs*, Lockhart did next to nothing to vet Berzin. A little digging into the colonel's history would have revealed that he led one of the massacres of Moscow's anarchists and was a staunch defender of the Bolshevik regime. For someone whose stock in Russia had been built on being well connected and well informed, this lack of basic research seems laughable. Unless one considers that by August 1918 Lockhart was cracking under self-inflicted pressure. By committing on several occasions to continuing his mission, the British Agent now had to deliver results to both Whitehall and to himself. His fist-on-the-desk demands for a massive intervention, his willingness to fling millions of roubles at subversives of varying reliability and his dramatic assertion to the Foreign Office that 'our whole fate in Russia now hangs on a hair' evidence a man who appreciated the height of the stakes he had set. By August 1918, reasoned thinking and thoroughness had no place in Lockhart's clawing quest for victory at whatever cost.

Cockiness also played a part in Lockhart's miscalculation with the Latvians. Years in Russia had bred in him a sense of contempt for intelligence services, be they Boyce's MI6 or Dzerzhinsky's Cheka. Despite his initial suspicions of Schmidkhen and Bredis, Lockhart struggled to believe that the 'terrifying but far from clever' Cheka could pull off such a slick infiltration of his team. As always, contradictions tore Lockhart asunder. His assuredness that he was the sharpest man in the room combined with his fear of mission failure robbed him of common sense. This mindset was fuelled by the counter-revolutionary groupthink created by Reilly, Grenard and Poole, which ensured that Lockhart felt unjustifiably confident in the

Riflemen scheme even as it gathered a dangerous momentum he couldn't hope to control. Hostage to a drama of his own making, the British Agent was inescapably committed to the disastrous plot that would come to bear his name and haunt his legacy.[16]

For his part, Reilly escaped the consequences of this ill-judged gambit. With false identity papers provided by Hill, he fled Petrograd and arrived in London on 8 November. He survived the subsequent accusation from an embittered Poole that it was he rather than Marchand or the Latvians who had betrayed the plotters. Not only was he clearly anti-Bolshevik, but his pledge to return to the hornet's nest he had stirred and continue fighting Lenin deflected Poole's criticisms and persuaded MI6 and Winston Churchill, one of his most influential admirers, that the 'Ace of Spies' was on the level.

Such evasion and rehabilitation proved elusive for Reilly's 'captain'. Sharing his boss's disdain for Lockhart, the Chekist commander Malkov was delighted to be given the honour of arresting the haughty British Agent. Arriving at 2 a.m. on the morning of 31 August at Number 19 Bread Lane, Malkov led a team of Chekists up the stairs to apartment 20, the door to which was reluctantly opened by Moura and Hicks. As his men detained the pair and searched them, Malkov stalked towards Lockhart, pointing his pistol and declaring that he was now at the Cheka's mercy. This reality was made clear to Lockhart twenty minutes later when he was dragged into a sparse interrogation room at the Lubyanka, within which his tour guide for the massacre of the anarchists, Jacob Peters, was sitting emotionless behind a desk. His face a study in blankness, Peters waited for Lockhart to be placed by the guards into the chair opposite him before ostentatiously placing a revolver on the desk between them. He then fixed dark eyes on his prisoner and pointedly asked: 'Do you know Konstantin [Reilly]?' What little confidence still remained in Lockhart melted away. The message that the Cheka knew what he had been up to was clearly sent, and the unsubtle threat of this revelation understood. The gamble that had ended Lockhart's mission, it seemed, would now cost him his life.[17]

CHAPTER 9

MISSION'S END

'Your career is finished. Your government will never forgive you.
Why don't you stay here?'

– Jacob Peters

'Lockhart arrested,' Britain's ambassador in Copenhagen cabled the Foreign Office, 'condemned to death'. Likewise, Francis in Archangel received word that 'Lockhart was in prison' and, given that Uritsky's murder and the attempt on Lenin had 'been attributed by the Bolshevik authorities and the Bolshevik press to French and English' agents, it was 'quite possible that all now under arrest at Moscow and Petrograd would be shot'. The Dutch consul in Moscow, William Oudendyk, confirmed these dire tidings in a report to Washington. As a neutral party, Oudendyk had tried interceding with the Bolsheviks on behalf of the consular staff, informers, couriers and other British, American and French nationals swept up by Dzerzhinsky's men. The hue and cry of the 'red terror', however, drowned out Oudendyk's pleas, leading him to conclude that the position of the prisoners was 'most precarious', and the 'question of whether to shoot or release them has not yet been decided'. This included Lockhart. With Lenin severely wounded and the Cheka having destroyed the remaining sinews of normality in Anglo-Bolshevik relations by killing Cromie, Lockhart's safe conduct passes were no longer worth the paper they were printed on.[1]

When the diplomatic chatter over Lockhart's plight reached the British press an outrage narrative quickly formed. The *Telegraph* railed at the lawless Bolsheviks who, driven to paranoid violence by the attempt on Lenin, were now rampaging 'un-checked, and without acknowledgement of responsibility to anybody'. In addition to Lockhart being detained and the mass round-up of British and French citizens, '512 so-called counter-revolutionaries', reported another newspaper, had been shot in Petrograd as a precautionary measure against further attacks on Bolshevik officials. Those enemies spared execution were imprisoned in medieval conditions, crammed like cattle into the stone-bleak cells of the Peter and Paul Fortress, wherein they were forced to use buckets for toilets and rely on black bread and filthy water for sustenance.

This was not journalistic hyperbole. Neutral diplomats confirmed the appalling state of the prisoners' incarceration in their reports to Whitehall, while the Bolshevik foreign affairs commissar, Chicherin, conceded to the Americans that over 500 people had been shot in Petrograd. Reports on the aftermath of Cromie's failed attempt to defend the British embassy also reaffirmed the idea that the Bolsheviks were now operating at the level of beasts. 'His corpse,' reported *The Times*, 'was treated with the worst indignities, and permission to say prayers over his body was refused to an English clergyman.' Oudendyk confirmed this story, reporting apologetically to Whitehall that after some wrangling with the Cheka he and his Danish counterpart managed to retrieve the fallen attaché's body from the cellar into which it had been callously flung. The consuls convened a hasty funeral, but with no Union Jack to hand they had to drape Cromie's casket with a Danish flag.[2]

The leaking of these disturbing details to the press embarrassed the British government and put its bedevilled Agent in an unwelcome public spotlight. A furious *Daily Mail* op-ed suggested that to spare Lockhart from Cromie's fate, the government had to decree 'that if an Allied subject is killed, 5 or 10 Bolsheviks, to be selected from the Lenins and the Trotskys and not from the miserable rabble which serves as their dupes, shall suffer death' once the revolution was inevitably snuffed out. More soberly, *The Times* opined that the Bolshevik leaders needed to be made to understand – preferably through diplomatic exchanges rather than murderous threats – that they would be held personally liable for any harm that came to Lockhart or the other British prisoners. The Foreign Office agreed with this sentiment and tried to stir neutral diplomats in Russia to issue such a declaration. Given the Bolsheviks' violently unpredictable actions against foreign nationals, however, the neutrals were unwilling to escalate things with the Kremlin. The British government did have one remaining ace up its sleeve, which it quickly threw on the table – ordering the detention of the Bolshevik minister in London, Maxim Litvinov, and over twenty other Russian nationals attached to his mission. The stage was now set for an exchange that could end the diplomatic stand-off and save the lives of those in Cheka custody – Litvinov and his people for Lockhart and the other Britons.[3]

This decision to take Russian hostages was not made solely to spare Lockhart a bullet. The British Agent's brief required him to work within the realms of plausible deniability. This is evidenced by Whitehall's repeated refusals to define the parameters of Lockhart's mission and its muted endorsement of his backing of Savinkov's violent plans for regime change. The details of Lockhart's operations were not as important to his political masters as his ability to be discreet about how he conducted them. With *The Times* now reproducing articles from *Pravda* (the Bolsheviks' propaganda newspaper), which spoke of 'the connexion of various counter-revolutionary organisations with the British government and the British embassy', Lockhart had violated this unspoken standing order. Lindley added to British anxieties by confirming that *Pravda* wasn't spinning a yarn. Having done some digging following the Cheka's raids, he reported that Cromie's 'plans may very well have included [the] destruction of certain bridges as [the] Bolsheviks declare'. Worse still, it seemed that lists of saboteurs and equipment confirming this violent intent had been seized by the Cheka from the British embassy. The question vexing Whitehall in the first days of September was how much more the Bolsheviks might find out about what Lockhart and his team had been planning. In musing on this, some officials raised the spectre of the British Agent's supposed flakiness, warning that the lightweight would crack under interrogation and 'disclose something damaging to England'. Arguably, this concern over Lockhart spilling the beans was as pressing to Whitehall as any fears for his safety.[4]

This unease over Lockhart's reliability was not assuaged when he refused the chance to extract himself from danger. A day after their arrest on 31 August, Lockhart and Hicks were released from the Lubyanka. This reprieve was owed to both a protest from Chicherin – who was one of the few friends Lockhart still had among the Bolsheviks – and the failure of Peters' interrogation methods. After revealing to his prisoner that he knew about Reilly and the Latvians, the Chekist put Lockhart back in a cell with Hicks where, knowing that their captors were listening in, the pair confined their talk to trivialities. Unable to draw any details of the conspiracy out of his tight-lipped prisoners, Peters next had an emaciated woman with a dead-eyed stare brought into their cell. This was Dora Kaplan, the would-be assassin of Lenin. Her presentation to Lockhart and Hicks was an attempt by Peters to elicit a flicker of recognition in either party's eyes, which would confirm a connection between the Britons and the Russian counter-revolutionaries who wanted Lenin dead. When no exchange occurred, the near catatonic Kaplan was removed from the cell and shot in the back of the head by Malkov. Under pressure from Chicherin and frustrated with the lack of progress in his investigation, Peters reluctantly decided to let his British prisoners go.

Fighting exhaustion and nervous tension, Lockhart and Hicks dragged themselves back to the Bread Lane apartment, which they found empty of life and thoroughly despoiled. Wallpaper had been stripped, upholstery slashed and furniture broken apart. The Cheka, however, had not found anything more incriminating than a stash of money and some pistols. This was suspicious but, in the Moscow of 1918, guns and ready-to-hand cash were not out of the ordinary possessions. Indicative of either Lockhart's luck or his captors' ineptitude, the Cheka also missed the notebook he had in his jacket pocket when he was arrested. This was a more damning piece of evidence than anything in his apartment, as it contained a record of the monies he had given to the Riflemen, the Socialist Revolutionaries and the Whites. Realising that he had carried this incriminating document into the Lubyanka, Lockhart gained permission from his guards to go to the toilet, where he flushed the notebook's pages down the bowl.

This opportunity to cover his tracks, combined with Peters' decision to release him, should have left Lockhart feeling relieved that he had, yet again, scraped through a tough situation. This satisfaction was robbed from him, however, by a single tormenting thought – what had become of Moura? She had been seized with him and Hicks yet had not been released like them from custody. Indeed, Lockhart had not seen her since he was bundled into a car bound for the Lubyanka. Was she being held hostage? Had she been executed like Kaplan? These and other worries assaulted Lockhart's mind, more so when Oudendyk visited the Bread Lane apartment to inform him of Cromie's murder. If the Cheka were willing to kill a British officer, what would they do to a Ukrainian well-to-do who had conspired with their enemies? In a stupor of worry and confusion Lockhart neither followed Hill and Reilly into hiding nor joined Hicks in seeking sanctuary at the American consulate with Grenard, Lavergne and the others. Instead of fleeing his enemies, the brazen Scot went to their front door. On 4 September, three days after being released from the Lubyanka, Lockhart marched into its reception hall and demanded an audience with Peters. Amused and delighted by this turn of events, the Chekist granted this request. Clearly, Moura's ongoing detention had rattled Lockhart, who appeared before Peters looking every bit the despairing love-sick fool he was. More than that, he had the mien of a custom-wrapped gift. 'You saved me some trouble,' Peters smirked. 'I have a warrant for your arrest.'[5]

This visit to the Lubyanka ended Lockhart's brief chance of fleeing Russia and began his second stint of incarceration at the Cheka's pleasure. This time, however, the charges on which he stood accused had been fleshed out with dire details. In the three days that Lockhart had been at liberty, the Bolshevik press had run outraged reports of his puppet-master role in an Allied conspiracy to blow up trains and bridges, bribe 'troops with the object of capturing the Council of People's Commissars' and proclaim 'a military dictatorship at Moscow'. With this coup accomplished, so the stories went, Lockhart intended to falsify documents that would re-start the war between Russia and Germany, in the hope that Bolshevism would be annihilated and tsarism restored. It was serious stuff, but even the narrators of this state-sponsored indictment had to concede that hard evidence had yet to be uncovered. It was with the aim of rectifying this problem of absent evidence that Peters had ordered the British Agent's rearrest. He also wanted a public confession out of Lockhart that could justify the 'red terror' and confirm the Kremlin's narrative that it was beset by enemies within and without. Aside from these prospective political gains, damage control also played a part in Lockhart being taken back into custody. The international backlash against Cromie's murder had been significant. Official protests had been lodged with the Kremlin by Allied and neutral diplomats. Even the German government issued a condemnation, in solidarity with its wartime adversaries. As Poole put it in his report to Washington, while there was 'some foundation of fact for [the] charges respecting Lettish troops', there was none 'regarding destruction of trains and other demolitions'. Lockhart, therefore, had been rearrested 'prematurely without conclusive proofs in order to befog [the] issue growing out of Cromie's murder'.[6]

Lockhart's second round of detainment was a carrot-and-stick affair, defined by mind games, creature comforts and the lingering threat of execution. He was initially held in a sparse cell at the Lubyanka, denied sleep and sent for by Peters at all hours of day or night for repetitive yet unfailingly polite interrogation. During these sessions, Lockhart was told that Grenard and Lavergne had confessed all (neither had been taken into custody) and was made to watch former members of Kerensky's government being executed by firing squad in the prison yard. Staring vacantly out of the window of Lockhart's cell as these men were gunned down, Peters explained how the nail-pulling torture meted out to him by the Okhrana decades earlier meant that he now felt pain in his hand every time he signed a death warrant. Like his show of indifference to the bloody scene at the House of Anarchy, Peters was letting the British Agent know he was swimming with sharks.

Lockhart swallowed his inner fear and presented himself as unrattled, refusing to sign anything implicating the British or any other Allied government in the plot. Accepting that the threaten-and-frighten approach wasn't working, Peters changed tactics. On 8 September – notably, two days after Lenin's doctors confirmed that he would survive his wounds – Lockhart was moved to the Kremlin. A far cry from his Lubyanka shoebox, Lockhart's new 'cell' was a three-room apartment with an ensuite bathroom and views of the garden. Though the changing of the guards woke him at all hours, Lockhart was provided with a servant to bring him newspapers and prepare his meals and was allowed an hour of daily exercise. Other than being a prisoner, the only sour point in Lockhart's new detention was that the guards gave him daily updates on what odds their betting pool was offering on his time at the Kremlin ending with a bullet and an unmarked grave.[7]

One wonders if Peters put the guards up to telling Lockhart this. Such psychological warfare was in keeping with the Chekist's approach to breaking his prisoner. He had started with the basics. Deploying a classic ruse, shortly after Lockhart was rearrested Peters had Schmidkhen, AKA Sprogis, brought into his room. Lockhart realised the Latvian was a stool pigeon, and so kept the discussion as bland as he had with Hicks. Peters was thwarted but far from defeated. After removing Schmidkhen from the game he deployed his secret weapon – Moura. She had been spared execution, but the socialite-cum-spy had still paid dearly for her love of the British Agent. On the night of their arrest, Moura had been separated from Lockhart and Hicks and driven to Butyrka prison. This was a hellish fortress of nineteenth-century vintage, within the walls of which generations of revolutionaries had perished from starvation and disease. There, Moura languished in pestilential conditions and was fed on thin soup, black bread and the occasional chunk of horsemeat. This led to her growing physically weaker with each day spent in what one similarly starved British detainee likened to the Black Hole of Calcutta. This deprivation doubtless contributed to the stress Moura felt when informed by the guards that her lover had been sent to the Kremlin, as it was known as a place from which prisoners never returned alive. Malnourished and wracked with anguish, Moura miscarried her and Lockhart's child. She had no time, however, to process the trauma. Two days later, Peters appeared in her cell with a twinkle in his eye and a letter from Lockhart in his hand. Adding a sneer of surrealism to the proceedings, he handed the precious piece of paper over to Moura while flashing a cheerful smile and suggesting she would be allowed to write back to her lover. Moura all but snatched the pen and paper out of Peters' hands and hastily scrawled out the first of many prison missives to her 'dear, dear, baby'.[8]

Owing to Moura's work for the Cheka in Ukraine and his monitoring of Lockhart since the spring, Peters knew the extent of their affair. He exploited this emotional bond to its fullest. Once he had established correspondence between the lovestruck prisoners – all the letters were, of course, read by Peters – he released Moura from the Butyrka with a promise that she could send her man gifts and perhaps even visit him. Moura duly bombarded the Kremlin with packages of food, clothes, shaving accoutrements, books and letters, in which she declared her undying love. Alone in his gilded cage, Lockhart took solace from Moura's outpouring of affection, which helped to distract him from the fear of summary execution. Further comfort came when Moura was finally allowed to visit him on 22 September. Their reunion was bittersweet. In addition to the meeting lasting less than twenty minutes and being conducted under Peters' watchful eye, Moura took the opportunity to inform Lockhart of her miscarriage. After a day spent processing the fact that he had once again lost the chance to be a father, Lockhart scrawled in his prison diary that 'I am much upset and wonder how everything will end'.

This despondency was stifled, however, by further visits from Moura, who was looking far better to Lockhart's eyes than she had any right to, given her ordeals and torment at the Butyrka. Her actions during one of these Peters-chaperoned meetings further lifted Lockhart's spirits. As the Chekist regaled the pair with a story from his revolutionary days, Moura surreptitiously slid a piece of paper into one of the books she had sent her lover, who managed a nod of acknowledgement that their captor failed to notice. Once Moura and Peters left, Lockhart rushed over to the book and read the note – 'Say nothing. All will be well.' He hadn't a clue why Moura was so sure of things, but Lockhart believed in her and trusted her judgement. The tension ebbed from his body and a flicker of confidence returned to lighten his weighty thoughts. Maybe his future would not involve staring down the barrel of a Chekist's gun?[9]

Lockhart was less confident that his future wouldn't involve prolonged incarceration. Peters told him with glee that a public trial was being prepared, at which the details of Lockhart's conspiracy would be revealed to the world. And it was by now *his* conspiracy. During subsequent meetings at which Peters allowed the pair to converse in private, Moura informed Lockhart that Reilly and Poole had successfully escaped Dzerzhinsky's dragnet and that the other conspirators were sheltering beyond the Cheka's reach in the American consulate. This left Lockhart under no illusions that he alone would be the star of Peters' show trial, paraded like a hunting prize to damn the Allies and score the Bolsheviks a propaganda win. As an unwilling tool in these proceedings, Lockhart would further the revolution he had tried to snuff out. From inside the American consulate, Hicks cabled a message back to Britain warning of this situation. He pleaded with Whitehall to both accelerate its plans to hand over Litvinov and, if 'necessary to liberate in exchange many and possibly all prisoners taken by the Allies in [North] Russia' to sweeten the deal and get Lockhart released before the trial.[10]

As Hicks laboured to save his boss from humiliation or execution, Peters pulled his final trick. Realising he was in a race against time to avoid Lockhart being exchanged for Litvinov, he laid a compelling proposal before his prisoner. Ignominy and derision awaited Lockhart in Britain but in Russia he had Moura and, if he played ball, the respect and protection of the Bolsheviks. 'Capitalism is doomed anyway,' Peters asserted, as he offered Lockhart a cigarette. Why hurry back to its crumbling bastion when 'you can be happy and make your own life' in Russia? It was not as mad a proposal as it sounded. Russia had given Lockhart the life of adventure he craved and a brief but invigorating career, the challenges of which had left him cynical about his government and his work in its service. More than anything, the land of revolution and discord had given him Moura, the 'heroine of my Russian life', who aroused Lockhart's passions in a way that Jean never could.

And yet, the lovestruck Russophile could not accept Peters' offer. It was not just the insulting transparency of the ploy. Lockhart had seen too much blood and paranoia from the Bolsheviks to trust his future to a life under their protection. Though he agreed with Peters that the failure of his mission meant his career was all but dead, the 'all but' gave Lockhart pause. He had achieved resurrection twice already. Surely he could rise again? Against this hope was stacked a certainty that if he chose to bask in the workers' paradise with Moura rather than return to Britain, his career would be over and with it all aspects of life as he knew it. Jean would be lost and so too would his family and friends. In the eyes of Britain's government, its press and its public he would be a traitor no better than Marchand, whose finger-pointing tales of Western skulduggery were all over the Bolshevik press at this time, much to Lockhart's disgust. Wretched as he felt for the way things had ended, Peters' offer of oblivion was too absolute for Lockhart to stomach. After months of playing the most dangerous of games in Russia, the British Agent finally decided to remove himself from the field.

In truth, the decision was made for him. Peters' final attempt to craft a propaganda coup from Lockhart's imprisonment was prompted by news that Whitehall and the Kremlin had agreed to exchange their respective hostages. Such was the level of distrust, however, that both sides demanded that the handover occur simultaneously, with Litvinov and his party boarding a ship bound for Russia at Bergen in Norway at the same time that Lockhart and his people crossed the Russo-Finnish border via train. With his quarry now officially on the road to freedom, Peters showed his softer side. He allowed Moura to spend the last two days of Lockhart's incarceration in his suite, granting them a modicum of privacy. In return, Lockhart agreed to carry a letter home to Peters' English wife, whom he had married during his time on the run from the Okhrana. Moura was also allowed to return to the Bread Lane apartment and arrange Lockhart's things in preparation for his departure, which was scheduled for 1 October. There was little for Moura to pack. The Cheka had stolen Lockhart's cufflinks, shirts and tie pins and emptied the once formidable wine cupboard. Even the butter had gone. Peters apologised for the looting and, in a final acknowledgement that their battle of wits was over, granted Lockhart's request that Hicks be allowed free passage out of both the American consulate and the country. The relieved captain was even permitted to marry his Russian girlfriend before the pair were put on the train to Finland.[11]

There was no such happy ending for Lockhart and Moura. While Hicks was a bachelor at liberty to wed, the prospect of the married Lockhart returning to Britain with a Russian mistress on his arm was dubious. This was not only for reasons of impropriety. Moura had two children, a sister, an ailing mother and a husband – a status that would persist until April 1919, when bandits murdered Djon in the forest outside Yendel. Though deeply smitten with Lockhart, Moura accepted that her personal circumstances made relocating to Britain near impossible. That was *if* the authorities agreed to let her in. In the scramble to assign blame for the plot's unravelling, those unconvinced of Reilly's nefariousness cast accusatory stares at the mysterious countess. Without doubt, she knew about the plot. Moura had been involved in her lover's machinations for months and when Robin Bruce Lockhart spoke to her in the 1960s while researching his Reilly biography, she complained about his father being depicted as little more than the 'cash box in the cloak and dagger affair', which she confidently asserted to Robin was 'doomed from the beginning'.

Certain members of Britain's intelligence community were convinced that Moura had betrayed her knowledge of the plot to the Cheka or had proposed 'various schemes more or less wildcat [in] nature' to Lockhart, including the 'Lettish Rifles' idea. The notion that Moura was either an *agent provocateur* or had 'directly informed the Soviets of these schemes' was furthered by odious rumours that she bought her way out of Butyrka and secured Lockhart's freedom by sleeping with Peters. Her reputation as a seductress aside, it is doubtful that Moura's feminine gifts would have been enough to convince Peters to release the architect of the most dangerous plot yet uncovered against the regime he loyally served. At most, she might have agreed to play the 'lure' role in Peters' plan to keep the British Agent in Russia, for this outcome would have given the Chekist his propaganda victory and Moura a life with the man she loved. Her unwillingness to pen a memoir and her thoroughness in destroying personal papers, however, means that these theories will always float in the realms of speculation. Lacking any firm evidence to the contrary, there is little to suggest that Moura betrayed her 'baby boy'.[12]

Lockhart didn't suspect her. Determined to leave his mission as he started it – by marching to the beat of his own drum – he delayed his departure for twenty-four hours to spend more time with Moura. It was a decision that Lindley derided as 'incredible' given the British Agent had just defied death by walking free from the Kremlin.

The pull of spending a further day with his beloved was not the only reason Lockhart took his time in bidding Russia farewell. Once back at the Bread Lane apartment, Lockhart had a meeting with the Swedish consul Claes Asker, whom he regarded as one of the most sound and reliable diplomats in Russia. The Swede had agreed to take charge of British affairs in the country now that Lockhart and the other officials were leaving. Though coy in both his memoirs and his report to Balfour about what he discussed with Asker, it is likely that Lockhart was making sure his tracks were well covered. During his time at the Kremlin, Lockhart made a note in his diary – scrawled in Malay for reasons of secrecy – that Moura had informed him 'all the letters were taken to the big Dutch house in the city'. This was most likely a reference to incriminating documents from either the British consulate or his office being given to the Dutch consul Oudendyk for safe keeping. Lockhart's meeting with Asker was probably a way of confirming that the trusted diplomat would keep any other evidence that might crop up out of the Cheka's hands. If this was his plan, then Lockhart's judgement was well placed. Weeks after returning from London, he could report with confidence to Balfour that 'the Bolsheviks have little actual evidence against us and practically no written evidence'. As Peters told him with grudging respect on the day he walked free from the Kremlin, he was 'either a fool or very clever'.[13]

Lockhart was both. The fool had authored a plot of follies but by burning his ciphers and making sure his documents stayed out of the Cheka's hands, Lockhart had demonstrated some of the savvy that led to his appointment as British Agent in the first place. He had left behind nothing to incriminate either himself or the British government and for this reason Peters was unable to get his man. Nor was Moura. On 2 October, she and a smattering of well-wishers gathered to see Lockhart, Hicks, Tamplin, Lingner, Boyce and fifty other British and French officials and their families board the train that would evacuate them to Finland. As the shadows lengthened and the railway platform's fluorescent lighting flickered to life, Lockhart and Moura shared idle reminiscences. The weight of anything else was too heavy to raise. The torture of their long and awkward goodbye lasted hours as the stationmaster waited for news of Litvinov's departure to come through. Moura stayed until this confirmation arrived at 2 a.m. When the whistle to board blew, Lockhart finally surrendered to his feelings. He sighed deeply and watched for what seemed like an eternity as the cold mist of his breath evaporated between him and the woman he loved. Taking her gloved hand in his, Lockhart affixed his eyes on Moura's and told her to 'remember that each day is one day nearer to the time when we shall meet again'. It was unclear if he meant in this life or the next, but Moura took heart from the sentiment all the same. This tender moment was then abruptly ended when a score of Latvian Riflemen – perhaps Peters' final jab at his adversary – began shouting and herding Lockhart and the other evacuees into the carriages. Steam rose, the sound of metal-on-metal cut the air and within a minute he was gone, leaving Moura alone on the platform telling herself to be strong. Despondent to the point of numbness, Lockhart silently withdrew himself from the pack of relieved outcasts who cheered and embraced as the train spirited them away from danger. He found a quiet seat away from the throng and pressed his face against the window, staring in blank silence as Russia – and the last six years of his life – retreated into a collage of eerie blacks and moonlit greys. His mission, his romance with Moura and his great adventure had all come to an end.[14]

CHAPTER 10

A NIGHT WITHOUT DAWN

'In Prague lies the wreckage of the last years of my youth.'
– Robert Bruce Lockhart

On 11 November 1918, the Great War finally ended. Amid the sighs of relief across Europe, however, a sense of disquiet prevailed, for battlefield losses alone had not brought the *Kaiserreich* to its knees. Days before the German delegation arrived at Compiègne to sign the armistice, sailors inspired by the Bolshevik revolution mutinied at German naval bases along the Baltic coast. This spark immolated the war-weary nation. Soldier and worker councils aping the Petrograd Soviet were formed at Kiel and Wilhelmshaven. Similar groups soon arose in Bavaria, and in Berlin police were disarmed by 'socialists with red and white armlets'. Fearing a full-blown descent into Bolshevism, moderate leftist politicians seized the revolutionary moment and declared the end of the *Kaiserreich* and the founding of a new republic on 9 November. 'All over Germany,' reported a *Times* correspondent, 'dynasties and powers are disappearing from view' and 'nominal control of the Empire, for what that at the moment is worth, has passed by very rapid stages from the Kaiser to a predominantly Socialist government'.

Germany was not alone in swapping the sufferings of war for the drama of revolution. In the months following the armistice, discontented workers and radicalised soldiers agitated everywhere, from the docks of Belfast to the barracks of Budapest. All pondered the war's purpose and, now that peace had been declared, sought alternatives to a trudging return to the *status quo ante bellum*. In search of this new dawn, many craned their necks eastwards. The Bolsheviks were consolidating their hold on Russia, both by fending off the incessant Whites and by eschewing the results of a Constituent Assembly vote that they lost to the Socialist Revolutionaries. Suffering from his gunshot wounds yet still burning with zeal, Lenin responded to the vote against Bolshevism by ordering the Constituent Assembly dissolved and the deployment of soldiers and Chekists to stop anyone defying his decree or questioning his rule. By the winter of 1918–19 one thing seemed clear to observers both within Russia and without – against all odds, the Bolsheviks' revolution was holding. Had the Allies underestimated these radical dreamers? Were Lenin and Trotsky really the liberators of the world's oppressed? Was Bolshevism the best model on which to base the reconstruction of war-battered Europe? It was with the hope of having these questions answered that hundreds of people crammed into the main lecture hall at King's College London on the evening of 14 January 1919 to hear what Britain's former Agent in Russia had to say.[1]

When asked by the college to deliver a talk on Bolshevism and its future, Lockhart initially demurred. Suffering from what was probably Spanish Flu, he had arrived back in London on 19 October after two weeks' travelling through the creeping cold of the Scandinavian autumn. No sooner had he disembarked at Paddington Station than Lockhart was set upon by journalists hungry for details of his time at the Cheka's pleasure. Despite illness and exhaustion, he duly obliged. This ensured that the story of Lockhart's prison stint shared column space next to articles on 'Rumours of the Kaiser's abdication' and the 'Allies view of the enemy's cry for armistice!' The thrill of being mentioned alongside reportage of the Great War's denouement meant little, however, to the now ex-British Agent, whose ego was too bruised by failure to swell with pride. The wound was given no time to heal. After the journalists came Whitehall officials, who assailed Lockhart with questions of varying sensitivity about his activities in Russia. Those whom he trusted, like Rex Leeper, seem to have been given specific details. To most, however, Lockhart stuck to the narrative he laid down in early November in his secret report to Balfour – yes, a surrender of the Riflemen was discussed, but it wasn't until Reilly went against orders and tried to orchestrate a coup that things went awry.[2]

Lockhart even received a royal summons. King George V had devoured his reports from Russia and was fascinated by the twists and turns of the British Agent's tale. Suppressing his nagging cough, the sickly Scot pulled on a mothball-reeking coat and reported to the palace gates. He came away impressed with his sovereign, who seemed to have 'a surprising grasp of the situation' in Russia and 'a wholesome dread of Bolshevism'. Lockhart was less enamoured of his Whitehall colleagues, to whom he presented himself like a black sheep returning meekly to its flock. He quickly deduced that his principal 'enemies' were the permanent under-secretary Lord Hardinge and Lord Cecil, who had been one of his most consistent critics in the War Cabinet. The public nature of Lockhart's failure meant that these and other detractors could shift from a campaign of disapproving whispers to one of outright insults, in which Lockhart was derided in the halls of power as a misbehaving schoolboy who had gotten messed up in a drama beyond his station. Even his benevolent former boss Buchanan expressed dismay at Lockhart's counter-revolutionary bungle. 'It is perfectly obvious,' the ex-British Agent confided to his diary, 'that apart from the relief of having rescued me from the Bolsheviks, the Foreign Office is not in the least interested in my account of things.' Ruefully, he concluded that 'I may even have difficulty in obtaining another job.'[3]

This despondency grew when a pseudo-job offer arrived from the 'Ace of Spies'. Seemingly oblivious to the fiasco from which they had barely escaped with their lives, Reilly wrote to Lockhart about his vision for continuing the battle against Bolshevism. 'The salvation of Russia,' he declared, 'has become a most sacred duty, which we owe not only to the untold thousands of Russian men and women' killed by the Bolsheviks, 'but to ourselves'. Surveying the rising revolutionary tides across Europe, Reilly implored Lockhart to support an ill-defined international declaration to fight

communism at the upcoming Paris Peace Conference, with the hope that
this would pivot Europe from war against Germany to a crusade against
the Soviet Union. Naturally, Reilly believed he should lead this battle for the
world's soul. And yet, even a megalomaniac of his calibre had to concede
that he couldn't do it alone. For this reason, Reilly expressed to Lockhart
his earnest wish to 'serve under you' once more in the struggle to come.[4]

This time, Lockhart couldn't summon a laugh in response. He had just
received news that he, Reilly, Verthamon and Grenard had been tried *in
absentia* at the Revolutionary Tribunal that Peters had promised would be
convened. Their sentences were unambiguous. All were found guilty of
espionage and conspiracy and would be shot if they dared set foot again on
Russian soil. The verdict was a gut-punch that confirmed Lockhart's separation from both the country and the woman who had captured his heart.
This separation, however, was not total. From the moment she returned
to the ransacked Bread Lane apartment, Moura had penned Lockhart
letters, sometimes more than one a day. The thematic thread of this correspondence was her pledge to 'always remember what you said to me at the
station – each day is one day to the time when we shall meet again'. Moura
fantasised about them overcoming geography, her family situation, the
judgements of others and the watchful eye of the Cheka to reunite. Lonely
and crestfallen, this was a hope Moura nurtured to 'give me the strength to
go on with this beastly life', for 'the thought of a future without you leaves
me cold and numb with terror'.

These letters provided Lockhart with great comfort in the bleak
autumn of 1918, during which he struggled with both the failure of his
mission and, like many others who served, with the thought of having 'been
exalted in rank by the war and reduced to where we started by the armistice'. After receiving his death sentence, however, Moura's talk of resuming
their romance struck Lockhart as outlandish, on a level comparable to
Reilly's plans to annihilate Bolshevism. His responses to her tailed off over
the winter, prompting Moura to complain that 'it is like writing into the
darkness'. In February, she asked 'Do you remember how you used to say:

"our love must stand a 6-month test?", well, do you think yours is going to stand it?' By April 1919, her frustration flared into rage as she pleaded 'for god's sake, be frank with me'. He wasn't. Instead, Lockhart let his parting promise of reunion fade as he tried to block out all thoughts of both Russia and Moura. He still loved her, but he couldn't summon the courage to officially end their relationship. Better, he thought, to silently move on.[5]

In search of this clean slate, Lockhart travelled to Tomintoul at Christmas 1918 to clear his head and exorcise his Russian ghosts. This return to the ancestral homelands, however, proffered more cause for angst than blessed relief. Age was transforming Robert senior from a rugged outdoorsman to a bookish grey-hair. Still in shock at the loss of Norman, the typically outgoing Florence was alarmingly withdrawn and, to Lockhart's guilty mind, each time she looked upon him she saw 'a reflection of my own consciousness that the best had been taken and the worst left behind'. Naturally, the Rubber Queen chastised Lockhart for once more returning to Scotland with his career in tatters. Jean showed greater empathy by treating him like the released prisoner he was. She did her best to refrain from judging him for his career missteps and weathered the humiliation of his affair with Moura being one of the worst kept secrets in London. Desperate to move on, Jean tried to get Lockhart focused on repairing their battered marriage and leaving the travails of Russia to memory. It was an impossible mission. His 'physical body' might have returned to Britain, but his 'thoughts were back in Moscow'.[6]

This was why Lockhart accepted King's College's offer to speak – it would provide a much-needed opportunity to order his muddled thoughts on Russia and draw a line under his life there. He prepared thoroughly for his lecture on 'Social Conditions in Russia under Bolshevism', for which he trawled through the few notes he had managed to bring back from Moscow. Though keen to include insights that only one who had dined with Trotsky and been imprisoned in the Kremlin could provide, Lockhart was mindful that he was still technically employed by the Foreign Office. This meant that, in addition to omitting all mention of rouble-packed suitcases and

Latvian Riflemen, attendees were informed that Lockhart would not be answering questions. The lecture went well to the extent that Lockhart felt 'smugly satisfied' about his performance. And then, as the applause faded, the inevitable happened. From the back of the hall a 'Communist band' rose from their seats and demanded to know why Lockhart had plotted, using 'secret service money to secure the persons of Lenin and Trotsky by means of Lett soldiery'. As Lockhart stood listless at the lectern pondering how to proceed, the hall was consumed by a cacophony of shouting and the waving of fingers from the impassioned youth of the audience, while the professors and government officials rushed to the exit doors as fast as their spats could carry them. Dragging a millstone of regret for ever thinking the lecture a good idea, Lockhart grabbed his hat and coat and followed in their wake, leaving the fracas he caused to rage.[7]

Whether it was Reilly's anti-Bolshevik crusade, mandarins musing on Lenin's mindset, *The Times* asking him for biographical sketches of the Bolshevik leaders or student radicals declaring that the future belonged to communism, the Soviet Union was all anyone seemed interested in now that the *Kaiserreich* had been vanquished. This prevented Lockhart from moving past his time as Britain's Agent and made finding a new job that didn't involve Russia challenging. The offers were there. Lord Milner remained a fan, insisting to Lockhart that his knowledge and abilities were such that there would always be a place for him at the Foreign Office. Another of Lockhart's supporters, Arthur Steel-Maitland, offered him the job of First Commercial Secretary at the Warsaw consulate. Proving that beggars could be choosers, Lockhart turned the idea down on the grounds that Poland was too close to Russia for comfort. He responded similarly to another suggestion that he go to southern Russia as the government's liaison to the White general Anton Denikin, whose army was still being backed by Britain despite diminishing returns on the investment.

This refusal was justified. Traipsing back into Bolshevik territory was both dangerous on account of the death sentence and disastrous for Lockhart's hope of weening himself off his Russia addiction. The fact that this offer was made, however, suggests that some in Whitehall were happy to feed his habit. It also shows that Lockhart's reputation was not as damaged as he initially supposed. Indeed, given the post-war panic over Bolshevism in Britain – which heightened in the first months of 1919 as the country was beset by strikes, riots and mutinies by returning soldiers with an interest in revolutionary ideas – the man who had conspired to bring down Lenin looked like a good soldier in the fight between capitalism and communism. Lockhart, however, had little interest in going to war. Unlike Reilly, he had learned his lesson from the Latvian conspiracy's unravelling and, having worked with the Whites, saw them as a dead-end prospect. He declared in both internal correspondence to the Foreign Office and an anonymous *New Statesman* article in late 1918 that the Bolsheviks had consolidated their rule. Unless launched immediately and on a massive scale involving the Americans, the French and anyone else who could be mustered, further British intervention would lead to the loss of many lives for no good purpose. To Lockhart's mind, the war was over and the Bolsheviks had won. Whitehall's insistence to the contrary and its placing of faith in the likes of Denikin simply confirmed to the ex-British Agent that he had no place at the Foreign Office.[8]

Fate thought otherwise. By the summer of 1919, public interest in Lockhart's Russian adventures was waning and, with it, the prospect of commanding payment for lectures and interviews. This window of opportunity closed, moreover, just as Jean announced that she was once again pregnant. To provide for his expanding family Lockhart had to grasp the only offer remaining from the employer he resented – commercial secretary in either Belgrade or Prague. He made his choice based on the memory of a Czech teacher at Fettes who struck him as being charmingly exotic and a belief that 'for those who still regard the pursuit of the trout as the highest branch of the angler's art', Prague was at the 'centre of a veritable paradise'. On this asinine basis, Lockhart set off for Czechoslovakia in November 1919 with a mind to fish, hunt and forget. This last could not be attempted without a final tip of the hat to his days in Moscow. A week

before departing for Prague, Lockhart attended a private party in London
with Hill, Reilly, Leeper and some MI6 officers attached to anti-Bolshevik
operations in Russia. With gallows humour, it was dubbed the 'Liquidation
Lunch', in commemoration of the one-year anniversary since the death
sentences had been passed on the conspirators.[9]

This could have been a moment for joyous reflection. Though marked
for death in Russia, Lockhart had a new life before him in Czechoslovakia,
which was one of the better places in post-war Europe for a man of his
talents and interests to wash up. Built from the detritus of the shattered
Austro-Hungarian Empire and the treaties that ended the First World War,
Czechoslovakia was a new-born nation rich in untapped mineral and industrial potential, boasting a population of over 14 million Czechs, Slovaks,
Magyars, Jews and other ethnic groups. Its cultural diversity was matched
by its geopolitical importance to Europe's new order, acting as a buffer
state between vanquished Germany and revolutionary Russia. The British
viewed the fledgling nation as a *tabula rasa* on which a Central European
economic powerhouse could be built. For this reason, the Bank of England
had invested heavily in Czechoslovakia, while the Foreign Office set up
a formidable diplomatic presence in the capital. Housed within Prague's
Thun Palace, the legation to which Lockhart was assigned had at its disposal
ballrooms, private gardens and three floors of well-appointed offices, all
built in an aesthetically pleasing manner that blended into the ramparts and
cobblestones of the city's old town. It was a far cry from the stuffy apartment
consulate that he and Buchanan had manned in Moscow. Between the Thun
Palace's splendour, the Bank of England's money and the possibilities that
pulsed through Prague, Czechoslovakia was a place for the adventurous
and ambitious to stake a claim to Europe's post-war future.[10]

Lockhart, however, no longer felt a part of this go-getter caste. When he
arrived in Moscow in 1912, he had ingratiated himself with the city's elites
via three days of drinking and hobnobbing. Invited to attend a party for
Prague's movers and shakers on his first night in town in 1919, Lockhart
'pleaded tiredness. Unpacked my belongings and went to bed'. Low energy

and a bad attitude informed his first impressions of the city. While in time Lockhart grew to adore Prague and its people, the hastily erected post-war buildings of cheap concrete depressed him. The basics of modern life like clean water and a consistent energy supply were as wanting as they had been in rural Russia, while culturally Prague seemed unfathomably duller to Lockhart than decadent Moscow. He struggled to summon enthusiasm for his work, the scope of which was eclipsed by the energy and aptitude of his colleagues. In addition to the heavy-hitting chargé d'affaires Charles Gosling, the legation's third secretary, John Latter, was a rising star of Britain's diplomatic corps, possessed of the drive and vigour that Lockhart now lacked. The antithesis of the ailing Buchanan, the British minister at the legation, George Clerk, was a man of great energy and ambition, who took his brief to build Prague into a business mecca very seriously. He and Gosling did most of the legation's work. True, Lockhart contributed to their annual reports, commenting on the reserves and dividends of the Czech banks with whom the Bank of England had partnered. He also sent the odd intelligence assessment, like those that had forged his reputation in Moscow, analysing the political views of both important Czechs and visiting dignitaries and the spread of radical movements across Central Europe. Notably, these reports were not sent by Lockhart personally but as enclosures to Clerk's own missives to Whitehall – such was the ex-British Agent's disempowerment. The work was neither stressful nor onerous, yet it was a poor replacement for the thrilling peril of anti-Bolshevik plotting.[11]

The nearest Lockhart came to recapturing the spirit of Moscow was when Savinkov and Reilly visited Prague in September 1920 in search of support from the Czech government for their anti-Bolshevik operations. This was not a fanciful idea. Czechoslovakia's inaugural president, Tomáš Masaryk, had been instrumental in forming the Czech Legion that had turned on the Bolsheviks in 1918 and his foreign minister, Edouard Beneš, saw his country's future laying in the West rather than the East. Both men were concerned about communist agitation in Czechoslovakia, which they feared could destabilise their efforts to create a strong democratic state.

Amid the malaise he felt in Prague, Beneš and Masaryk piqued Lockhart's interest. Their devotion to the post-war order of stable government and international cooperation dovetailed with Lockhart's own thoughts, and their openness towards him personally helped to soften his initially harsh view of his life in their capital. Owing to his budding friendship with the Czech leaders, when Reilly and Savinkov arrived at the Thun Palace like shifty salesmen looking to pitch a risky counter-revolutionary venture, Lockhart claimed to have balked. Instead of organising a meeting with Beneš and Masaryk, he took his erstwhile colleagues to lunch, reminisced on his old life and then sent the schemers on their way.[12]

This was not the whole story. Contrary to his later claims, Lockhart did send Reilly and Savinkov to meet Masaryk and Beneš who, though wary of the pair, offered some support for their anti-Bolshevik operations, a key aspect of which involved raising money for the Whites. Lockhart played an important role in this venture. In September 1921, he brokered a deal for Reilly to acquire radium from Czechoslovakian mines on behalf of the Imperial and Foreign Corporation of London. Radium was a valuable commodity in the 1920s, essential to the manufacture of everything from illuminated clocks to bogus health cures – it was an ideal money-spinner for a cash-strapped spy in need of funding for subversive operations. The question is, did Lockhart get involved with Reilly beyond smoothing the way for the radium scheme? Jean thought so, hinting to her son years later that his father and Reilly continued working together for the British government on various projects related to the fight against Bolshevism into the 1920s.[13]

Lockhart's diaries show that he met with MI6 officers after returning from Russia in 1918, but details of what they discussed were not recorded. He also provided Whitehall with reports on Kerensky's work with the Whites after the deposed prime minister visited Lockhart in Prague at the start of 1921. Beyond the radium deal, the archival record of Lockhart's dealings with Reilly at this time is sparse, but it is clear that Leeper sponsored the spy's journeys across Europe in 1920, issuing him with the cover story of being a commercial agent working for the Board of Trade, while also providing liaison in Whitehall for Hill's related efforts to back the Whites. While in Prague, Reilly sent coded messages to MI6 from the Thun Palace, which was something that Lockhart would have most likely arranged. Finally, the fact that Lockhart, Reilly, Hill and Leeper all attended the 'Liquidation Lunch' suggests that the ex-British Agent remained attached in some way to his old comrades and their schemes.[14]

Whatever connection Lockhart had to his government's secret war against Bolshevism, it was not strong enough to disturb his pedestrian existence in Czechoslovakia which, in the spring of 1920, became a shared concern. On 13 April, Jean gave birth to their son Robert (known as Robin) and brought him to Prague. Having finally become a father, Lockhart acquired a large flat close to Kinsky Garden in the old town and tried to engender a comfortable family existence, employing servants, a chauffeur and a cook who, he fondly recalled, 'taught my son to gurgle in Czech'. These stable foundations for a marriage reset, however, rested on a quagmire into which Lockhart was fast sinking – his insatiable love of nightlife. By 1920, the miserable washout of war was ebbing across Europe and a tide of decadence was rising in the form of American-style bars and nightclubs. In the music halls and basement theatres of Vienna, Bucharest and Prague, one could also find troupes of gypsy musicians who had fled Russia to ply their trade beyond the reach of Bolshevik rule. Sometimes, Lockhart would hire out an entire venue so that these gypsies could entertain him and his friends, many of whom were themselves Russian émigrés. At other times, he would strike out alone to enjoy the nightlife on offer across the former Austro-Hungarian Empire.

In doing so Lockhart courted danger and partook of absurdity. One night in Belgrade, he survived a dance-floor misunderstanding with a violent Serbian gangster, whom he charmed to such an extent that the pair spent the rest of the night toasting each other's health. After booking a gypsy band to perform at the Thun Palace, a drunken Lockhart donned a wig and folkish garb, obscuring his identity from colleagues and guests as he joined the band mid-song. Less successful was Lockhart's attempt to

find work for his frequent drinking companion, a quick-tempered piano
player named Wolff, with whom he often played a game in which they
would balance themselves on upturned champagne bottles while imbibing. Lockhart's boss, George Clerk, was not impressed with this feat.
Reminding his subordinate that Wolff had once drunk himself into embar-
rassing oblivion with British-bought brandy at a Thun Palace event, Clerk
shot down the suggestion that the pianist be kept on retainer for future
functions. Given these misadventures, it's small wonder that Lockhart
earned a legendary reputation among Prague's drinkers and dancers, to
the extent that in certain haunts a double cognac could be ordered simply
by requesting a 'Lockhart'.[15]

Jean was not averse to indulgence and would occasionally accompany
her husband on his nights of revelry. However, for her the thrill soon wore
off. This left Lockhart to party alone or sometimes in the company of
'animer dames' – nightclub-appointed female companions. Accepting that
Prague's clubs were consuming her marriage, Jean left for London in July
1922, taking Robin with her. Still Lockhart chased the night. By this point
he could do little else. What had begun as a means of seeking joyful distraction from the monotony of his job had now become a coping mechanism
through which he numbed the pain of having fallen from the heights of
being Britain's Agent to the depths of being a third-string legation staffer.
His marriage cracked further under the weight of this despairing hedon-
ism. During one of Lockhart's returns to London in July 1923, he found
Jean 'very ill with severe hysteria', to the point that he had to call a doctor
to calm her down. Three years later, a 'nervous attack' led Jean to stay in
bed rather than spend time with her visiting husband.

Lockhart's wallet suffered no less than his marriage. The scale of
his nightclub addiction meant that even with the cost of clubbing being
relatively low in Prague, his salary was routinely obliterated by the outlay required for nights without dawn. When the Rubber Queen died in
1922 without leaving him a penny – loans had wiped out his inheritance
– Lockhart was forced to rely on his uncle to top up his bank account. The

rubber business, however, was as susceptible as any other to the slump into which Europe's economy fell once the post-war boom faded. By mid-1921, Lockhart's overdraft had ballooned from £700 to £2,000. In response, he accepted that his wage could never rebalance his accounts and, just before Christmas 1922, handed his resignation to Clerk. So ended, in what Lockhart conceded was a 'humdrum and undistinguished' manner, his decade-long career at the Foreign Office.[16]

For all that he had developed self-destructive tendencies, this was not a case of Lockhart jumping without a parachute. His intelligence reports on economic conditions in Czechoslovakia had caught the eye of Bank of England executives, who were impressed enough by his intuition and contacts to offer Lockhart a job with their Vienna affiliate, the Anglo-International Bank. The absurdity of this notion was not lost on the free-spending reveller, who by this time had resorted to money lenders to repay his debts. Thankfully for Lockhart, his new bosses were not after a number cruncher but an intelligence gatherer who could apprise them of political developments and big business deals across Central Europe. And so, in 1923, the rubber planter turned consul cum British Agent joined the Anglo-International Bank as an economic intelligence gatherer.[17]

Like Prague, Lockhart's new home, Vienna, was brimming with late-night temptations. So too were London, Cologne, Berlin, Sofia and a host of other European cities caught up in the smoke and jazz of the roaring twenties, which he visited on the bank's behalf to shake hands and analyse the intentions of everyone from the King of Serbia to Viennese cooperative groups. For this reason, whatever financial benefits Lockhart's new career offered were wiped out before they could accrue. He tried to supplement his income by writing articles for British newspapers on topics ranging from the relationship between Eastern Europe's peasants and its urban elites to the state of Anglo-Russian relations. Neither these forays into foreign correspondence nor his job with the Anglo-International, however, alleviated Lockhart's need for money lenders. As late as March 1928, he wrote in his diary of facing a 'critical week, as I must raise at least £750 in order to meet my debts'. There were also medical bills to pay. Nightly excursions in which Lockhart consumed 'two cocktails, melon, soup, lobster, cutlets, cold grouse, ice and savoury, sherry, champagne, port and brandy – and whisky!' put the once robust rugby-player in a wretched state, necessitating a visit to a Harley Street doctor to treat gout and exhaustion.[18]

The depths to which Lockhart had fallen were made uncomfortably apparent to him when, in the summer of 1924, Moura abruptly returned to his life. It had been a long six years for the once glamorous socialite. Her connection to the British conspirators meant that after the autumn of 1918, she was denied the freedom to leave Russia permanently and was monitored by the Joint State Political Directorate (OGPU) – the successor to the Cheka. Deprived of her wealth and status, the countess was also made to work for a living. Moura, however, rose to this challenge, becoming a translator and then secretary for the famous writer Maxim Gorky who, predictably, fell hard for her. Having become his mistress, Moura joined Gorky's commune-like household of bohemians, who addressed each other by nicknames and paid no mind to whether the sun was up or down. It was far removed from the polished splendour of Yendel but Gorky's home provided Moura with a welcome sanctuary from the attentions of the OGPU, for her lover was much admired by Lenin. This connection paid dividends when, in 1920, Moura tried to escape Russia by crossing the frozen waters of the Gulf of Finland, only to be apprehended by the border guards and thrown in jail. Her release was secured when another of Gorky's mistresses – who was involved in an art smuggling racket that was putting funds into the Bolsheviks' treasury – intervened.

Aside from wanting to flee the revolution's misery, Moura's other reason for trying to reach Finland was to hasten a reunion with Lockhart who, despite their lapsed correspondence, never left her thoughts. Had Moura known the divergence their lives' paths were taking, she might have thought twice about risking her life on the ice. Her dashing British Agent was becoming a debt-ridden drunk in thrall to past glories while Moura was emerging empowered from the catastrophe of 1918. She had survived life under the Bolsheviks through her relationship with Gorky and started a new career as first his translator and, later, his literary agent. She delved deeper into the book business through a dalliance with another famous writer, H. G. Wells, whose interest in Russia's revolution led him to visit Gorky in 1920. Besotted by Moura, the genius behind *War of the Worlds* and *The Time Machine* humiliated himself in the years that followed by repeatedly proposing marriage, only to be sharply rebuffed each time.

When Moura did countenance the altar, it was for purely pragmatic reasons. In 1923, she married an Estonian noble named Count Nicolai Budberg, who agreed to annul the union once Moura acquired the title of Baroness Budberg and an Estonian passport. This enabled her to reunite with her children and pursue a new life beyond Russia's borders. Moura's strategic seductions of Gorky, Wells and Budberg were driven both by self-interest and an acceptance that she had suffered a parting of the ways from the man she truly loved. Writing to Lockhart in 1921, she declared herself 'unable to live with the thought' that it was Jean rather than her who had borne him a son. In despair, Moura even mentioned 'little Peter' – the name they had chosen for the child she had lost in 1918. To her mind, the arrival of Robin marked the end of any thought that the former lovers might one day rekindle the flame.[19]

And yet, she couldn't let him go completely. When visiting her old friend Hicks – who, like Lockhart, had found a new non-government career in Vienna working for the Cunard line – in July 1924 Moura picked up the phone and called her erstwhile lover. At the sound of her voice, Lockhart's mind clouded with memories and his words were stolen by confusion. The more Moura spoke, however, the more the fog lifted and the old feeling stirred – the feeling that had once given Lockhart the confidence to view Bolshevik Moscow as his fiefdom. Moura was the custodian of his adventurous past and the jolt of inspiration he desperately needed. Two days later, when he finally laid eyes on her as she stood waiting expectantly at Hicks' front door, Lockhart was catapulted back to that winter's eve in Petrograd when they first met. Her hair was now bobbed in the fashion of the time and her face hardened by the wages of experience but, fundamentally, Moura looked and carried herself as she always had – as the shining light of any gathering, to whom all must pay fawning attention. As the heavier, more weathered Lockhart was forced to conclude, 'the change is in me – and not for the better'. This was not only in physical terms. When Moura talked of Cheka prisons, treks across frozen seas, her laissez-faire life with Gorky, her career in books and her relationship with Wells, Lockhart was as impressed as he was embarrassed that he had no comparable stories to share. When he stopped writing to Moura in 1919, he had done so with the aim of moving on. Instead, it was the wily baroness who had pushed her life forward as a lover of great men and an arbiter of their business affairs, while Lockhart drank away his days, dodged debt collectors and laboured in jobs that left him listless and uninspired.

Though he recognised the gulf that lay between them, sentimentality spurred Lockhart to try building a bridge. When they found a quiet moment away from their hosts, he began muttering about the pledge he had made on the train platform in Moscow that cold autumn night in 1918. Raising her hand abruptly, Moura urged him to speak no further and to keep the past in the past. In response, all Lockhart could summon was a half-smile and a nod of helpless agreement. After two further days spent drinking, playing games and talking long into the night with Hicks and his wife, the former couple crammed themselves into the crowded carriage of a train bound for Masaryk Station in Prague. Speaking in Russian to avoid eavesdropping from the other passengers, they reminisced about things only they knew. They were no longer lovers, but they were certainly companions – forever bonded yet destined to be apart. In this development, at least, Lockhart found comfort and experienced an important epiphany. Moura had her children, her work and her lovers. She had created a life apart from his. Lockhart's once dependable muse was not going to dig him out of the hole into which he had burrowed. For that, he had to rely on the one person whom he trusted least – himself.[20]

CHAPTER 11

HELL ON FLEET STREET

*'He will be a hard task master and you will find the work
pretty stiff'*

– George Clerk

ockhart sat at the head of a long dining table, clutching a crystal flute of flat champagne. It was the early hours of 22 February 1928, and he was staring quizzically at a 'strange little man whose make-up is two-thirds genius and one-third puckishness', who had just made him an intriguing offer. Max Aitken – Lord Beaverbrook or the 'Beaver' to Whitehall insiders – was a shrewd Canadian who had made his fortune investing in businesses, playing the stock market and, after running a propaganda department during the First World War, developing a newspaper empire. He commanded enormous power and influence. Politicians, generals, captains of industry and some of Europe's finest minds had sat at the same table over which Lockhart was now hunched. All had flocked to Beaverbrook's west London residence to pay homage to or ask favours of the man who controlled what was printed in the widely read *Evening Standard* and *Daily Express*.

Given the state of his life and finances, deference and pleas for assistance were also on Lockhart's mind. The dynamic between Beaverbrook and his guest, however, was beyond that of a supplicant to a benefactor. Since first meeting Lockhart in 1919, the Beaver had taken a shine to the brash young Scot. He saw promise beyond his career follies and character flaws, asserting with a journalist's flair for hyperbole that Lockhart was 'one

of the most brilliant men of this generation'. Appalled at the thought of
this brilliance being eclipsed by long nights and loan-sharks, Beaverbrook
summoned Lockhart to dinner to propose a plan that would rescue him
from further ruin.[1]

For all that he liked Lockhart, the Beaver was no altruist. If he was
going to invest in 'brilliance', he expected a handsome dividend. After
the port and cigars, he requested that Lockhart use his position at the
Anglo-International to acquire tens of thousands of pounds' worth of shares
for him. This agreed to, Beaverbrook poured out the last of the evening's
champagne in celebration, while raising a second idea that would utilise
Lockhart's ability to make friends, acquire information and arrange it
into engaging prose. For a starting salary of £2,000 per year, Beaverbrook
offered Lockhart the job of editing the Londoner's Diary, a daily feature
in the Standard that regaled readers with titillating stories of the famous
and infamous, interspersed with glib political commentary. The man who
once pitted his wits against the Cheka was now being asked to helm a
gossip column. Lockhart was wary. Apart from the position seeming like
a step down from life with the Anglo-International, Beaverbrook had a
well-earned reputation for being a relentless taskmaster who kept an iron
grip on his employees. He was, on paper, the worst possible boss for a man
of Lockhart's freedom-loving temperament to have.

As had been the case with his assignment to the Prague legation in
1919, however, Lockhart felt he had no choice but to throw in his lot with
the Beaver. Despite his personal problems, Lockhart had done his job
well at the Anglo-International and his name still carried enough weight
that, in 1927, he was made honorary Austrian consul-general in London.
It sounded impressive, but the position didn't pay. Rather, Lockhart was
expected to keep up appearances in London on Vienna's behalf without any
kind of stipend to support his efforts. This meant that despite being fully
employed, Lockhart was still struggling financially by the late 1920s and
with the banking business down and lay-offs at the Anglo-International
imminent, Beaverbrook's offer could not be refused. He duly accepted,

albeit on the condition that he receive eight months' grace before reporting to Fleet Street. This insistence was born of brutal self-reflection. Lockhart knew he needed time to conquer his demons, otherwise they would ride on his back from the bars of Vienna to the clubs of Soho. Not for the first or last time in his life, he pledged himself to clean living and resolved upon a fresh start.[2]

Having secured a golden handshake from the bank and an advance from Beaverbrook, Lockhart made the most of his eight-month sabbatical. He recaptured some of his old zest for life by trekking across Slovenia, Yugoslavia and Germany, where he spent Armistice Day wandering around the Berlin Palace, reflecting on all that had happened to Europe in the decade since the guns fell silent. He also broke the barriers of marital estrangement by reuniting with Jean, who had relocated to Geneva with Robin. Lockhart spent a little over a month there playing golf, fishing with his son and dining out with his wife, albeit without forging a full family reconciliation. Aside from his mother's death in May 1928 and the return to Britain this necessitated, Lockhart enjoyed his time off and stuck to his pledge to cut down on drinking. Years earlier in Prague, he had tried going cold turkey, only to relapse almost instantly. Now, he showed wisdom by limiting the scale of his revelry, rather than halting it completely. He also 'did my exercises' daily and kept the wheels of his brain turning by reading widely in German, French, Malay, Russian and Czech, as well as penning short articles on European politics and culture for Beaverbrook's press.[3]

By the time Lockhart officially started with the *Standard* in September 1928, he felt re-energised, the more so as he commenced this new career on the best possible foot by becoming the first British journalist to interview the ex-Kaiser, Wilhelm II. Exiled at the end of the war to the town of Doorn in the Netherlands, the former master of Germany was now a white-bearded gent of leisure, whose days were spent practising amateur archaeology and reading Greek literature. He also devoted time to nursing resentment over the way the war ended, and the treatment he and Germany had received from its victors. Outraged at the prolonged occupation of the Rhineland by Allied troops and post-war chants of 'hang the kaiser' from across the English Channel, Wilhelm had vowed never to speak to a British journalist. This was why, when Lockhart arrived at Doorn in November 1928, he was granted only a tour of the grounds from the ex-kaiser's butler. Through exchanges with his guide, however, Lockhart identified Wilhelm's Achilles heel – the yearning to rehabilitate his public image. This led to him writing a sympathetic story on Wilhelm's life in exile for the *Standard*, in which the former emperor's love of dogs and the adoration of 'his personal attendants, who cannot speak too highly of his thoughtfulness and consideration for others' was emphasised. This had the desired effect. On 14 December 1929 Lockhart got his interview.

The next two days were spent discussing the world's affairs with the ex-kaiser, who impressed upon Lockhart the view that he and his country had been wronged by the Great War's victors. Under the terms of the Versailles Treaty, defeated Germany was forced to admit guilt for starting the conflict and accept a suite of restrictions on its military and economy, the latter facilitated by a sizeable reparations bill from the Allies. German territory was also ceded to the war's victors and the ex-kaiser was labelled an offender of 'international morality and the sanctity of treaties' who needed to be put on trial. Though this never happened, Wilhelm took the insult and humiliation to heart, blaming Britain for branding him a war criminal.

When the interview was published in the *Standard*, Lockhart tried to rectify his subject's image problem. In the name of moving past Anglo-German bitterness – something Lockhart personally felt was necessary for a stable post-war Europe – he emphasised quotes of praise from the ex-kaiser for the behaviour of Britain's 'well-disciplined' troops in the Rhineland and his hope 'that these two great peoples [Britons and Germans] will live to see the day when, with a real understanding of each other, they will tread the common path of genuine friendship'. The article was in keeping with Beaverbrook's remark to Lockhart that Wilhelm was 'a fine figure in history, and we must do him well'.[4]

Buoyed by this spectacular start, Lockhart settled into his new life in London, which required a modicum of social adjustment. He had, after all, spent more of his life on the continent than in the British Isles. It was not that he found London and its inhabitants unfriendly; they were just more uptight and guarded than the people of Vienna or Prague. To Lockhart's mind, the average Londoner had 'more genuine politeness than the citizen of any other capital' and yet, they showed 'no curiosity about your family, your business and your income. He is the least inquisitive man in the world and, for this reason, the most difficult to make friends with.' In the *Standard*'s offices on Shoe Lane, however, Lockhart found a vibrancy he struggled to locate in the streets beyond. He got along well with most of his colleagues and enjoyed the tales of gossip and scandal they spun. He loved that being a journalist meant needing to adapt to the challenges of an entire morning's labours being wiped out by the sudden death of an important political figure or the outbreak of a war. The more regimented side of his work also appealed, for after his travels and travails on the continent even Lockhart's restless soul yearned for normalcy. 'My hours,' he noted with satisfaction in his diary, 'are from 9:30 to 1:15, during which I am working at full pressure.' The release valve for these focused mornings came in the afternoon and evening, when the 'Londoner' descended on the capital's clubs, theatres and restaurants to gather gossip for the next day's 'Diary'.

This was where the trouble started. The impetus to wine and dine London society in search of column content drove Lockhart into familiarly dangerous places of overindulgence and debt, wiping out the gains he had made on both fronts during his sabbatical. As early as March 1929, the refrain 'feeling rather seedy after last night' began to creep into his diary entries, alongside the bleak assertion that 'this life is hell!' Battered by cocktail parties, long lunches and even longer evenings spent at Soho's notoriously debauched Club 43, Lockhart developed gout and insomnia which, when not clubbing, he tried to soothe by playing billiards alone until dawn. Two years after commencing work at the *Standard*, he was in a perpetual state of feeling 'ill, depressed and miserable'. The fresh start had failed.[5]

He could at least take satisfaction in his work. After the ex-kaiser scoop, Lockhart secured an interview with the German statesman Gustav Stresemann, with whom he found himself in agreement on the need to strengthen Anglo-German relations and heal the old wounds of war. Aside from these high-profile interviews, the success of Londoner's Diary offered Lockhart opportunities to mingle with the capital's elites. In March 1929, he was accosted by Winston Churchill, ten years after the future prime minister had invited the ex-British Agent to lunch to discuss the progress of the Whites in the Russian Civil War. Far removed from that time of high drama, Churchill now complained about how Lockhart had used the Londoner's Diary to declare him the worst-dressed man in Britain. He then denounced Lockhart's column as mindless rot, albeit while confessing through a cheeky grin that he never missed a chance to read it.

There was much to keep Churchill's interest. Under Lockhart's stewardship, Londoner's Diary became more than a digest of daily gossip, instead reflecting his eclectic range of interests, sharp wit and keen political insights. In the space of a page, Lockhart covered everything from infighting among Britain's political parties to the rise of cinema 'talkies' and the threat they posed to stage plays, the uninspiring design of new postage stamps, the splendour of Paris's Sacré Cœur and predictions for rugby showdowns between Oxford and Cambridge. Amid the irreverent froth, Lockhart also kept a running commentary on Russia, opining that 'although Bolshevist persecution of the Jews is probably more anti-religious than anti-racial, Stalin himself is not above earning a cheap popularity by exploiting anti-Semitism', and converting 'numerous synagogues into workingmen's clubs'.

Closer to home, he was no less barbed in dissecting the various economic policies floated by politicians and industrialists for dealing with the end of the post-war boom. He even found space for prophecy. Having heard rumours of a new coin-operated machine from New York that 'shouts at the offending human in robot-like tones' when bad coins are inserted, Lockhart predicted that, 'if the scheme is effective, we are likely to find loudspeakers everywhere commanding the public to "keep to the left", "wipe your feet", "beware of pickpockets", "do not smoke" and so forth'. Future 'life in the great cities', he warned, 'will become noisier than ever'.[6]

Seeing that his gamble on Lockhart had paid off, Beaverbrook doubled down. In July 1929, editing responsibilities for Londoner's Diary were taken over by the former diplomat turned journalist Harold Nicolson, opening the way for Lockhart to assume two important posts in Beaverbrook's empire – liaison between the latter and the editors of the *Daily Express* and leader-writer for the *Sunday Express* and the *Standard*. The Beaver also tasked Lockhart with producing propaganda for a new political party he had established to promote trade between Britain and her colonies. While Lockhart was forced to crow in the *Standard* about Beaverbrook's 'Empire Crusade', privately he struggled to muster enthusiasm for his boss's protectionist attitude and related opposition to Britain's membership of the League of Nations. Established in 1919 as a means of preventing another catastrophic war, this supranational organisation had been left for Britain and France to lead after President Woodrow Wilson failed to persuade congress that the USA should join. Beaverbrook thought the League was a toothless tiger and the Versailles Treaty it was meant to enforce was unduly harsh on Germany. The problems of this post-war order convinced Beaverbrook that a second conflagration between Europe's great powers was inevitable, and that Britain had to retreat into protectionist economics and political isolation to avoid being dragged into the carnage. Lockhart agreed with Beaverbrook's criticisms of the League. However, the well-travelled Europhile and innate internationalist found 'something immoral about his wish to destroy it' and 'put nationalism in its place'.[7]

A difference of opinion with his boss, however, was a luxury Lockhart could ill afford. Now one of Beaverbrook's right hands, the warnings of indentured servitude he had received from friends after signing up with the press baron seemed to be coming true. Despite his growing seniority in the Beaver's empire, Lockhart's pay hadn't gone up much since working on Londoner's Diary. This forced him to work even harder to clear his debts by producing additional columns and searching out scoops, which required keeping his ears open at nightclubs and dinner parties. For this reason, a year after formally stepping away from Londoner's Diary, Lockhart was still whiling away his evenings at Club 43 and spending money he didn't have. This self-defeating cycle was exacerbated by the fact that the more Lockhart laboured for Beaverbrook, the more he struggled to start work on a project that could restore his parlous finances and, possibly, free him from Fleet Street's shackles for good – a blockbuster memoir of his time as Britain's Agent.

Having abandoned the folly of trying to forget Russia, Lockhart had begun thinking about writing a memoir in 1924 when Lenin, debilitated by strokes, died. The revolutionary juggernaut's demise sparked a new wave of curiosity about the Soviet Union he founded, the more so when the brutal yet enigmatic Joseph Stalin assumed control at the Kremlin. Interest in the revolutionary motherland and its leaders was so high that in 1928 Lockhart was approached by the Hollywood producer Sam Goldwyn, who pitched the idea of depicting his 1918 escapades on the silver screen. Caught off-guard by the suggestion that he sell off the most important chapter of his life, Lockhart rejected Goldwyn's offer and with it a new and much-needed revenue stream. Instead, still in the honeymoon period of his employ with Beaverbrook, Lockhart stuck with compiling Londoner's Diary. By the time he came to resent his life on Fleet Street, the film offer had vanished and Lockhart had taken on too many jobs to countenance starting work on the book.[8]

The dysfunctionality of Lockhart's personal life also sapped whatever reserves of energy remained in him after a long day labouring for Beaverbrook, who once quipped that, 'but for women, Bruce would have been prime minister and certainly foreign secretary by now'. In addition to Moura and his various nightclub dalliances, Lockhart was deeply involved with two women other than Jean during the interwar years. The first of these relationships to develop was with Pamela Chichester, the wife of the honorary attaché to the British legation in Bucharest and Prague, whom Lockhart first met while working there. When the Chichesters' marriage collapsed in 1924, Pamela and Lockhart's relationship intensified, to the extent that she insisted he divorce Jean and cease his other extramarital relationship with the well-connected socialite Countess Vera Mary of Rosslyn, known to Lockhart and other intimates as 'Tommy'.

Second to Moura, Tommy was the woman who had the greatest impact on Lockhart's life and career. They met in 1923 during one of his visits back to London for the Anglo-International, embarking on an affair that Tommy's husband, the Earl of Rosslyn, seemed at first oblivious to and then accepting of. Whenever Lockhart returned to Britain the two were seldom apart, dining in the finest restaurants and attending parties with society heavy hitters whom Tommy called friends. This paid dividends for Lockhart when he started on Londoner's Diary, the columns of which he crammed with gossip from the circles into which Tommy had smoothed his entry. These circles were eclectic and elite. Lockhart partook in golfing weekends with the Prince of Wales and drinking sessions with Churchill's son Randolph who, despite being 'very egocentric and conceited and therefore very unpopular', amused Lockhart such that they became friends – Randolph even took on the 'Londoner' mantle from time to time. Tommy also did much for Lockhart's spiritual life. In an echo of his willingness to submit to Islam for Amai years earlier, on 6 June 1924 the Presbyterian-raised Scot followed Tommy into the Catholic faith. The irony that this conversion was born of infidelity didn't seem to trouble the pair, who continued their affair openly even as Lockhart persisted in his relationship with Pamela.[9]

Lockhart's marriage suffered accordingly. It was no coincidence that from 1923 onwards his diary became peppered with references to Jean's 'nervous attacks', bouts of 'hysteria' and myriad marital quarrels. Jean's state of mind was likely not helped by the fact that in the summer of 1929 Moura finally accomplished her decade-long mission to relocate to Britain.

Her unclear involvement in Lockhart's plot and suspicions that she worked for the OGPU raised eyebrows at the Home Office and MI5, prompting the former MI6 chief in Moscow, Ernest Boyce, to personally assure the authorities that she wasn't a security risk. With her visa finally granted, Moura started her new life in London in typical style, ingratiating herself into the capital's literary and political circles. She also kept up her contacts in Germany, Estonia, Italy, France and the Soviet Union, to which she regularly travelled throughout the 1920s and 1930s, reaffirming MI5's impression that she was 'a politically suspicious character'. She made efforts to obscure her activities on these trips, requesting that Lockhart edit all mention of her 1928 visit to Moscow out of his memoirs.

Maybe she was working for the Russians. Maybe she wasn't. As always with Moura, the evidence is inconclusive – particularly in this instance as Boyce was later accused by a Soviet defector of being a double agent, the inference being that he used his influence to set Moura up in Britain as a spy for the Kremlin. What cannot be doubted is that she used her web of contacts on both sides of the Channel to feed Lockhart material for Londoner's Diary on everything from Gorky's changing opinions on Bolshevism to the progress of Benito Mussolini's fascist experiment in Italy. She also acted as a sounding-board for Lockhart's worries and a cheerleader for his stalled efforts to start his memoirs. The old bond – that of sharing information and confidence – was restored and, doubtless with it, Jean's ire fuelled.[10]

In December 1930, the strain of managing his wife, muse and mistresses brought Lockhart to breaking point. During a dinner date in which 'she was miserable, and I was miserable', Pam insisted that he had to leave Jean and Tommy or lose her. Despairing at the ultimatum, Lockhart dropped Pam home in favour of a solo nightclub binge, which concluded with the breaking of dawn and the rueful self-assessment that he was now a 'nervous and physical wreck'. Recognising the worsening state of his right-hand man, Beaverbrook granted Lockhart's request for a break from Fleet Street, during which he visited Jean in Geneva and made a last-ditch attempt to save the marriage. The fact that he waited expectantly on letters from

Tommy and Pam during this sojourn indicates that a genuine reconciliation was beyond Lockhart's capabilities. He added further strain to the proceedings by telling Jean that he was going to ignore her demands to redact the stories of his romances with Amai and Moura from his planned memoir. Still, he refused to end the marriage, admitting to his diary that 'I am in love with Pam' and 'I love and adore Tommy', yet 'I cannot abandon Jean and Robin'. Sighing through his pen, Lockhart concluded that the 'whole outlook is almost hopeless'.[11]

Burdened by a complex love life, an empty bank account and a demanding boss, the man who committed 200,000 words per year to his diary for most of his life took nearly four years to complete his first memoir. However, when it was finally published in November 1932, *Memoirs of a British Agent* proved to be worth the wait. The book was a critical and financial success, more so when it was made into a Hollywood film. Staring Leslie Howard as the dashing Stephen Locke, *British Agent* dramatised and distorted the events of 1918, recasting Locke's lover – Elena Moura – in the guise of a conflicted Cheka agent and having the characters based on Lavergne and Verthamon mercilessly slain by the Bolsheviks. Creatively, Lockhart was dissatisfied with a film that 'bore little or no resemblance to my narrative' but was nonetheless pleased that it 'brought a much needed, if temporary, relief to my strained finances'. Though Moura was put off by the oversentimentalisation of their relationship in the *Memoirs*, she was unfussed by her portrayal in the movie. Indeed, safe in the knowledge that no one would take the outrageous tale seriously, she revelled in the notoriety it gave her.[12]

Where the film fell down artistically, the book soared critically. The *Telegraph* approved of how *Memoirs* revealed the 'truth about the Soviet outrage' in which Cromie had been gunned down, urging its readers to pick up 'the most talked about book of the year'. Writing for *The Times*, Lockhart's old comrade Arthur Ransome declared that 'no better picture of those tense, galloping weeks of the summer of 1918 in Moscow has been or is likely to be painted', while the *London Illustrated* noted how 'the story, in its personal aspect, is one of lost opportunities and incomplete achievement'.

Sympathising with Lockhart's post-1918 plight, the reviewer concluded that, 'as the villain of the "Lockhart Plot"', the former British Agent 'became a symbol of Albion's perfidy' to Russian minds. Lockhart was the victim of his own story. The *New York Times* followed this thread when it lauded the 'very human' aspects of Lockhart's tale, forgiving its author's missteps in Moscow by declaring that he had 'been thrown into a world crisis which no diplomat, probably, could have handled successfully'.[13]

As a business venture and a means of reputational restoration, *Memoirs* served its author well and announced his gift with the pen to the world. This led Lockhart to conclude that he could forge a life beyond Fleet Street as an author, which seemed an ideal career move for a compulsive writer and lover of literature who was instinctively resistant to being under anyone's thumb. Motivated by this prospect, two years after *Memoirs* was released Lockhart produced its sequel, *Retreat from Glory*, in which he chronicled his inglorious return from Moscow, his fall from grace in Prague and the start of his new career in journalism with a 'frankness' that was applauded by the *Times Literary Supplement*. Other reviewers were not so kind. By revealing details of his extramarital affairs and the debauchery of Prague's nightclubs, the *Sunday Times* questioned whether Lockhart – 'an artfully artless sort of enfant terrible' – was being too candid for the reader's own good. Mostly bereft of the derring-do that made *Memoirs* a page-turner, the *Telegraph* likewise judged Lockhart's second offering to be 'not quite so successful' as his first.

Lockhart was less concerned with the barbs of critics than with the opinions of friends. Harold Nicolson thought *Retreat* superior to *Memoirs* and the novelist and politician John Buchan applauded Lockhart for pioneering a 'new kind of autobiography' that was 'self-revealing without being self-conscious'. The ex-kaiser – with whom Lockhart had maintained a friendly correspondence since 1929 – wrote to him in praise of *Retreat* and the recounting of their interview in it. Even Beaverbrook thought it equal to Lockhart's first offering, albeit with a grumble that *Retreat from Glory* was a lesser title than *Memoirs of a British Agent*.[14]

Beaverbrook's support was vital. Buoyed by the success of his first two books, at the end of 1934 Lockhart requested and received time off from the press baron to work on a third tome which he hoped would be successful enough to justify him quitting journalism for life as a full-time author. As Lockhart's diary entry for New Year's Eve 1934 reveals, the need to disentangle himself from Beaverbrook's web had grown pressing. Entering his forty-eighth year 'fatter, lazier, and definitely worse in health' than ever, Lockhart was convinced that Fleet Street life was killing him. Rather than pick the bones of this bleakness for material, Lockhart decided that his next book would be a travelogue that would chronicle his reacquaintance with the land that had kickstarted his life of adventure – Malaysia. As the perceptive Beaverbrook concluded, this was not simply Lockhart trying to break the mould of his previous offerings. He was also yearning to revisit a happier past and, as the Beaver quipped 'search for the pair of shoes' Amai left on the porch when the doomed lovers parted decades earlier.[15]

As Lockhart made clear in *Return to Malaya*, the goal of reuniting with Amai was key to the book's conception. In this respect, the memoir was a mid-life crisis in print. It was also the tale of a journey through a world that, despite post-war hopes for renewal, seemed to be changing for the worse. Starting in spring 1935, Lockhart chronicled his journey through a France gripped by economic depression and fears of German revanchism into an Italy where Mussolini was thumbing his nose at the League of Nations and planning an invasion of Abyssinia. From Genoa, Lockhart took a ship to Singapore, where he beheld new art deco buildings, sealed roads and the adoption of Western-style dress by its once exotic inhabitants. This encroachment of modernity bothered him and so too did the fact that the island hummed with war concerns and suspicions of spies. The sun-bathed bastion of easy commerce was now consumed with fears over battles to come, and its coastline peppered with gun emplacements. With the Japanese on the march in China, gone were the days, Lockhart rued, when British troops saw a posting to 'Singapore as an exotic and not unpleasant interlude in the ordinary duties of soldiering'.

Lockhart's reflections on a world in troubling flux make up the bulk of *Malaya*. The narrative hook, however, was the promise of its author's reunion with Amai, who was first introduced to Lockhart's fans in *Memoirs*. Unfortunately for both the writer and his readership, their reacquaintance was awkward and anti-climactic. Having confirmed that rumours of Amai's death were false Lockhart set out for Pantai, where he discovered that she had married the local muezzin. Undaunted, Lockhart arranged a meeting which, owing to the wariness of Amai's husband, was not permitted to happen in a private house. The former lovers instead reunited on the grassy edge of a rice paddy under a baleful sky of near-black clouds. Her ageing features creasing into an uneasy smile, Amai spoke to Lockhart with little emotion or sentiment, offering him a stilted exchange of questions and answers concerning what had become of their lives since they parted in 1909. Her only noteworthy contribution to the proceedings was to point out how many extra pounds Lockhart had added to his once boyish frame. Embarrassed and accepting the situation for what it was, Lockhart shook his first love's hand like he was concluding a business meeting, then took his leave. As one reviewer put it, Lockhart's Pantai had become 'the living cemetery of a romance that was dead'. Lauded elsewhere as an interesting travelogue that was 'mature and sagacious, humorous and true', *Malaya* did well enough to encourage Lockhart to delve further into his past with *My Scottish Youth*. Released in 1937, this memoir of Lockhart's upbringing was acclaimed, like all his books, for its 'anecdotes, its enthusiasm, the odd scraps of information, the snapshots of great men' and, above all else, 'the author's disarming frankness about his own affairs'.[16]

It was this aspect of Lockhart's storytelling that drew his long-beset marriage to its inevitable close. Hurt by her husband's willingness to publicise his infidelity and worn down by years of bickering, in February 1937 Jean informed Lockhart that she had been having an affair of her own since 1935 with another Scot, Loudon MacNeill McLean. On this basis, she demanded Lockhart divorce her and end their shared misery. To make clear her seriousness, Jean then started removing items and furniture from their apartment in London. It was 'an unsavoury business', Lockhart wrote in his diary, made more so from his perspective by Jean 'making a broadcast of it to her friends'. If the irony of this complaint were not enough, given that Lockhart had sold thousands of copies of books detailing his passions for Moura and Tommy, the fact that their divorce papers imply it was Jean's infidelity that caused the rupture marks a fittingly bizarre coda to their unhappy union.[17]

The ending of his marriage prompted Lockhart to confront another problematic aspect of his life – working for Beaverbrook. Reasoning that he had to 'leave Fleet Street even if I starve', Lockhart assessed his finances and figured that if he quit journalism and continued writing at the pace he had set since completing *Memoirs*, he could just about keep his head above water. He seemed popular enough to sustain a readership. When publicising *Malaya* and *Scottish Youth*, Lockhart appeared on several BBC radio shows, delivered many invited talks at universities, received fan mail from women who wanted to fix his broken soul and was even approached by Scottish nationalists to see if he would publicly endorse their crusade to secede from Britain. Tommy and Moura urged him to take the plunge and become a full-time author, the latter imploring him repeatedly to cease wasting his potential under Beaverbrook's thumb. Finally, mere weeks after finalising his divorce in the summer of 1937, Lockhart tendered his resignation to the press baron. Beaverbrook granted this wish, giving Lockhart a parting gift of two months' salary, an acknowledgement that he had surpassed all expectations in running Londoner's Diary, and the promise of an open door should he ever wish to return to the fold. For all his outward callousness, Beaverbrook had sympathy for Lockhart's state and valued the contributions he had made to his media empire.[18]

Lockhart's departure from Fleet Street and divorce from Jean were supposed to open the door to a new life in which he would write on topics of his own choosing, for sums he felt appropriate and in forms he enjoyed. Crashing towards his fifties with a renewed sense of self-worth, Lockhart was excited about his future for the first time in years. However, while living through the experiences that filled the pages of *Retreat* and *Malaya*, he saw things he sensed might eclipse this blissful new dawn. Lockhart had grimly noted the Royal Navy dry docks under construction in Singapore and felt unease at the 'fascist guard who watched my effects while I ate' on a train ride through Italy. During trips to Germany on behalf of the Anglo-International, he had watched post-war resentment rise with the worship of militarism and nationalism, culminating in the founding of the Third Reich in 1933. That year, he realised that his golfing friend, the Prince of Wales, was 'quite pro-Hitler' after he breezily told Lockhart that it was 'no business of ours to interfere in Germany's internal affairs either re: the Jews or anything else'. Even as Lockhart plunged into a personal abyss of long nights and longer bar bills, he was not blind to the fact that Europe was beating its own path to self-destruction. Lockhart wanted to be an author. He wanted to be carefree. But as the 1930s wore on, the swelling sound of war drums became too loud for him to ignore.[19]

CHAPTER 12

WHITHER EUROPE?

*'I have been right too long about
the Nazis . . . and that is fatal'*

— Robert Vansittart

'The Hitlerist terror is worse than anything that ever happened in Russia or Italy,' Moura declared. Lockhart reclined, snuffed a cigarette in the ashtray and called for the bill. It was March 1933, four months after Adolf Hitler had been appointed chancellor of Germany. Prompted by Moura's outburst to muse on the budding Führer, Lockhart searched the recesses of his overstuffed memory and recalled a business trip he made to Munich in 1922. Walking down the Kellerstrasse, he happened upon a 'little black-haired man in riding boots and a cheap brown water-proof' haranguing a crowd of about a hundred people. Lockhart hadn't thought much of the firebrand at the time, though he was prompted to reflect on this first encounter with Hitler when, in 1931, he was again in Munich, this time pursuing an interview with Germany's rising political star. The days of street-level soapboxing behind him, the Nazi Party leader was now too busy campaigning to give a Fleet Street muckraker the time of day. Instead, Lockhart was given a tour of the Nazi Party headquarters – the Brown House – by Hitler's chief theorist, Alfred Rosenberg, who put on a show for his guest. The Brown House's expensive furnishings were on full display, and so too was the order and discipline of the *Sturmabteilung* (stormtroopers) who guarded it. The swastika was omnipresent, emblazoning everything from clock faces to floor rugs. They were crass and ostentatious, but Hitler and his people seemed impressive.[1]

Lockhart was not blind to the realities of Nazism. Despite leaving Whitehall officially in 1922, in the years that followed he remained connected to diplomats, ministers and spies, from whom he acquired information on this new and unnerving ideology. Fleet Street correspondents in Berlin gave Lockhart character sketches of Heinrich Himmler and Hermann Göring. He also spent many evenings at Beaverbrook's main residences – Stornoway House in London and Cherkley Court in Surrey – in the company of the likes of Stanley Baldwin, Ramsay MacDonald, Winston Churchill and the man who appointed him Britain's Agent in 1918, Lloyd George, all of whom possessed varying degrees of insight into fascism and the implication of its rise for Europe's future. Though he initially assumed that Nazism was little more than a re-vamped form of the Prussian militarism that had underpinned the kaiser's regime, Lockhart soon understood its more dangerous, cult-like elements and in particular the importance of the iron bond between Hitler and his followers. First-hand accounts of *Sturmabteilung* street violence also gave Lockhart an appreciation of paramilitarism's centrality to the Nazis' rise, prompting him to run a story in the *Standard* in which the party faithful were referred to as 'Hitler's Fascist Army'.[2]

The Nazi leader's quirks, however, provided too much of a distraction for Lockhart to fully appreciate the depths of the menace. When Moura visited Germany, he always asked her to seek out stories about Hitler, particularly if they pertained to his sexuality. He loved the German journalist Hans Wilhelm Thost's talk of Hitler's vegetarianism and boyish love of motor car racing, to the extent that Lockhart had Nicolson reproduce this gossip in Londoner's Diary. He also commissioned mocking tales of the former Austrian corporal's attempts to acquire German citizenship by appointing himself a professor, and his inability to 'imitate Mussolini and march on Berlin'. Guided by Beaverbrook's indifference – he waxed and waned between seeing the Nazis as a good or a bad thing for Germany – and the need to titillate readers, during the 1920s and early 1930s Lockhart viewed Hitler as a demented curiosity who could sell newspapers rather than a danger to the global order. This was why, when Moura insisted to Lockhart that horrors unseen in either of their memories were unfolding in Germany, he dismissed her claims as 'rot'.[3]

This attitude was not uncommon in Britain prior to the war. For many conservatives, the arrival of a militantly anti-communist regime in Berlin provided a welcome bulwark against the Soviet Union, which had been entrenched as Europe's bogeyman for over a decade. Some Britons who were concerned with the impacts of the Great Depression hoped that Nazi economic policies would light a beacon to guide the world out of the slump. Others refused to accept that Hitler was as bad as he seemed, writing off *Mein Kampf*'s myriad references to the 'Jewish Problem' and the need for war to address the sins of the Versailles Treaty as its author blowing hot air. Even those who took Hitler's rantings at face value found it hard to countenance the thought of *Mein Kampf*'s nightmares becoming reality. Numbed by the notion of war returning to Europe and dictatorship consuming democracy, the option to stick one's head in the sand and hope for the best was all too tempting. Worse than denial, some Britons agreed with Hitler, welcoming his takeover of Germany as the dawn of a new age that would revitalise Western civilisation.[4]

In Lockhart's case, there was an extra element to his initially hubristic take on the Nazis – life experience. He and Moura had personally suffered the consequences of Lenin's 'red terror', while Cromie, Garstin and, more recently, Reilly and Savinkov, had met their ends at the hands of the Bolsheviks, the latter two having been executed by the OGPU in 1925 during their last ill-conceived attempt to foment a counter-revolution. Weighed against this heavy ledger of violence and pain in the Soviet Union, Lockhart's experiences of Germany were weird but harmless. He had his recollections of a young Hitler waving his fist on the Kellerstrasse, and the *Sturmabteilung* rabble that accompanied him in the early 1920s. The well-appointed Brown House gave the Nazis a veneer of normality and

Rosenberg's talk of racial struggle was, for the time being, just that – talk. Whispers of Hitler's odd eating habits, perverse sexual proclivities and childish mood swings rendered him small beer in Lockhart's mind when compared to the likes of Dzerzhinsky, Lenin and his menacing heir, Stalin.[5]

Even when fascism came to Britain, Lockhart kept a cool head. This was partly because he knew its representative well. Oswald Mosley was a First World War veteran turned member of parliament, who had jumped between the Conservative and Labour parties in the 1920s, habitually dissatisfied with both sides' policies and frustrated by his lack of influence on them. After the stock market crash of 1929 and the Great Depression that followed, Britain's unemployment levels rose, prompting Mosley to posit himself as the man who could get workers back their jobs and set the economy on the road to recovery. In 1931, he formed the New Party and declared a crusade to establish a protectionist Britain. Like Beaverbrook's Empire Crusade, however, the New Party fizzled out after a poor showing at the 1931 general election. Smarting from the humiliation, Mosley turned further to the right of the political spectrum, donning a black turtleneck that aped Italy's fascist paramilitaries and delivering Mussolini-like lectures on the state of Britain's economy, in which Jewish bankers were singled out as the culprits. This turn culminated in Mosley founding the British Union of Fascists (BUF) in 1932, with the aim of fighting 'red terrorism' and engendering a fascist takeover of Britain.[6]

Mosley was one of the celebrities with whom Lockhart dined and partied while working on Londoner's Diary. Through these social interactions, the cynical Scot watched the privileged braggart develop his various public personas, concluding in a pithy remark made next to Mosley's name in one of his notebooks that 'political polygamy has its limits'. Amusing as Sir Oswald was to Lockhart, he had no illusions about the man's ambitions, noting in July 1929 that he 'intends to be Prime Minister of England'. To achieve this, Mosley recruited Lockhart's journalist friend Nicolson into the New Party and ingratiated himself with Beaverbrook to receive positive press coverage. Mosley assured Lockhart that he opposed deploying fascist tactics like street-fighting to the detriment of democratic processes. This pledge, combined with his experiences of Mosley's big talk around bottle-strewn dining tables, left Lockhart feeling that he was little more than an energetic political opportunist. Moreover, Mosley was a contact from whom Lockhart could get scoops like the New Party's manifesto, which he printed in the *Standard* two days before its public announcement in December 1930. Lockhart was, after all, a journalist, not an activist.[7]

Put off by Mosley's growing obsession with 'shock troops and the roll of drums around Westminster', Nicolson left his employ in spring 1932. Lockhart, however, continued to keep Mosley's company even after the BUF was formed. Between this affiliation and his generally light-touch coverage of Hitler, some of Lockhart's friends accused him of making the *Standard* pro-fascist. It speaks to his ideological ambiguities that these accusations were made at the same time that Lockhart was mentioned in an MI5 report as having been 'at one time, very closely in touch with [Communist] party leaders here and had been regarded as a possible recruit to intelligentsia circles'. The truth in both cases was more benign. As a more prosaic MI5 officer put it, by the 1930s Lockhart was well past flirting with communism. The 'financial advantages' of life under Beaverbrook had 'won over Lockhart once more to the side of capitalism' – clearly MI5 were not informed of their subject's struggle to achieve the capitalist imperative of wealth creation.[8]

Regarding accusations of being pro-fascist, Lockhart's relationship with Mosley was an instance of him engaging in the same practice he had followed in Russia and in Central Europe – mingling with political figures to collect information. As he had with Trotsky and Lenin, Lockhart came to perceive Mosley, Hitler and their disciples not as horrors to be spurned but as curiosities to be understood. To this end, Lockhart inquired after Mosley's plans for the BUF, which he recorded in his diary as being 'Mussolini in policy but Hitlerite in organisation'. Its leader, Lockhart concluded with alarm, thought that 'England is the country best adapted to fascism!', the arrival of which in Westminster was 'inevitable'. As he pondered the implications of Mosley's words, Lockhart also raised the BUF in conversation at London's private clubs and at Beaverbrook's dinner parties, deducing that Mosley was 'obviously gaining some converts' in certain circles, while leaving a 'very divided' view in others. Lockhart was not turning to fascism. He was simply trying to understand the impact it was having on Britain.[9]

These inquiries brought Lockhart into contact with some unsavoury people. As he kept an eye on Mosley, Lockhart returned the favour of playing host to Rosenberg during the latter's visit to London in December 1931. When Lockhart visited Berlin in 1932 he met with the head of the Nazis' Foreign Organisation, Hans Nieland, and on multiple occasions entertained Fritz Randolph, an attaché from the German embassy who promoted Anglo-German cultural links and whom Lockhart thought 'quite brainless'. Still in search of an interview with the Führer, Lockhart also corresponded with Hitler's press secretary Ernst Hanfstaengl, who offered apologies for the leader of the Third Reich's perpetual unavailability. One wonders how such a meeting would have gone, for even an apolitical charmer of Lockhart's calibre struggled with the viciousness of Nazi fanaticism. Enraged at a less than laudatory *Standard* article on Hitler, in September 1933 the German journalist Thost barged into Lockhart's office and accused him 'of having a Jewish secretary and England having Jewish watch-dogs in all important posts'. Lockhart tried to take the incident in his stride, recording phlegmatically that Thost's verbal assault left him 'bored'. Not so bored, however, for the unpleasantness to pass easily. After Thost stormed away, Lockhart retreated into his time-honoured method of escapism from that which he found difficult to process – he went to a club and stayed out late.[10]

More disturbing than anything from Thost's mouth was the intelligence Lockhart received from the German diplomat Albrecht von Bernstorff. Though he had worked for Hitler's government, Bernstorff was appalled by the extremists within it and the anti-Semitic policies they enacted. Bernstorff saw a well-connected journalist and widely read author like

Lockhart as a conduit through which to warn the British public, and so fed him information on everything from the scale of German rearmament to the primacy of the army in political decision-making. He also reported on the rising persecution of the Jews and the role played in it by the Nazi-controlled press. As Bernstorff told it, when a Jewish teenager killed an escaped lion from Berlin Zoo he was not praised as a hero but demonised as an 'insolent Jewboy' at the Reichsminister for Propaganda Joseph Goebbels' direction. This led to an outburst of anti-Semitic violence to which the police turned a blind eye. Disgusted as he was with the Nazis, Bernstorff was not eager for war with them. He believed the solution to the Hitler problem was to bring the regime down from within, and that the German people would do so once they realised the depths of the Nazis' crimes. He suggested to Lockhart that an international boycott of the 1936 Berlin Olympics would 'show the German masses who hear nothing in the controlled press, what the world says and thinks of their political masters'. Even after this initiative went nowhere, Bernstorff continued supplying Lockhart with information until the attentions of the Gestapo forced him to stifle his correspondence. He was imprisoned in Dachau in 1940 and executed as the war drew to its end in 1945.[11]

Bernstorff's alarming intelligence coincided with a series of international events that hardened Lockhart's views on fascism. Mussolini's invasion of Abyssinia in October 1935, Hitler's reoccupation of the Rhineland in March 1936 and the willingness of both dictators to send soldiers and war machines to aid their fellow fascist Francisco Franco in the Spanish Civil War confirmed Bernstorff's assertions that warmongers were in the ascendancy and that Britain had to prepare accordingly. Lockhart despaired at this thought. An Anglo-German clash would lead to another war which, he felt, Britain could not win. Informed by his contacts in Whitehall and the generals and admirals with whom he kept table, Lockhart concluded in 1937 that 'very little is being done' on national security and rearmament and, most worryingly, 'nothing for defence from air attack'. The commander of the territorial army did little to assuage

Lockhart's concerns, telling him that 'we could not go to war now. The army has nothing, and the organisation is chaotic'.

Lockhart's fears were heightened by a personal dimension of the looming conflict. Robin was now old enough to serve his country and had taken an interest in joining the Royal Navy. In vain, Lockhart asked Nicolson to convince Robin to pursue a safer life behind a desk at the Foreign Office, but this idea went nowhere. As Nicolson noted, the son was much like the father – 'far too sensitive and intelligent' for a career in Whitehall. This was an astute observation. Robin worked for Naval Intelligence during the war and later followed in his father's footsteps into Beaverbrook's employ, after which he became an author.[12]

Lockhart's interest in fascism and the gathering war storm in Europe caught the attention of a figure from his past. Since providing diplomatic support for the British Agent in 1918, Rex Leeper had settled into the life of a beige civil servant. His 'flat, deliberately unemotional voice' and reputation for being reliably inoffensive had assured him the kind of stable Whitehall career that Lockhart had forsaken. By the mid-1930s, Leeper was running the Foreign Office's news department and had access to intelligence from across Europe. As a contemporary recalled, this made Leeper an 'early prophet of the Nazi menace'. He shared this intelligence with Lockhart and picked his brains for ideas on how to halt fascism's onward march. Both men recognised the crucial role that propaganda played in Hitler and Mussolini's success, turning failures like the Beer Hall Putsch of 1923 into a celebration of martyrs and propagating the myth of Il Duce's courageous 'March on Rome' in 1922, despite the fascist leader staying far from the Eternal City during this takeover of the Italian state. Leeper's vision was to highlight these and other fascist lies via the British Council, which he had established in 1925 to champion British culture and values overseas. It was an under-funded body that had little backing from a government that saw British cultural superiority as self-evident and not in need of active promotion. Hitler's consolidation of power and the Reich's territorial expansion in the mid-1930s, however, led to the British Council's budget being increased to £30,000 per annum. With these funds, Leeper sought to weaponise the British Council into a medium through which to spread anti-fascist, pro-democracy propaganda. Who better to help with this campaign, Leeper thought, than a well-informed raconteur who, after years in the book-writing wilderness, was primed by concerns over fascism to get back into political work?[13]

This work was not solely concerned with propaganda, the dissemination of which provided cover for what Leeper really wanted Lockhart to do. A month before departing on his first British Council-sponsored lecture tour of Europe in 1937, Lockhart was issued further instructions on who to meet and what to report on by the Foreign Office's permanent under-secretary, Sir Robert Vansittart. As an advocate for rearmament and a staunch critic of those who believed in appeasing Hitler, Vansittart – 'Van' to intimates – was Whitehall's detester-in-chief of the Third Reich. When not irritating colleagues with outbursts over their timidity towards Germany, Van spent the 1930s constructing a private network of informants who gathered intelligence on fascism's growing influence. This network included not only Leeper and Nicolson but also probably Moura, who became associated at this time with Jona 'Klop' Ustinov (father of the actor Peter Ustinov), a Russian-born press attaché at the German embassy who worked for Van. Though her contributions to the latter's intelligence network are unclear, Moura was both 'a tireless champion of the victims of Nazi persecution' and compulsively drawn to collecting information during her travels across the continent.[14]

Lockhart was tasked with the same job, which he relished. Not only was he back in the intelligence-gathering game but he was also getting to revisit his old stomping grounds of Prague, Vienna, Sofia and Bucharest, which he had missed greatly during his time behind a typewriter on Fleet Street. At universities and embassies in these cities Lockhart delivered lectures over the course of a five-week tour, in which he shot down Hitler's claims that Britain and the USA had been softened by decadence. He argued that nationalism of the brutal form found in Italy and Germany was a diabolical tangent from the patriotic, democratic form of nationalism practised in the more civilised world. Further tours followed to Scandinavia, Yugoslavia and the USA, where Lockhart was generally well received. In the USA, the 'urbane and gregarious' speaker was lauded in the press for his insights into European politics, while in Czechoslovakia he was treated warmly by attentive audiences, albeit with a few walkouts from attendees who despised the Beaverbrook press and were unwilling to listen to one of its affiliates, irrespective of what he had to say.

The 'observe and report' aspect of Lockhart's mission confirmed his and Leeper's fears. He reported to Van that the one significant change in Europe since he had lived there was 'the effect of a re-armed Hitlerian Germany on the policy and on the psychology of all the countries which I visited'. This effect, Lockhart concluded, was 'best described as a combination of fear and admiration'. In Czechoslovakia, this manifested in lines of anxiety carved into the face of Lockhart's old friend Edouard Beneš. Having quizzed the Czech president on his army's fighting capacities, Lockhart came away unconvinced that Czechoslovakia could resist a German invasion but, ever enamoured of Beneš personally, noted that he could be relied on as an ally of Britain come what may. No such potential existed in Romania, where Lockhart observed that the quasi-fascist Iron Guard movement was comprised of angry young men possessed of a 'mysticism mixed with a certain amount of gangsterism', underpinned by a violent strain of anti-Semitism. The Iron Guard, Lockhart predicted, would rally to the swastika once the time for fighting came.

That dreaded hour was fast approaching. On 12 March 1938, Lockhart was attending a luncheon with government officials in Zagreb when a messenger burst through the banquet hall's doors, bearing news that Hitler had marched his troops into Austria. The life drained instantly from the party and a numbed silence descended. The anxious chatter and ill-informed speculation that broke out seconds later was not enough to satiate Lockhart's curiosity. Having apologised to his hosts for an abrupt departure, he hastened from the building and caught the next train to

Vienna. Three days later, Lockhart joined the crowd on the Heldenplatz who were watching Hitler crow about this latest territorial coup. As the Führer barked triumph and menace, Lockhart turned his gaze skywards to where scores of swastika-emblazoned warplanes were flying in ominously well-ordered formation. In the streets below, *Wehrmacht* soldiers marched with unfaltering discipline through the garlands of flowers flung at their feet by well-wishers who, Lockhart concluded, were ordinary Viennese of various classes and ages sharing in the delight of being brought 'home' to the Reich. Much had changed and nothing for Europe's good, since Lockhart had last set eyes on Hitler.[15]

Aside from its seismic geopolitical significance, Hitler's incorporation of Austria into the Reich was a victory that bolstered Goebbels' main propaganda theme – fascism was Europe's future. Everywhere he travelled, Lockhart saw signs of this narrative taking hold. Aides to King Boris of Bulgaria informed him that the Italians and the Germans were spending big money disseminating fascist propaganda in schools and offering scholarships for Bulgarian students to visit the Reich and receive ideological education. In Belgrade, Lockhart noted the sense of admiration that flooded over cinema audiences when presented with footage of Nazi stadium rallies. In early 1938, Lockhart attended one such rally at the Berlin Sportpalast, where he beheld the brains of the Nazis' propaganda operation in full flight. Preaching from behind a dramatically lit podium in front of a colossal swastika banner, Goebbels – the 'little demagogic wizard', as Lockhart described him – electrified the thousands before him with bile-laced talk of war and revenge. Stunned by the obedient cheers and waves of *seig heil*s the reptilian-like Goebbels received, Lockhart came away in no doubt that he had witnessed the 'greatest master of propaganda the world has ever seen'.[16]

This was a bitter compliment that depressed Lockhart greatly to bestow. He knew from his time in Russia that control of information was among the most powerful weapons in the arsenal of dictatorships, and that the propaganda produced by totalitarian states was of an order above anything Britain could devise. This was confirmed to Lockhart when he made a modest attempt to attack Hitler's regime through the *Standard*, to which he briefly returned in 1937 at Beaverbrook's request. The piece he penned mocking the Nazi foreign minister Joachim von Ribbentrop for his prior career as a champagne salesman was thrown into the bin by Beaverbrook, who feared it would harm Anglo-German relations. As this meagre effort to propagandise through the press was shut down the British Council's funding was cut, despite Lockhart's warnings about the money Berlin and Rome were splashing around Europe to preach the fascist gospel. It was a worrying blind spot in Whitehall's capacity to reckon with Europe's dictators.[17]

Frustrated by the Beaver's squeamishness and the government's lack of vision, in 1938 Lockhart wedded his concerns over fascism with his career as an author in his fifth book, *Guns or Butter*, in which he chronicled the perturbing details of his recent European travels. The book was a departure from the scandal and self-focus of Lockhart's previous works, in which he heeded the advice Leeper gave him after reading *Retreat from Glory* – 'it is time you got away from writing about yourself, because you have powers of writing which can carry you further than that'. Lockhart turned this page at the perfect time. *Guns or Butter* hit the shelves days after Prime Minister Neville Chamberlain's infamous flight to Munich in September 1938 where, in a meeting with Hitler, Mussolini and the French prime minister, Édouard Daladier, an agreement was made to hand the Czechoslovakian Sudetenland over to the Führer in return for peace. It was not for nothing that the *New York Times* dubbed Lockhart's latest offering 'an informed and successfully prophetic' record of his 'journeys to the trouble countries'.

Guns or Butter's initial run of 10,000 copies sold so quickly that a further 5,000 were ordered within weeks of its release. This success, however, did little to temper Lockhart's disgust at what had happened in Munich. He felt shame at his government's part in betraying the wishes of Beneš and the Czech minister in Britain, Jan Masaryk (son of the president who died in 1937), with whom Lockhart had formed a friendship based on their shared love of democracy and detestation of demagogues. After Chamberlain's return to London the crestfallen Masaryk visited Lockhart in tears, declaring that 'your people have finished us – let me down'. The Czech-loving Scot could only nod in silent agreement. Writing in the *Standard*, Lockhart pointed out to the British public that a sizeable minority of German-speaking democrats, Jews, Catholics and others opposed to Nazism lived in the Sudetenland. He posed an ominous question to readers who supported Chamberlain's appeasement policies: 'Are these people to be handed over to the same fate as the anti-Nazis in Austria?' When this inevitably happened, Lockhart cut the mien of a man whose time had come. A man who understood that Hitler would not stop until he was made to.[18]

Unlike Lockhart – who was a private citizen – Vansittart's voicing of the same opinion led to his demotion in Chamberlain's government from permanent under-secretary at the Foreign Office to the ceremonial position of chief diplomatic advisor. This attempt to kick Van upstairs did nothing to silence him. Over the winter of 1938–39, he bombarded the Foreign Office with demands for a robust anti-fascist propaganda campaign that would exceed the British Council's humble efforts. Van wanted anti-fascist films, pro-democracy radio programmes and the assigning of anti-appeasement figures to key diplomatic posts, all to the tune of £500,000. Unsurprisingly, it was not until Hitler broke the Munich Agreement and invaded the remainder of Czechoslovakia in March 1939 that this idea for a propaganda onslaught was cautiously entertained by the British government, albeit on a budget that was one fifth of what Van had requested. As he awaited this middling response to his grand plan, the disempowered diplomat despatched Lockhart to America once more.

The situation there was concerning. 'Surprise and annoyance' at Britain's refusal to confront Hitler at Munich, Lockhart reported, was expressed to him by everyone from senators and tycoons to line-cooks and schoolteachers. And yet, he also sensed 'little enthusiasm, even in New

York's radical circles, for any active American participation in a European war'. Anti-Semitism was also on the rise and, with it, crowing vitriol from a vocal minority of pro-Nazi Americans. As for Britain's most valuable potential ally in the war to come, Lockhart noted that while 'among the rich and business circles criticism of the President is much more violent than it was in 1933–1934', he 'found little to no anti-Roosevelt sentiment among the under-dogs'. Still, his overall impression was that the USA was a long way off being ready to join the global struggle between democracy and totalitarianism.[19]

While Van wanted Lockhart to bring him news from abroad, Leeper was more interested in what his old friend could do for the cause in Britain. At the height of the Munich crisis, Leeper proposed that in the event of war Lockhart should rejoin the Foreign Office and head up its intelligence desk on Eastern Europe. This would put him in the Political Intelligence Department (PID), which Leeper had worked for during the First World War and had been blowing the mothballs from since 1935 in anticipation of a bloody reprise. Leeper's war plan called for PID to supply intelligence on political, economic and social conditions across Europe to the Ministry of Information (MOI), which would then use it to craft propaganda that could boost morale on the home front and attack the Third Reich's ideology and war aims.

Having gained an appreciation of propaganda's importance through his European tours, Lockhart liked the idea. Not as much, however, as the thought of putting his exhaustive knowledge of Eastern Europe and his array of contacts there to good use by joining an embassy in the Balkans once war was declared. In this scenario, Lockhart envisioned his wartime role as a renewal of the intelligence work he had done in Moscow prior to the revolution. The problem was the changed circumstances of the bright-eyed vice-consul of the First World War, and the old rogue who was staring into the abyss of its sequel.

Before the Munich Agreement, Leeper had tried to get Lockhart appointed as an advisor to Lord Runciman's diplomatic mission to

Czechoslovakia, the purpose of which was to investigate Hitler's claims that Germans in the Sudetenland were being maltreated by the Czechs. Lockhart, however, had worn his affection for Beneš and the Masaryks on his sleeve in *Retreat from Glory*. On this basis he was disqualified from inclusion in Runciman's mission by the Foreign Office, who felt that the Germans would object to his bias. This exemplified the problem Lockhart faced. Through his books he had revealed to the world his anti-Bolshevik plotting, his love of the countries Hitler coveted, his advocacy of rearmament and his connections to power brokers across Europe. This, combined with the savagely honest way he had discussed his problems with drink and women, made him less attractive than ever for a public-facing job, let alone for a position gathering intelligence at a foreign embassy. He was too much of a public figure and too notorious a personality. For this reason, Lockhart accepted Leeper's offer to work for the clandestine yet pedestrian PID once war returned to Europe.[20]

His part in the coming drama confirmed, in the summer of 1939 Lockhart abandoned the anxious buzz of London for the soothing tranquillity of Tomintoul. Safe from war talk in the shadow of the Cairngorms, Lockhart took to the banks of the nearby River Avon to fish away his fears and await the ingress of the inevitable. It was in this idyll by the reeds on the morning of 1 September that a runner from the village pub informed him that important news was breaking on the wireless. Dragging himself into the Richmond Arms, Lockhart gathered with the locals to listen in numbed silence to reports of Hitler's panzers streaming into Poland. He sighed deeply and let the odd blend of apprehension and catharsis wash over him. Accepting that his 'selfish ambitions and desires were now of no importance' and that he was to become one of the many 'cogs in Britain's ponderous, relentless, war machine', Lockhart shuffled into the pub's back room and called Leeper.[21]

Robert Bruce Lockhart, the boyish rubber planter, circa 1909.

An example of the anonymous writing Lockhart used to busy his mind and bolster his finances in Russia, 1913.

Baroness Moura
Budberg – the love
of Lockhart's life.

Lockhart's faithful
'lieutenant', Sidney Reilly.

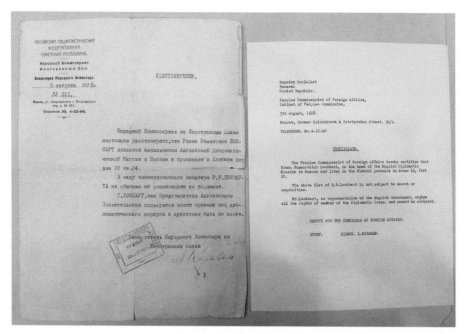

Lockhart's safe conduct pass, issued in early August but useless to him by the month's end.

The British Agent's nemeses – Jacob Peters and Felix Dzerzhinsky.

The arbiters of Lockhart's destiny – Anthony Eden (top) and Lord Beaverbrook (bottom).

Opposite page: The British Agent strikes a pose (top right). Lockhart's *Memoirs of a British Agent*, sensationalised in print (top left) and on the silver screen (bottom).

A PWE leaflet from 1942 that brought home the reality of Germany's changing war fortunes.

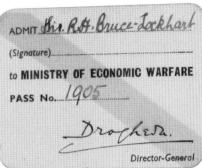

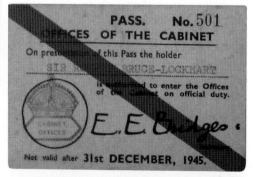

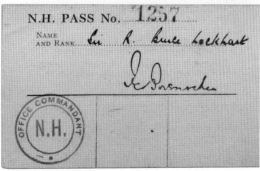

Man about Whitehall –
Lockhart's various Second
World War security passes.

Sefton Delmer, PWE's star propagandist.

The adventurous rogue turned retiring writer – Lockhart in his later years.

CHAPTER 13

FIGHTING 'PHONEY'

'This government will never win this war.'

– Lord Beaverbrook

There was something ominously laboured about the start to Lockhart's Second World War. Two days after Chamberlain declared Britain's entry into the fray, Lockhart left his apprehensions about rejoining the Foreign Office at Tomintoul and headed to London. Along the way, he saw young soldiers mustering on train platforms and Bristol Blenheims roaring through the skies. The sadness he felt at these portends of conflict was muted by the sense of steel they proffered. By the time Lockhart arrived at Paddington Station he was galvanised in a way he hadn't been for decades – Britain was at war, and he was going to do his bit to ensure victory.

This resolve soon took a hit. Upon reporting to Whitehall, Lockhart was told to wait four days for his PID position to commence. Given that Poland was fighting for its existence and the first British soldiers were arriving on French soil at this time, these orders struck him as concerningly unhurried. From what he had observed of the capital, however, they were not out of place with the prevailing mood. Some Londoners had gas masks on their belts and in Hyde Park barrage balloons were being fumbled into the air, but otherwise the city seemed blissfully detached from the drama unfolding across the Channel. Shoe polishers in Piccadilly Circus plied their trade and the clubs were full of drinkers and dancers. Women were shopping with their children and businessmen in well-cut suits were trading playful barbs over expensive lunches in Mayfair. Few Londoners seemed to be spoiling for a fight with Hitler.

Tired of walking the untroubled streets, Lockhart dropped into the St James's Club, a members-only institution he had joined in 1936. Rooms there were Lockhart's primary residence in London and the associated mailbox the connection to his many friends and acquaintances. Rifling through the piles of personal correspondence and fan mail for *Guns or Butter*, he found a letter from MOI addressed to 'Captain R. H. Lockhart' – a rank he had never held. The missive declared that Lockhart had been selected to join MOI and was not to engage in any other form of wartime service. Whitehall's *enfant terrible* let out a bitter chuckle. He enjoyed the novelty of being in demand but was perplexed by the honorary rank and disturbed that MOI seemed unaware he had been assigned to PID since September 1938. Confusion in government, it seemed, reigned with the apathy of the capital's governed.

After four days of frustrating stasis, Leeper appeared at the St James's and bundled Lockhart into a car that drove them through the Bedfordshire countryside to Woburn Abbey, the residence of the Duke of Bedford. To maintain operational secrecy away from London, Leeper had acquired the abbey's outlying buildings for use by PID and the propaganda organisation with which it was partnered, Department EH, so called as it was initially established at Electra House in East London. In a deviation from Leeper's original plan, MOI had been tasked with home-front propaganda, while EH would direct its efforts against Germany. Informed by PID's intelligence summaries, EH's propaganda would be distributed across Europe via fake newspaper articles, air-dropped leaflets and radio broadcasts, with the aim of undermining German morale and promoting Allied war aims. The PID–EH operation was the sum of Leeper's years spent preparing to wage psychological warfare on Germany, and yet Woburn was still a work in progress when Lockhart arrived. His office and adjoining living space was a small attic in an old barn, bereft of carpets, heating or even a chest of drawers. Embarrassed upon presenting the room to his friend, Leeper sheepishly asked Lockhart to return to the capital until the renovations were completed. Between the travel time from Tomintoul, the four days waiting in London and the construction delay at Woburn, Lockhart did little but kick his heels for the first two weeks of the Second World War.[1]

By late September Woburn's rooms were finished and its propagandists and intelligence analysts were in situ. Still, Lockhart couldn't shake the thought that he and the abbey's other denizens were stranded on an island of irrelevancy. Fifty miles from London's foreign embassies and service departments, PID struggled to get good intelligence in a timely manner. This affected Woburn's reputation. Lockhart was explicitly told by a Foreign Office staffer that until PID and EH were relocated to London, no one in Whitehall would take their work seriously. Even if Leeper's people moved to the city, Lockhart doubted they would be well received. Woburn's rooms were packed with an eclectic mix of journalists, businessmen, schoolmasters, authors, barristers and university dons, most of whom had been conjured from Leeper's personal address book. Lockhart was impressed by some of his colleagues, such as the historian of Germany E. L. Woodward, the former *Standard* journalist Robert Carvel and Kinahan Cornwallis, a former director of the propaganda producing Arab Bureau in Cairo who had an encyclopaedic knowledge of the Middle East. The others, however, struck him as a collection of 'freaks, some genuine antiques, several fakes and a few geniuses', peppered with socialist intellectuals and celebrity anti-Nazis like Nöel Coward.[2]

These were the kind of quirky outcasts that appealed to Lockhart on a personal level – creative types who loved to read, drink and talk freely. However, he knew from experience that Whitehall officials would look down on such people, which they did, referring to the Woburn operation as 'Leeper's sleepers'. Their secretive base in the countryside also fed rumours that cars brimming with champagne and prostitutes set out nightly from London to entertain what one minister assumed was a 'den of socialists'. These accusations obscured the reality that politically and culturally Woburn was a house divided. As a visitor to the abbey recalled, it had an 'atmosphere highly charged with personal rivalries', in which those with pretences to professionalism and those who revelled in wordplay and tomfoolery often clashed. The propagandist Ellic Howe was probably referring to Lockhart when he derided PID as a wheeze cooked up by Leeper to provide 'genteel employment' for Whitehall rejects. Cognisant that at least one minister thought he was 'a fascist once, with Mosley' and that the shadow of 1918 still hung over him, Lockhart likely agreed with Howe's assessment.[3]

The fruits of Woburn's dysfunctional labours were also questionable. PID's intelligence summaries were criticised for their bias, with Lockhart's talking-up of Czech resistance to the occupying Germans prompting one Whitehall official to complain about the 'disproportionate space' devoted to reporting on Czechoslovakia by someone with 'a facile pen'. The propaganda side of Woburn's operation invited similar criticism. Techniques for subverting the enemy through words and ideas had been pioneered during the First World War by Crewe House, a clandestine organisation run by Beaverbrook's rival press baron, Lord Northcliffe. After the war, Northcliffe's deputy Campbell Stuart penned a laudatory account of Crewe House's work, in which he argued that propaganda had been decisive in bringing down the *Kaiserreich* and that he had played a central role in engineering this triumph. This led to Stuart being made head of Department EH when it was established as Crewe House's successor in 1938. Once the war began, it didn't take long for the truth of Stuart's limitations to show. Dashing in his chauffeur-driven Rolls-Royce between brief meetings at Woburn and long lunches in London, Stuart presided over a propaganda operation that ignored the success of Hitler's *Gleichschaltung* (coordination) policy, which had created a *Volk* (a 'people') that either through devotion or fear was unified in thrall to its Führer. Instead, EH worked on the assumption that if British voices simply pointed out to the German people that Hitler was insane and his leadership questionable, then the Reich would implode. This ill-informed notion guided Britain's first propaganda salvoes against Germany.[4]

Hours after Chamberlain declared war, EH leaflets were fluttering through the skies over Germany, Czechoslovakia, Poland and Switzerland. This was one of the Royal Air Force's first 'raids' of the conflict. As such, Stuart could have claimed a propaganda victory by broadcasting into Europe that, contrary to Göring's boasts of the *Luftwaffe*'s strength, British planes had easily penetrated the Reich's airspace. Instead, Stuart emphasised the quality and effectiveness of the leaflets themselves to the War Cabinet. The 'comebacks' (intelligence reports on the reception of propaganda) told a different story. MI6 assets in Europe indicated that few recipients took the leaflet's attacks on Hitler's competency seriously. Even fewer had time for the German translations of Chamberlain's dull speeches, in which Britain's entry into the war was presented as a noble corrective to the brutal lawlessness of Nazism. The fact that British pilots had risked their lives to disperse these tame ideas – rather than, say, explosive ordnance – was viewed as being 'well mannered', 'feeble' and a 'typically mad and English thing to do'. Trying to find a silver lining, the British consul-general in Zurich recommended that the leaflets continue to be dropped, if only to busy German soldiers with gathering them up. Faced with this criticism, even Stuart conceded the obvious point that the people he was trying to turn against Hitler 'condemn the leaflet because it is not a bomb'. Lockhart felt likewise. Reflecting on Poland's losing battle against the *Wehrmacht* and the Red Army – the latter had also invaded Poland in accordance with a secret pact between Hitler and Stalin – he despaired that Britain's only riposte was to drop pieces of paper conveying ill-informed ideas.[5]

Sensing his friend's disaffection, Leeper arranged for Lockhart to assume another role in addition to his Woburn job – Whitehall's liaison to the Czech officials who had escaped to Britain after the Germans occupied their country in March 1939. Chief among these refugees was Beneš, who wanted to form a government-in-exile that could continue the fight against Germany from London. This aspiration was sound on paper, but the terms of the Munich Agreement didn't permit Beneš and his officials to be recognised as conquered Czechoslovakia's governing body. This left

Lockhart with a similarly murky diplomatic status to the one he had in 1918, prompting one colleague to suggest that he assume the title of 'British Agent' to the Czechs. Lockhart winced at the thought. Not only did it stir bad memories, but he knew that Goebbels would make a propaganda feast of the situation, using Lockhart's history to sour Anglo-Soviet relations. When offered the Agent moniker, therefore, he opted for 'Representative'.

The title was not as important as the job itself, which interested Lockhart more than anything he did at Woburn. Czechoslovakia may have been the wellspring of his years of spiral, but Lockhart's affection for the country and its people never faltered. He dreamed of getting the hated Munich Agreement torn up and full recognition given to Beneš' government-in-exile, as a precursor to an independent Czechoslovakian state being re-established once the Nazis were vanquished.

The first problem Lockhart faced in achieving this goal was among the trickiest for him to solve – Beneš himself. Resentful of Munich and enraged at how his country had been swallowed by the Reich while Britain and France stood by, Beneš had earned a reputation in Whitehall for being unbending and irascible. Given that the fugitive ex-president had few military assets at his command, most British officials also saw Beneš as a burden rather than a boon to the war effort. 'I insist always that the Czechs can help us during the war,' Lockhart scrawled in his diary, 'but no one listens. No one cares.' As in 1918, Lockhart was backing an unpopular cause for which he earned a derisive reputation.[6]

His support for Beneš was not the only reason Lockhart felt once more like an outsider in the government he served. Woburn's sorry state and London's lack of war-mindedness struck him as symptoms of a serious underlying issue – Chamberlain wanted to get out of, rather than get on with, fighting the war. This hunch was confirmed to him in November 1939, when Woburn's proposal to drop leaflets exposing Nazi corruption and war profiteering was scotched by the foreign secretary, Lord Halifax, on the grounds that the propaganda would implicate the notoriously crooked and self-indulgent Göring. Tipped off by Vansittart and friends in MI6, Lockhart knew that this moratorium on slandering the Reichsmarschall was owed to 'some private negotiations going on'. These had begun weeks earlier when Göring started sending peace feelers to Lord Halifax through intermediaries. The possibility of extracting Britain from the war via a secret settlement with Germany caused the government to drag its feet rather than prepare for a long fight. While dining with the intelligence officer, and future creator of James Bond, Ian Fleming and the soon-to-be-infamous commando Fitzroy Maclean, Lockhart was told that 'the atmosphere in Whitehall (wasn't) serious, not warlike, full of intrigue'. Nicolson shared similar views and revealed to Lockhart that he and Anthony Eden – who had resigned as foreign secretary in February 1938 – were part of a clique to oust Chamberlain. The comfort these like-minded voices gave Lockhart was not enough, however, to quash his feeling that Halifax's peace negotiations would bear fruit before a more war-minded occupant moved into Number 10.[7]

Lockhart's mood was lifted on 1 May 1940, when he attended a dinner at Beaverbrook's Stornoway House. The Beaver had endorsed the Munich Agreement in 1938 and, once war began, argued that a peace needed to be brokered that would preserve the British Empire while satisfying Hitler's lust for *Lebensraum* (living space). He also championed the anti-war rhetoric of America's ambassador in Britain, Joseph Kennedy, and had his newspapers highlight the threat of German invasion and the 'much grimmer phase of war' that was coming. After Britain's disastrous attempt to land troops in Norway in April 1940, however, Beaverbrook was hit by one of his idiosyncratic mood swings, penning an article for the *Express* in which he declared that 'the whole nation is now fixed and settled in its purpose to fight the war to a conclusion'. Lockhart knew well the influence Beaverbrook wielded and had faith that his old boss's changed mind would have a political impact. This faith was repaid quickly. Days after Beaverbrook unveiled his revised opinion on the war at Stornoway, Chamberlain's government collapsed and Churchill became prime minister, with Beaverbrook brought into the War Cabinet. Lockhart was elated but felt that the new premier needed to 'cut down his alcohol and curb his temper' to be successful. The hypocrisy of this statement revealed itself five days after Churchill's appointment when Lockhart, Beaverbrook, Randolph Churchill, Clement Attlee and Arthur Greenwood drank into the early hours in celebration of Britain's new, more bellicose, prime minister.[8]

Churchill's ascendancy and the ending of the war's 'phoney' period raised Lockhart's spirits, but not enough to distract his worried mind from the fact that the country remained under the sword. As the Battle of Britain unfolded in the skies above, Lockhart found himself musing with increasing pessimism on the prospect of a German invasion and subsequent occupation. He wasn't aware that both he and Moura were on the Nazi 'blacklist' of those to be executed during Hitler's proposed conquest, but even so he despaired at the thought of being in London when the worst happened. Like most residents of the capital, Lockhart had a terrifying taste of German intentions. While attending a dinner party at the United Services Club in October 1940, a bomb fell into the garden just beyond the window where Lockhart was sitting. The explosion shattered glass, dislodged chandeliers and threw him across the room. Seconds passed like hours as the frightened guests huddled under a cloud of dust and detritus. Gingerly, Lockhart rose to his feet, picking shrapnel from his forearms as he did so. In that dazed moment he beheld the otherworldly sight of a naval captain standing resolute amid the smoke and panic with a glass of impressively un-spilled port in his hand. Inspired by this stoicism, Lockhart took his leave from the blast-shattered party and embarked on a bizarre nerve-strengthening pub crawl to the Sports Club, the Landsdowne and finally back to the St James's Club, even as bombs continued to rain down on London.

Aside from the danger to life and limb it posed, Lockhart remained concerned that the Blitz was keeping the prospect of a negotiated peace alive. In late June, he recorded a rumour that while wielding the stick of the *Luftwaffe*, Hitler had proffered the carrot-of-peace terms to anti-Churchillites in the government through Francisco Franco. The deal was simple – 'Hitler to rule Europe, we to rule the seas . . . Winston to go. Lloyd George to be our Pétain'. It was a story, Lockhart noted, that was 'all over London'. Churchill's public displays of bombastic defiance in the House of Commons were stirring and his orders for Whitehall officials to abstain from peace talks with the Germans were reassuring. However, thinking like a propagandist, Lockhart felt that if deeds were not forthcoming to back Churchill's fighting words, then his government would soon stop listening. The will to resist would be lost and talk of negotiating a settlement with Hitler would return.[9]

This impetus for action, combined with his crusade to improve Beneš' reputation, led Lockhart to make his first operational proposal of the war – a campaign of guerrilla attacks in occupied Czechoslovakia (re-christened by the Germans as the Protectorate of Bohemia and Moravia). In 1939, resistance fighters in the Protectorate established a secret radio channel with Beneš through which to receive orders and request guns, explosives and other materiel from Britain. At Beneš' urging, in the spring of 1940 one of these resistance fighters smuggled himself out of the Protectorate for a meeting with Lockhart, for the purposes of discussing the next phase of the fightback against Nazi occupation. Having arrived at a hotel in Putney just after dawn, Lockhart was led upstairs by officers from Czech intelligence to a room they had booked out for the secret rendezvous. The suite's sole occupant was a gaunt-looking thirty-something, who unsmilingly extended his hand to Lockhart and introduced himself as the head of the Protectorate's main resistance group, the Czech Maffia. He assured Lockhart that the Maffia was a professional outfit, structured in a cellular fashion that maintained tight operational security among its ever-growing membership. They had guns and explosives, experience and fortitude. They were ready to lay down their lives to free Czechoslovakia from its oppressors. Summarising his two-hour meeting with the determined Czech, Lockhart offered an uncritical assessment to the Foreign Office, reporting that the Maffia's 'military preparations were complete', and its fighters were 'ready for a general revolt', provided that British backing was forthcoming. Energised by what the Maffia chief told him, Lockhart was once again getting into the insurrection business, albeit this time to dislodge occupying Nazis rather than bring down revolutionary communists.[10]

Lockhart's contact talked a big game, but there was little evidence to back his claims about the Maffia's readiness. An uprising by Czech university students in October 1939 had failed dismally, leading to the execution of participants and the arrests of thousands more. Enthusiasm for a reprise was stifled across the Protectorate in the months that followed by further acts of Nazi oppression. As the British guerrilla warfare expert General Colin Gubbins reported after carrying out a reconnaissance of the occupied territories in early 1940, 'prospects for sabotage in Poland and Czechoslovakia are hopeless'. Lockhart's refusal to accept Gubbins' assessment and his willingness to buy what the Maffia chief was selling indicate that his adventurous spirit and romantic view of the Czechs trumped his common sense. As late as 1942, when the Czechs pulled off their most infamous act of rebellion by assassinating SS Obergruppenführer Reinhard Heydrich, the resistance movement was still small and ill-prepared for a sustained guerrilla campaign. Indeed, part of Beneš' motivation for issuing the order to kill Heydrich was to prove to other Allied leaders that the Czechs could offer tangible resistance to their oppressors. The fact that it took until 1942 for this demonstration to take place indicates the hollowness of Lockhart's assertions about the Maffia's preparedness in 1940.[11]

Lockhart's advocacy of the Maffia and his pestering of the BBC to give more airtime to Jan Masaryk so he could broadcast morale-boosting messages into the Protectorate earned him the ire of some Foreign Office officials, who responded by avoiding meetings with him. Despite this, Lockhart managed to achieve a diplomatic breakthrough on behalf of those he affectionately referred to as 'my Czechs'. On 23 July 1940, Churchill officially recognised the Czech government-in-exile with Beneš as its president, at the expense of his Slovak rival for the title, Milan Hodža. Lockhart played a key role in shutting Hodža out. With help from Masaryk, he dug into Hodža's background and reported to the Foreign Office that the would-be Czech leader had embezzled money from Prague's treasury and that placing him on a pedestal would reflect poorly on the British government. While he didn't get his guerrilla campaign, the acknowledgement of Beneš and his government-in-exile was claimed by Lockhart as a personal victory from his ten months of struggle with colleagues who paid the Czechs no mind. It was one of the few triumphs he enjoyed in 1940.[12]

As he laboured for Beneš, Lockhart continued working at Woburn, producing weekly intelligence reports and getting increasingly involved in propaganda. One area to which he contributed was the creation of rumours – known as 'sibs' to the propagandists, from the Latin word *sibilare*, meaning to hiss. Disseminated through fake newspapers, radio broadcasts or via the chatter of MI6 assets, sibs were designed to undermine German morale by raising anxieties and inciting fear. Some sibs effectively walked the line between sounding alarming yet credible, such as the rumour that a disease spread by pigs had been detected on livestock ships in the Baltic and, as a consequence, the *Volk* could not trust the safety of the Reich's pork products. Rumours of a new British incendiary bomb with a delayed detonation prompted fears that hours after an air raid had taken place, German civilians might be blown apart by what they thought were duds. Likewise, a sib concerning a British weapon that could set fire to the seas had a psychological impact on *Luftwaffe* pilots who, in the interrogations that followed their capture in the Battle of Britain, spoke of the terror they felt at the thought of being immolated after ditching into the Channel. Other sibs, a Woburn staffer recalled, 'bore the signs of having been thought up after a good lunch'. An exemplar of this was the rumour that Britain had imported sharks from Australia for releasing into the English Channel as a deterrent to German invasion. Similar silliness abounded in sibs that were disseminated in the mosques of West Africa, where the faithful were told that 'when Germans swear, they use the word "*scheisse*", which is their way of pronouncing Satan, who is their god'.[13]

When not brainstorming sibs, Lockhart penned pro-Beneš leaflets for dispersal over Prague and broadcast messages via the BBC to the people of Zagreb, recalling his love of the city and the need to defend it from fascists within and without. He also helped Moura's lover H. G. Wells develop a leaflet for dropping over France, the objective of which was to encourage resistance amongst the liberal middle classes, by appealing to their reason and intelligence. This scheme was born out of one of the many lunches Lockhart shared with Moura who, as she had in revolutionary Russia, adapted and thrived amid the drama around her. At the start of the war, Moura was briefly employed as a propagandist at MOI, before questions over whether she was working for either the Soviets or even the Germans were raised. Having been recruited by MI5 to spy on her, Moura's old friend Klop Ustinov assured his bosses that the baroness was not pro-German. Her shady reputation, however, and the existence of a photo of her next to Stalin was enough for MOI to cut Moura loose. In the end, Ernest Boyce once again intervened to suggest that Moura's intellect and work ethic made her an asset to the Allied war effort, provided that she stick to work 'unconnected in any way with the intelligence department'. This led to Moura penning articles for *La France Libre*, the propaganda magazine produced by General Charles de Gaulle's French government-in-exile. As Lockhart was pestering Beaverbrook at this time to get the Home Office off Moura's back, it is likely that he pulled the necessary strings to land her this uncontroversial job working alongside Britain's close ally. Certainly, Lockhart benefited from her being embedded with de Gaulle's people, from whom Moura extracted stories on the state of their administration and conditions in France itself, the details of which ended up at Woburn.[14]

Neither his dealings with Moura nor the production of leaflets sufficed to satisfy Lockhart's fighting spirit, which had been stirred by the miraculous evacuation of 300,000 soldiers from the beaches of Dunkirk in June 1940. Still stewing on the rejection of his Czech Maffia idea, Lockhart complained to Beaverbrook that when it came to innovative ways of combatting Germany, he felt he was banging his head against Whitehall's wall of 'extreme caution and indecision'. He reflected that 'twenty-two years ago, I should have reacted violently. Today, I adopt gentler methods, but I still have something of the lust of battle in my blood'. Campbell Stuart's dismissal from Woburn shortly after Dunkirk seemingly gave Lockhart the chance to indulge this combative mindset. Acknowledging the dysfunction in Leeper's operation, Churchill ordered that EH and PID should be incorporated into the propaganda wing of a new clandestine organisation, tasked with the mission to 'set Europe ablaze' through subversion and sabotage – the Special Operations Executive (SOE).[15]

Owing to his relationship with Beneš and experiences in secret operations, Lockhart was given the Czech section of what Whitehall insiders called 'Dalton's show'. This referred to SOE's head, Hugh Dalton, a Labour politician into whose hands Churchill placed control of Britain's economic warfare, propaganda and sabotage operations in July 1940. The prime minister detested Dalton on a personal level but appreciated his hatred of fascism, even if it rubbed other people the wrong way. Possessed of an ability to pontificate and alienate in equal measure, SOE's head was habitually 'offensive and got people's backs up', usually by suggesting that anyone who didn't froth at the mouth in loathing of Hitler was two steps shy of being an appeaser.

Members of SOE's intelligence wing grumbled about serving under Dalton, who was soon written off by influential figures close to Churchill as a 'windbag' who couldn't accomplish anything. This further damaged the reputation of SOE's propagandists and saboteurs, who were already looked down on as rank amateurs by many in MI6 and the military. It didn't help that SOE was beset by internal quarrelling over who was supposed to do what in any given operation. 'Hours, days and weeks are wasted on these personal questions,' Lockhart lamented, 'and no work is done.' In Lockhart's opinion, the organisation's impotence was further driven home on the evening of 13 September 1940, when the *Luftwaffe*'s arrival over London sent him scrambling for an air-raid shelter with his colleagues. Amid the thud and crash of the bombs, a knock rang out from the shelter door. Once it was opened, a 'little Czech girl, about sixteen' shuffled over the threshold, politely asking who Mr Lockhart was and waving a letter she had carried across town from Beneš. While the men who were meant to set Europe ablaze cowered, a teenager had fearlessly walked through London's exploding streets to do her job.[16]

The Czech girl became a living, breathing epiphany to Lockhart. Aside from acting as an agony aunt for his colleagues – his likeability generally kept him above the fray – Lockhart spent most of his time at SOE producing intelligence reports on conditions in the Protectorate. Knowing that for all his faults he had more to offer, in December 1940 Lockhart wrote to Dalton to request a change of assignment. He highlighted his 'wider, longer and more varied personal knowledge of European countries and leading figures than most people in Whitehall' and declared that he would no longer 'waste my time collecting and writing reports on housing conditions, food prices, wages, transport and other statistical data'. He needed a job that would make a difference. Dalton agreed that Lockhart's talents were being wasted at the Czech desk and that he was among the 'most well informed on discussions between ministers and officials' in Whitehall, particularly on matters that were 'supposedly secret'. This led to Dalton giving him a unique floating position in SOE, in which capacity he could interject himself into whatever matters he saw fit, be it intelligence, propaganda or the organising of anti-Nazi resistance groups.[17]

Lockhart was no fool. He knew Dalton's offer was more a sop to his ego than an actual position – the memory of Van's reduction to the impressive-sounding but meaningless position of chief diplomatic advisor was still fresh in his mind. In early 1941, therefore, Lockhart explored other employment options. Among them was the suggestion of a role in MI6. Mindful of his limitations as a spymaster, Lockhart declared that 'nothing on this earth would induce me to accept' the position 'even if begged'. As always, Beaverbrook buzzed with ideas. Aside from his standing offer of a Fleet Street return, the Beaver suggested that Lockhart become minister of information and cooked up a scheme to send him to Washington for an unspecified propaganda role which, given that Britain was without a major ally in the spring of 1941, was likely aimed at encouraging the USA to enter the war. Beaverbrook also recommended Lockhart to Anthony Eden – restored to power as foreign secretary and secretary of state for war in Churchill's government – as the man who could fix Britain's propaganda problem. In doing so, Beaverbrook once more became the arbiter of Lockhart's destiny.[18]

Eden was as fed up with Dalton as anyone and, knowing the rot over which he presided could be traced back to Woburn, he ordered Lockhart to undertake a comprehensive review of Britain's propaganda campaign since its inception. Lockhart relished this opportunity to crystallise eighteen months of frustration in print, noting that the 'confusion, over-lapping and lack of organisation' was 'greater than I had believed possible'. He identified the multiple fingers in Britain's propaganda pie as a key issue and recommended that 'the proper solution to this problem is to put all forms of enemy war-zone propaganda under a single control'. A new department, comprised of propagandists from SOE and MOI, controlled by one director and with one purpose – to undermine German morale through methods of psychological warfare – had to be created. Eden agreed and on 8 August 1941 the Political Warfare Executive (PWE) was signed into creation by Churchill, after which it began operating in secret under the cover of being the latest iteration of Leeper's PID. Despite Lockhart's assertion that a single leader needed to take charge, PWE was initially run by a committee of which he was a member. Predictably, this committee imploded under the weight of the egos involved, leading to Lockhart finally being given the title of PWE's director-general on 20 March 1942.[19]

It is tempting to interpret this sequence of events as Lockhart's skilful execution of a self-promoting coup. His concerns for Britain's propaganda campaign were real enough, but so too was his dissatisfaction at the dead-end state of his career and, as always, his money troubles. Lockhart had two books nearing completion in 1939. However, his return to the Foreign Office at the onset of the war meant that neither was published. This left him reliant on his wages from PID and SOE which, at a little over £1,000 per year, were too low to meet his ever-indulgent spending habits. Citing Tommy's volunteering for the Red Cross and Moura's preoccupation with working for de Gaulle, Lockhart later claimed that his social life fizzled out during the war. In truth, he still hosted expensive lunches and dinners with old friends and new contacts and, like many government officials, imbibed frequently as a means of coping with the stress of life in Blitz-hit London. As late as October 1941 he was facing his latest 'week of destiny', in which he had to find £250 to pay off debts. This habitual need for money was likely at the back of Lockhart's mind when he told Eden that the propaganda campaign needed a major-domo. It was certainly the impetus for his insistence that to become PWE's director-general, he should also be given the financially lucrative position of deputy under-secretary at the Foreign Office.[20]

Any manoeuvring on Lockhart's part for financial gain should not discount the sincerity of his grievances over Britain's propaganda campaign or his appropriateness to lead it. Between his time in Russia, his work in Central Europe, his careers as a journalist and author and his labours on behalf of Van and the British Council, there were few in Whitehall with Lockhart's breadth of experience in the activities that constituted psychological warfare. His friendship with key figures in the Foreign Office was also a boon for Britain's unloved propagandists. A lifetime of being politically connected and working in the realms of half-truth and subversion was about to pay off. The confidence this career experience gave Lockhart was caveated, however, by his infinite capacity for critical self-reflection. He refused to believe Beaverbrook's assertion that he was a problem-solving magician. Rather, Lockhart saw himself as a prop in the show 'produced, like a rabbit out of a conjurer's hat' to fix the mess created by Leeper and Dalton. He also realised that reconceptualising Britain's propaganda war and managing the madhouse that waged it would push him to his limits. Having accepted Eden's offer to become PWE's director-general, Lockhart shared a drink with a colleague in Beaverbrook's employ. This friend admitted that he was 'being murdered' by the demanding press baron's schedule but, poking a finger into Lockhart's chest, asserted to him that in assuming control of PWE 'you've committed suicide'. Lockhart smiled wanly and downed his scotch. 'Metaphorically true,' he replied. 'Literally, a future possibility.'[21]

CHAPTER 14

CANCEL THE REVOLUTION

'This attempt to convert the Germans to rebellion against Hitler by argument and appeal was a waste of breath and electric power.'

— Sefton Delmer

The German people were guilty. Since 1933, they had cheered a false prophet and basked in the glory of his brutal triumphs. They would soon reap the whirlwind. Hitler's conquests had prompted an 'awakening of England and of the Empire', the citizens of which were possessed of the 'freshness, youth, inexhaustible vigour and aggressiveness' that was ebbing from war-burdened Germany. Already tasked with occupying France, the Low Countries and the Balkans, the Reich's overstretched legions were now sinking into the quagmire of the Soviet Union, which Hitler had ordered his *Wehrmacht* to invade in June 1941. This foolish decision had achieved that which was once unthinkable – the uniting of the British Empire with the Soviet Union against a common foe. Now, the Führer's days were numbered but so were those of the *Volk* who had supported him. The 'responsibility of the German people for the continuation of the war' was obvious, but they had one slim chance for redemption. If they did their bit to hasten Germany's defeat by refusing to work and committing acts of sabotage they might yet wash the stain of the swastika from their person. To encourage this, the 'ultimate purpose of every news item, of every broadcast, of every word addressed to the Germans' from

Britain via radio, leaflet or deliberately spread rumour had to be one thing only – revolution.[1]

Lockhart, eyes sore and head spinning, slumped into his chair and placed the proposal atop a messy stack of papers on his desk. He folded his hands over his waistcoat and gazed upwards, losing himself for a blissful moment in the ornate brilliance of the Locarno Room's vaulted ceiling. He liked his base of operations. Having relocated permanently from Woburn at the end of 1941, Lockhart now spent most of his time at the Foreign Office building – the place he had first entered as a bright young thing in 1911. Then, he was nobody. Now, he convened daily meetings with Eden, Beaverbrook, ambassadors who fed him intelligence on occupied Europe and the minister of information, Brendan Bracken, with whom he had struck up an instant rapport. Lockhart's relocation to London also meant more time with Moura who, not content with working for de Gaulle, had followed her former lover's lead in charming her way into the confidences of Whitehall's power brokers. Such was Moura's reach, even Bracken thought it 'better to feed the tigress' whatever intelligence she wanted, rather 'than be pulled out of his bath in the morning to answer what his butler had told him was an urgent, secret call' from her. Like his well-connected muse, Lockhart was enjoying a position of influence greater than any he'd held since being Britain's Agent. This heightened status, however, came with a burden in the form of a difficult question – what was PWE's mission and how could its propagandists complete it?[2]

In pursuit of an answer, Lockhart spent long days hunched over his desk in the winter of 1941, trying to block out the sound of coughing and background chatter that seeped through the paper-thin walls of the other office cubicles that filled the Locarno Room. With cigarette in hand and confusion on his face, Lockhart siphoned through the various psychological warfare schemes that had been cooked up at Woburn since 1939. There were sibs about Hitler attending a performance of Richard Wagner's apocalyptic *Götterdämmerung* on the eve of the invasion of the Soviet Union, there were proposals for news bulletins on Britain's preparedness for a long war that Germany wasn't up to fighting, and scripts for a subversive radio programme called *Gustav Siegfried Eins (GS1)*, which had been broadcasting into the Reich since May 1941. This last one caught Lockhart's eye. The man behind *GS1* was a Berlin-born journalist named Sefton Delmer, who was known for thinking outside the box when it came to propaganda. An exemplar of this was a suggestion paper he submitted to Lockhart, calling for sibs about the spread of venereal diseases through the *Wehrmacht*'s ranks to be printed on cigarette wrappers and toilet rolls that were destined for German barracks. In addition to his fertile imagination, Delmer also had a reputation for being able to 'think not only like a German, but like a Nazi official'. This was owed to his first-hand experiences of travelling with Hitler as a foreign correspondent in the 1930s. Observing how the aspirant Führer manipulated his people, Delmer concluded that the best way to speak to the *Volk* was to command their respect while appealing to their baser instincts – what Hitler described to Delmer as his people's 'inner pigdog'.[3]

To this end, Delmer invented a character to host *GS1* who would be both a figure of authority and a titillating entertainer who could draw the German listener in with violent talk and sexual innuendo. The twist was that he wasn't spouting straight-up anti-Nazi propaganda. Instead, Delmer's radio character – Der Chef – was a traditionally conservative Prussian general who loved his country and wanted it to win the war. The problem was that Der Chef had no faith in the Nazis' ability to achieve this. Through expletive-filled rants, Der Chef bemoaned the sexual depravity of Hitler's inner circle and the rampant corruption of the SS officers, sowing seeds of doubt in listeners' minds over the character and capabilities of the Nazi leadership. Sophisticated in its conception and successful in its subversion, comebacks revealed that *GS1* had a wide listenership across the Reich. Indeed, a German prisoner interrogated in 1941 reported that Himmler had despatched his men to find Der Chef, in the mistaken belief that Delmer's creation was a real person transmitting bile from within Germany itself. This story probably influenced Delmer's decision to have the Gestapo dramatically burst into the radio station and gun down Der Chef on air in 1943, when it was decided that *GS1* had run its course.[4]

GS1 was one of the few bright spots Lockhart noted in the propaganda campaign he now led. Having completed his review of two years' worth of good, bad and bizarre ideas, he concluded that PWE and its antecedents had spent an inordinate amount of time producing propaganda that had no strategic purpose. The material that did have a purpose, moreover, was designed to achieve what Lockhart thought unachievable – convincing 'good Germans' to rise up and overthrow the Nazis. In the war's first months, this belief that the *Volk* were alive to the criminality of Hitler's regime and ready to act against it was popular in Whitehall. This was partly owed to Halifax's discussions with moderate conservatives in Germany, who muttered about their intentions to depose Hitler by force. Like the foreign secretary's concurrent peace negotiations with Göring's emissaries, this talk of a coup led by 'good Germans' ebbed after Churchill came to power, in part because there was still no clear policy from the War Cabinet about how to handle anti-Hitlerites. Some cabinet members believed they needed to be courted, while others thought the notion of 'good Germans' was oxymoronic. This indecision affected Britain's propaganda campaign. When Lockhart rose from his desk at the Locarno Room to attend strategy meetings in Eden's office with the likes of Bracken and Dalton, he beheld 'fantastically rude duels' between those who believed PWE should damn the *Volk* in its entirety and those who thought it should tailor messages of encouragement to Hitler's internal enemies. This propaganda conundrum was a microcosm of the wider problem in Allied policy, which was hazy on the issue of whether victory in the war constituted the destruction of Germany or simply the removal of the Nazis from power. Bereft of clear guidance from his government, Lockhart was left at relative liberty to figure out what message PWE should send to the German people.[5]

This lack of instruction and relative autonomy conjured memories of 1918 in Lockhart's mind. PWE's director-general, however, was not the adventurous British Agent of twenty years prior. The passing of time and the pain of experience had bred a caution in Lockhart that his younger self would have scoffed at. For this reason, despite the earnest hope of some of his subordinates, Lockhart rejected the idea that 'good Germans' were scattered across the Reich and that PWE's mission was to stir them to revolt. The failure of his previous foray into regime change was not the only reason Lockhart felt this way. His pre-war observations of Germany and the information conveyed to him by Moura, Bernstorff, Delmer and others who had visited the Reich convinced Lockhart that the bond between Führer and *Volk* was too strong to be broken by words and ideas. Even if the German people could be moulded into rebels by British propaganda, the outcome would be dire for all concerned. Lockhart believed that psychological warfare had to be 'the handmaid of official policy and of military strategy'. The War Cabinet's policy towards Germany may have had its ambiguities, but the strategic situation could not be clearer. Neither Britain nor its new allies, the Soviet Union and the USA – which had entered the war after the attack on Pearl Harbor in December 1941 – were in a position in 1942 to put boots on the fatherland's soil. If PWE advocated revolution in Germany without Allied military support, Lockhart feared he would be handing Goebbels ammunition to fire back at untrustworthy Britain, painting it as a nation that was happy to fight to the last drop of someone else's blood.

As his backing of the Czech Maffia shows, Lockhart was not averse to encouraging acts of violence and sabotage. In the case of the Protectorate, professional frustration and the impetus to improve Beneš' standing in Whitehall had driven Lockhart's support for this. When it came to backing resistance movements he was not personally invested in, however, Lockhart decided that PWE had to bide its time until a turn of Allied military fortunes made supporting rebellions more viable and propaganda highlighting Hitler's incompetence as a war leader more credible. This was the argument he brought before the chiefs of staff in May 1942, during a meeting at which he outlined his grand propaganda strategy and explained how, as the supposed 'fourth arm' of Britain's war effort, PWE could support the Royal Air Force, the Royal Navy and the army.

Knowing that the odour of Woburn's amateurishness wafted through the doors upon his entry, Lockhart opened his talk with a wry smile of self-deprecation, referring to PWE as the 'hot air' wing of Britain's armed services. The men in uniform sniggered good-heartedly and, with the ice now broken, Lockhart laid out his vision, stating that propaganda was no replacement for military success and that encouraging a premature uprising against Hitler was folly. PWE's mission was therefore clear – to 'undermine and to disrupt by overt and covert means the morale of the enemy' and 'to sustain and foster the morale and spirit of resistance in occupied territories' until such time as the Allies could offer a significant military riposte to the Reich. The miscreants of Woburn, Lockhart assured his audience of generals and admirals, were not on a fool's errand to find revolution.[6]

His speech was well received by those who had written PWE off as an assembly of dreamers. Realising that a key part of his job was to improve relations between PWE and the military chiefs, whose planes it needed to drop leaflets and whose embedded operatives it relied on to spread sibs, Lockhart came away satisfied from what was the first of many briefings he delivered to the chiefs of staff. Aside from boosting his organisation's reputation, Lockhart's displays of professionalism and even temperament were necessary to keep his detractors – and their long memories – at bay. A week before Lockhart addressed the chiefs of staff, Eden requested that the director-general be in the room for his upcoming meeting with the Soviet foreign minister, Vyacheslav Molotov. This request was flatly denied by the Russians, who had yet to rescind the death sentence they had passed on Lockhart two decades earlier.

This came on the heels of a leak from someone in Whitehall who named Lockhart as PWE's leader, despite both the organisation and his role in it supposedly being secret. To his fury, Lockhart's name was mentioned in the press and the House of Commons, prompting a Labour member to snipe that such 'a notorious anti-Soviet man' should not be running Britain's psychological warfare campaign at a time when London and Moscow were trying to get on the same page. The appointment of the Moscow conspirator turned Fleet Street muckraker reeked of the unserious amateurishness for which Woburn had become notorious.

Goebbels seized the moment to apply pressure on his opposite number. Nazi newspapers printed articles on Lockhart that focused on his anti-Bolshevik work in 1918, painting him as a master spy with a penchant for biting off more than he could chew. Goebbels ordered his fake news radio outlet – the New British Broadcasting Station – to run a story on Lockhart's supposed new book, *Inside Wartime Russia*, which detailed a recent trip he had made to the Soviet Union. The book wasn't real and the journey never happened. Still, Goebbels had all the details. In the autumn of 1941, Lockhart had travelled in secret to Archangel on board a Royal Navy cruiser and then entrained to Moscow. There he met with Stalin and his entourage, noting the gangster's-den atmosphere of the Kremlin and the odious personal habits of the Red Army's generals. The broadcast went on, speaking of how *Inside Wartime Russia* abounded in scandalous stories of Stalin's court, as well as revealing new details of the Allied plot to kill Lenin in 1918. Because of this, the British censor wouldn't allow the book to be published. Using fake quotes attributed to Lockhart, Goebbels reported his rival's protest that 'my book simply sets out my impressions of Soviet Russia at war and I can only assume that it has been banned because, in many cases, it shows up the Russians and their system in an unfavourable light ... perhaps if the British public knew the truth, they would be less inclined to welcome a Soviet victory in Europe'.[7]

Goebbels' attempts to discredit Lockhart with past deeds floundered, like those of his Whitehall critics, on the bulwark of professional reinvention. He still weathered the odd raised eyebrow as he bounced between meetings at the imposing MOI building and Whitehall. However, Lockhart's position as PWE director-general, his growing closeness to Eden and Bracken and the enduring support of his powerful benefactor, Beaverbrook, gave him a degree of immunity to the slights and assumptions that had long bedevilled his career. Even certain Russians now had a grudging respect for him. Molotov may have refused to have the

revolutionary wrecker sit in on his meeting with Eden, but the Kremlin's
ambassador in Britain, Ivan Maisky, wanted to keep Lockhart onside. The
pair met regularly to discuss tailoring propaganda to non-Western ears
and the development of a coordinated Anglo-Soviet psychological warfare strategy against Germany. In a moment of supreme irony, in 1943
Maisky invited the man who had tried to turn the Bolsheviks' elite troops
against them to a party at the Russian embassy to celebrate the Red Army's
twenty-fifth anniversary. Moreover, having read Lockhart's memoirs and
come to know his proclivities, Maisky presented him with a book on the
history of gypsy music as a gesture of friendship. Though some would
never get over the events of 1918, by 1942 most of the people with whom
Lockhart dealt had accepted that the scandalous British Agent was now a
Whitehall major-domo.[8]

To maintain this new status and be effective as director-general,
Lockhart accelerated his campaign to end PWE's era of amateurishness.
In addition to bringing the organisation under closer government control by getting approval for major propaganda offensives from Eden and
Bracken, in the first months of 1942 Lockhart had most of his propagandists
wrenched out of their bubble at Woburn and transferred to Bush House
in London, two floors down from the BBC. PWE's new headquarters was
a small and stuffy place from which to wage a war of words, being devoid
of adequate ventilation and crammed with two dozen desks tightly packed
together. Regardless, Lockhart descended into its maw. He moved out of
the Locarno Room and into Bush House, where he set up his office with
direct lines to various Whitehall officials, with whom he often conversed
long after Big Ben had struck its midnight chime. From then on, Lockhart
recalled his wartime world as being 'bounded by an ellipse of which the
four points of the compass were the East India Club in St James Square,
Whitehall, Bush House and the Ministry of Information'.

He shared this claustrophobic existence with his deputy, Brigadier
General Dallas Brooks. A Royal Marine who had initially been recruited
by Campbell Stuart in 1939 as a liaison between the propagandists and the

chiefs of staff, Brooks' role expanded under Lockhart's regime as he tried to recast PWE as a psychological warfare force multiplier to the regular armed services. This ambition required improvements in not just organisation but in the quality of propaganda, to which end Lockhart brought in a Cambridge University psychologist, J. T. MacCurdy, to advise PWE on how best to get inside German heads. Working on the premise that the German fighting man drew confidence from the Reich's advanced weapons systems, MacCurdy devised a sib about a sabotaged U-boat factory, with the aim of making German submariners fearful of loading torpedo tubes lest the ordnance explode in their hands.[9]

Setting up new offices and trying out fresh ideas was relatively easy. When it came to managing the people who had given PWE its infamy, however, Lockhart struggled, for beneath the pragmatic director-general, the free-wheeling rogue of old still lingered. His handling of the German-born *Manchester Guardian* journalist Frederick Augustus Voigt was a case in point. Voigt rejected the idea of encouraging a mass revolution in Germany but felt strongly that anti-Nazi allies could be found in the Reich's churches and in the manor houses of the Prussian gentry. A coup against the regime was possible, Voigt maintained, albeit 'not by the German scum but by the German elite', to whom PWE should tailor its propaganda messages. Voigt fancied himself as Woburn's best informed on all matters pertaining to the Reich. To Lockhart's mind, he was 'one of those complex megalomaniacs who dislike what they love' and was prone to boasting of 'the immense strength of the Germans – a compliment to his own blood', while simultaneously being 'angry with them for not behaving as he would like them to behave'. Voigt's belief that good Christian Germans could save his ancestral homeland was tolerated in the Woburn days but was incompatible with Lockhart's new vision for PWE. And yet, the director-general couldn't bring himself to move Voigt on. The latter's assertiveness and energy were too impressive and his willingness to fight for what he believed in doubtless struck a chord with the romantic in Lockhart. In the end, Voigt made the decision for his boss by quitting PWE in December 1941 with 'hurt feelings and considerable bitterness' towards Lockhart and the direction in which he was taking Britain's propaganda campaign.[10]

The man who took Voigt's chair behind PWE's German desk was the political antithesis of his predecessor, yet he gave Lockhart larger and more prolonged headaches. An Oxford professor and future minister in Harold Wilson's Labour government, Richard Crossman believed that 'good Germans' abounded in the Reich, particularly in its factories and on its farms. To speak to these working-class resisters, Crossman contacted London's émigré community of communist Germans and established a radio station called *Sender der Europäischen Revolution*, through which they could broadcast propaganda to their radical brothers and sisters in the Reich. The problem with this plan was that after years of Nazi persecution Germany's left-wing resistance movement was deeply fractured by the time the war began, with thousands of communist party members in concentration camps and only a smattering of cells remaining in the cities. Most of these cells, moreover, worked in an uncoordinated manner and in constant fear of violent suppression from the Gestapo.

For this reason, as a Woburn contemporary bluntly put it, Crossman's scheme to incite the Reich's communists was 'glorious twaddle' that had little to no impact on resistance operations in Germany. Moreover, given that *Europäischen Revolution* was broadcast from a house in the country where the émigrés dossed on the floor and Crossman ruled as a quasi-bohemian guru, the project smacked of the unprofessional indulgence that Lockhart was trying to eradicate. The problem was that Crossman – described by a colleague as 'often exasperating, sometimes dangerous but never boring' – reminded Lockhart too much of his younger self. Unwilling to cut Crossman loose, the director-general spent much time and energy trying to disabuse him of the idea of searching for 'good Germans' while deploying all his charm and influence to save the troublesome propagandist's job. Lockhart's greatest exertion to this end came in August 1942, when Crossman made an unauthorised broadcast to Germany warning that the Royal Air Force would pulverise its cities via round-the-clock bombing. Churchill demanded that he be fired but Lockhart went to bat for Crossman, working through Eden to change the prime minister's mind.[11]

Unwilling to remove bothersome 'good German' seekers from PWE, Lockhart created a greater workload for himself, which involved having to constantly scrutinise their schemes. Some of these schemes, like the 'Peasants' Revolt' campaign, had been running since 1940 to little or no effect. This had involved the BBC broadcasting a dawn programme for the ears of Germany's early-rising farmers, who were encouraged to question the Nazis' requisitioning policies and corrupt price-fixing measures. By building animus towards the regime, the show aimed to encourage pithy acts of rural defiance like spoiling grain consignments and putting potatoes in the exhaust pipes of army trucks. Comebacks, however, suggested that few farmers took the broadcast seriously and those who followed the BBC's suggestions did so in a manner that was ill-coordinated and ineffective. Still, the 'Peasants' Revolt' broadcasts had continued for nearly two years alongside the complementary 'Go Slow' campaign. This urged factory workers in the Ruhr, France and Belgium to damage the Reich's war machine by misplacing tools, showing up late for work, pocketing small but crucial tank parts from production lines and, if so inclined, smashing railway signals and loosening the wheels of *Wehrmacht* trucks.[12]

'Go Slow' and 'Peasants' Revolt' required little effort for PWE to run and, owing to their passive listenership, were middling in their effect. As such, Lockhart didn't pay them much mind. The 'V' campaign, however, was of an order of magnitude that required greater consideration from the director-general. It began on 14 January 1941 when Victor de Laveleye, a Belgian politician who had escaped to Britain after the Germans overran his country, broadcast a plea via the BBC for the letter 'V' – standing for *victoire* in French, or *vrijheid* (freedom) in Flemish – to be chalked on the walls of public spaces in Brussels. The proposal seemed trivial, yet in the days after de Laveleye's broadcast hundreds of 'V's appeared not just in the Belgian capital but also on the streets of Prague and Paris. Goebbels was spooked enough to launch a propaganda counter-operation, in which

German soldiers were told to put up gothic styled 'V's in occupied cities. This attempt to claim German ownership of the Allied campaign fizzled out quickly as more 'V's appeared on the doors of *Wehrmacht* barracks and Gestapo police stations. Even Churchill got in on the act, posing for the infamous photo in which he flashed a 'V' with his fingers.

Lockhart liked the 'V' campaign. It struck him as more subtle and wide-ranging in its appeal than the crudely propagandistic broadcasts targeting farmers and factory workers. The way it had evolved, however, troubled him. In the spring of 1941, the former *Telegraph* journalist turned BBC propagandist Douglas Ritchie invented a radio character named Colonel Britton to personify and expand the 'V' campaign. Crowing in a John Bull-like bluster, Ritchie barked orders to his European listeners to tap out the letter 'V' in Morse code on café tables in the presence of German soldiers, so as to 'unnerve the bastards and let them know that they are few and we are many'. According to comebacks from British assets and the interrogation of German prisoners, this put *Wehrmacht* garrisons on edge by creating the impression that a mass organised resistance was lurking in the shadows of the cities they occupied. Ritchie wanted to make a reality of this illusion. Linking 'V' to the 'Go Slow' campaign, Colonel Britton urged his more than one million listeners to engage in acts of sabotage. 'Slow down the wheels of production!' he demanded. 'Blunt the tools! Leave a screw loose! Form cells of your own!' More provocatively, the colonel also ordered listeners to take the names of German soldiers and draw up lists of collaborators in preparation for the day 'when the British government gives the word' to strike back and 'cause riots and demonstrations in every city in Europe'. Concerned by this escalation from encouraging passive resistance to ordering blatant acts of rebellion, in May 1942 Lockhart told Ritchie to silence Colonel Britton and wrap up the 'V' campaign.[13]

Charles Cruickshank, one of the earlier chroniclers of PWE's history, was critical of Lockhart for this decision. He argued that the director-general's scuttling of the 'V' campaign was symptomatic of his lack of creativity and dynamism. Like some of Lockhart's contemporaries and many historians since, Cruickshank fell into the easy habit of caricaturing him as a has-been who was out of his depth running PWE and, when faced with the imperative to take the 'V' campaign to a more confrontational level, chose caution over courage.

In truth, Lockhart was bringing measured judgement to a foolish plan. While he recognised the 'V' campaign's 'potential to prime the occupied territories for action against the Germans when the time of liberation comes', Lockhart felt that Ritchie's efforts had peaked too early. It was the spring of 1942. Britain and America were reeling from Tokyo's Far East *Blitzkrieg* in which Singapore, Hong Kong and the Philippines had fallen in quick succession. Having held the line against the *Wehrmacht* at Moscow over the winter, the Red Army was licking its wounds and was in no shape to launch a meaningful counterstrike against Germany. The Americans had plans to this end, however, not via an invasion of mainland Europe but of North Africa, where an operation was pencilled in for some point at the end of the year. The Allies' strategic situation in the spring of 1942 didn't align with Lockhart's policy of PWE encouraging insurrection only when significant military force was in play to back it up – a policy that was likely informed by his bitter memories of Savinkov's unsupported and ultimately futile uprising of July 1918. Aside from the prospect of operational failure, the risk of propaganda blowback was also high. As Lockhart explained to Ritchie, if thousands of brave Belgians, French, Poles and Czechs died heeding the words of 'Britons who are safely ensconced beyond the Channel' without any intention of landing troops on the continent, 'Goebbels will then have all he needs to turn the people of Europe against us forever'.[14]

Lockhart also appreciated – in a way few of his propagandists did – that Britain was fighting Germany as part of a coalition whose wishes needed to be considered. During a night out at the Carlton Club in January 1942, Lockhart ran the idea of Colonel Britton's uprising past intelligence officers, Foreign Office officials and the Allied diplomats with whom he was dining. The reaction was one of trepidation and disquiet. PWE's capacity to engineer such an operation and the ability of SOE to supply would-be insurgents with grenades and Sten guns were doubted. Even if everything went to plan, Lockhart's confidants thought that the gains would be negligible. 'There would be panic among the Germans at first,' Maisky reasoned, 'but, before long they would strike back and suppress them all.' The Dutch ambassador impressed on Lockhart the point he had already realised about Britons 'sitting at home and not doing anything active in the way of fighting', while egging on Europe's oppressed to risk their lives in the ill-timed shedding of German blood. To continue a campaign that was contrary to the wishes of Britain's allies was clearly bad politics that Lockhart wanted no part of.[15]

There was another possible reason why the man who had full-throatedly supported the Czech Maffia in 1940 was now baulking at the idea of unleashing Colonel Britton's 'V' army. As he mused on what to do about Ritchie's campaign, Lockhart was briefed on Operation Anthropoid – the long-awaited Czech effort to incite resistance in the Protectorate by assassinating its ruler, SS Obergruppenführer Reinhard Heydrich. Armed with this foreknowledge, it is likely that Lockhart decided to see how Anthropoid played out before taking PWE down a similar insurrectionary road. If this was part of Lockhart's reasoning, then he would have felt justified in killing off Colonel Britton. On 27 May 1942, two SOE-trained Czechs threw a grenade at Heydrich's car as it negotiated a sharp bend on the road to his headquarters outside Prague. The explosion sent shards of chair leather and scrap metal into Heydrich's body, wounding him such that he passed out, albeit not before scattering his attackers with errant shots from his Luger. Days later, the Nazis' blonde-haired *wunderkind* perished in the fevered grip of sepsis.

Anthropoid seemed successful, but its aftermath played out in a manner that confirmed Lockhart's reservations over the limits of unbacked resistance to German rule. Far from engendering an uprising, Heydrich's death brought a hammer down on the Czechs. Hundreds of civilians were rounded up and brutally interrogated or simply shot in a spasm of revenge. Distraught at his right-hand man's death, Himmler unleashed the full force of his Gestapo, whose agents murdered hundreds of people in the village of Lidice and deported hundreds more to concentration camps. The nearby village of Ležáky – at which components of an SOE radio were found – was razed to the ground.[16]

The disastrous wake of Anthropoid did much to quiet revolution-hungry voices in PWE, giving Lockhart the space to pursue his vision of aligning propaganda with regular military operations. It helped that, as he commiserated with Beneš over the fate of Lidice and Ležáky, Lockhart was informed by Eden that the Americans wanted PWE to launch a propaganda offensive in support of Operation Torch. This was the plan to land troops in North Africa with the aim of retaking the region from the Vichy French – the Nazi-aligned puppet government that had been established after France's defeat in 1940. Lockhart was excited. A welcome turn from talk of civilian-led uprisings, Torch would be 'the first genuinely positive military action to be taken by the Allies' in two years and would proffer the opportunity he had been waiting for to prove PWE's worth to its detractors. Instead of chasing an implausible revolution, PWE would enhance the fear the enemy felt when American warships appeared on the horizon by spreading rumours ahead of the landings of insubordination among the ranks of the Vichy defenders. This 'war of nerves' in North Africa would be complemented by PWE broadcasting narratives of hope to Europe's oppressed and warnings to its oppressors that the landings were the first act of the Reich's denouement. As Lockhart sorted through the torrent of Torch-supporting schemes cooked up by his propagandists, he received a phone call that injected further energy into the already feverish atmosphere at Bush House. Speaking from a secret site outside Woburn, the caller informed him that after months of wrangling and experimentation a new weapon of psychological warfare – one that would cement Lockhart's efforts to turn PWE into a genuine 'fourth arm' of Britain's fighting services – was finally ready for deployment.[17]

CHAPTER 15

WORDY WARFARE

'A deception, a Big Lie – was a military operation.
Political warfare was the machine used to project it to the enemy'.

– John Baker White

The wheels of the Rolls-Royce crunched over the gravel as it passed between the barbed-wire-topped gates. The barrier lowered in the car's wake and the armed guards settled the Alsatians at their feet. They then resumed their positions, peering into the treeline that separated the nearby village of Milton Bryan from the top-secret facility behind them. Peering through the rear window of his chauffeur-driven car at this scene, Lockhart allowed himself a satisfied smile. Much had changed since the first ramshackle days of the war at nearby Woburn.

The car stopped outside a brutally plain redbrick building, the roof of which was scattered with dozens of transmission masts and aerials of various shapes and sizes. At the building's front door stood a short, rotund man with a receding hairline and a welcoming smile. Sefton Delmer was proud of the clandestine fiefdom he was building on Milton Bryan's outskirts and was eager to show it off to PWE's director-general. The two men shook hands and exchanged pleasantries as Delmer ushered Lockhart over the threshold into a warren of studios in various stages of construction, which would soon be filled with German, French and Italian speakers broadcasting messages of despair, deception and vengeance into Europe via fake radio stations – known in PWE parlance as Research Units (RUs).

By blending intelligence-informed morsels of truth ('white' propaganda) with fake news and subversive suggestions ('black' propaganda) the resulting 'grey' material would, Delmer believed, undermine German morale by conveying a message that had replaced PWE's campaign to incite revolution – with Britain, the USA and the Soviet Union arrayed against it, Germany could not possibly win the war.[1]

Delmer had Lockhart's enthusiastic backing for his plan. He may have become a Whitehall boss beholden to policy memoranda and tasked with keeping PWE professional, but Lockhart still enjoyed the clever subversions and mischievous gallows humour that informed Delmer's work. This was why, when Delmer's *GS1* programme was criticised by the British ambassador in Moscow, Sir Stafford Cripps, for being vulgar and distasteful, Lockhart had protected him. Cripps' complaints centred on a *GS1* broadcast in which Der Chef graphically described an orgy involving a German admiral and the wives of U-boat submariners. Horrified by the pornographic details of Delmer's script, Cripps complained that PWE was producing morally reprehensible content that didn't align with British values. Privately, Lockhart wrote Cripps off as a 'religious maniac'. In his official capacity, however, PWE's leader trod carefully, mindful of the rumours that Cripps might replace Churchill at Number 10. He agreed with Cripps that Delmer had crossed the line into the obscene while defusing the episode with Eden, to whom he wrote half-jokingly that 'there is no European man so lecherous or so coarse in his lechery as the German', and on this basis Delmer's propaganda was on point. Delmer got a tepid wrap on the knuckles and Lockhart did little to halt Der Chef's onward march.[2]

Instead, Lockhart doubled down on his support for PWE's star propagandist. This included accepting with 'an alacrity amounting to enthusiasm' Delmer's proposal to have new studios and outbuildings for intelligence analysis built at Milton Bryan, so that it could become the base for a top-secret campaign of 'total radio warfare' against the Reich. This campaign would involve the dissemination of 'grey' material via the RUs and the hijacking of German radio wavelengths to broadcast 'black' propaganda that would sound to listeners as if it was official news from the Nazi regime. Under this veil of subterfuge, Delmer envisioned PWE declaring to the *Volk* that the war against the Soviets had ended in German triumph and that Stalin had been captured. When the truth came out that the *Wehrmacht* was still clawing and scraping with the Red Army, the German people would question future reportage from Berlin and have the hope of the war's cessation wrenched from their hands, sapping their morale. Lockhart relished the thought of bloodying Goebbels' nose and appreciated that Delmer's plan would stir discontent among the *Volk* without openly calling for them to take up arms against Hitler. The only problem he saw was that Milton Bryan's transmitters were not powerful enough to override German broadcasts in order to inject the 'black' material. Delmer had to wait until PWE had 'more radio guns' to fire at the enemy.[3]

The arrival of this new, more powerful broadcast ordnance was the reason why Lockhart took time out from preparing for Operation Torch to inspect Milton Bryan and consult with Delmer on the weapon that would give life to the RUs it housed. This weapon was a massive 600-kilowatt radio transmitter – known as the Aspidistra – the components of which had been purchased in the USA and shipped to Britain at great expense. To Lockhart and Delmer, any financial outlay was worth it. Aspidistra was strong enough to override the frequencies used by enemy radio, and its ability to switch frequencies in a split second gave PWE the capacity to seamlessly put words into Goebbels' mouth. Aspidistra could also boost PWE's regular radio signals. This meant that during the invasion of North Africa, PWE would have an enhanced capability to control how the story of the landings would be told to the listening public from Tangiers to Trondheim. As Lockhart reported to Churchill when the latter asked after this new weapon, Aspidistra could 'create confusion in enemy broadcasts in Western Europe' and 'overcome jamming in North and Western France'. Fascinated by gadgets and excited by innovation, Churchill impatiently asked Lockhart 'when will it work?'.

The answer to that question was the final week of October 1942 – a matter of days before Torch, which was scheduled for 8 November. This led to a rush within PWE to make Aspidistra part of its plans for the landings, which were crystallising after weeks of late nights and heated arguments at Bush House. The invasion was primarily an American operation. For propaganda purposes it was felt that this should be emphasised, as intelligence from North Africa informed PWE that the Vichy French garrisons would be more likely to surrender to the Americans than to their former British allies, whom they resented for 'deserting' France in 1940. This emphasis drew Lockhart into planning meetings with the American equivalent to PWE, the Office of War Information (OWI) and its SOE equivalent, the Office of Strategic Services (OSS). Small wonder that when Lockhart and Brooks were invited to brief the supreme commander of the Allied expeditionary force, General Dwight D. Eisenhower, the latter complained about the glut of acronyms involved in the operation. This grumble aside, Ike struck Lockhart as a man who grasped the essence of psychological warfare and welcomed the help PWE could give his troops. Caught up discussing propaganda for Torch over lunch one day, Eisenhower even suggested to Lockhart that PWE should produce leaflets featuring the Marquis de Lafayette, the French officer who had played a pivotal role in supporting George Washington's Continental Army during the American Revolutionary War. While this suggestion didn't make the cut – it was felt that French colonial subjects would be unfamiliar with Lafayette – the history of America and France's shared love of liberty and freedom was a recurring theme of the 25 million leaflets that PWE dropped over North Africa and France during the Allied invasion.[4]

Leaflet drops were not the only element of PWE's operations for Torch, the success of which led to Lockhart receiving an official thanks from Eden and a personal note from Bracken, who declared that PWE had 'done a better job than any other governmental publicity organisation in the world'. Hyperbole aside, PWE's participation in this first great Allied offensive of the war felt like a moment of validation for Lockhart, particularly when

Eisenhower asked him to select a team of propagandists to land with the troops. The director-general's ambition to marry psychological warfare with regular military operations was finally fulfilled. True, the field propagandist's deployment was far from smooth. As one of them recalled, 'with our faces duly anointed with soot and Vaseline, wearing American helmets, slung megaphones (the symbol of our trade) and combat boots', they were placed on a flotilla of four small boats that were meant to land off the Algerian coast. In the confusion of the landings, however, the flotilla broke apart, leading to only one of the boats reaching its target beach at the right time. Things quickly improved for those who landed. One of PWE's agents even received a commendation for capturing a German diplomat in Algiers at gunpoint.

The field propagandists' more regular duties involved securing radio transmission equipment, explaining the purpose of the invasion to the local population and furnishing American soldiers with guides on how to win hearts and minds by respecting Islamic beliefs and abstaining from causing trouble. For 'a brawl in a café or a street incident would give the Nazis just the ammunition' needed to undermine PWE's narrative that the Americans were liberating North Africa from oppression. Aspidistra was also used during the landings to boost the BBC's signal so that news of the Allies' success and speeches from Eisenhower and de Gaulle could be heard far and wide. This led to an incident in which the British Admiralty – which wasn't aware of the Aspidistra secret – assumed that the news it was broadcasting emanated from Rabat in Morocco, suggesting that the city had been captured by the Allies even though it was still under Vichy control. This was one of the few missteps in PWE's campaign to support Torch, but it was one Lockhart noted. For if Aspidistra could fool the British, then it could certainly fool their enemies.[5]

Delmer thought likewise. With works now completed at Milton Bryan, in the first months of 1943 he launched his 'total warfare' campaign by using Aspidistra to broadcast the *Atlantiksender* and the *Soldatensender Calais* programmes into occupied Europe. Crafted for the ears of German

troops, these RUs exemplified Delmer's attention to detail and inher-
ent grasp of human psychology. Each show opened with popular music
of the sort young men of the 1940s would listen to, sourced from either
records shipped from Europe or composed in the studio by remnants of a
German band that had been captured in North Africa while on a tour to
entertain the *Wehrmacht*. Once the introductory music had grabbed the
listener, Delmer's team of disc jockeys – an assortment of émigrés from
the Reich and German prisoners of war who had turned against their
Führer – regaled listeners with birthday wishes for individual soldiers,
reports of bombings on German cities and frontline updates that were
either true enough to be disparaging or slanted such as to embed doubt
about the Reich's prospects for victory. The reports were very convincing,
as Delmer used intelligence gathered from either German news broadcasts
or prisoners of war to get soldiers' names and precise information on the
haunts they favoured in their home cities. Blending subtle falsehoods into
factual narratives, collectively *Atlantiksender* and *Soldatensender Calais* was,
according to an OWI visitor to Milton Bryan, 'the best piece of propaganda
I have ever listened to'. The Aspidistra-powered operation also represented
an important step forward in Lockhart's mission to make PWE a serious
part of Britain's war effort. As Delmer later reflected, 'for the first time in
the department's history, Bruce Lockhart was able to tell his ministers that
a fighting service had proposed an operational task'.[6]

While Delmer ushered in this new phase of PWE's radio warfare campaign, Lockhart was informed that he was to be knighted in the 1943 New
Year Honours List. He assumed this was a reward for reforming PWE but
was later told by Churchill that the honour wasn't bestowed solely for his
wartime work, but in long-overdue recognition of his labours as Britain's
Agent. Time and circumstance had officially erased the blot of 1918 from
his record. This crowning moment of professional rehabilitation came on
2 February 1943 when Lockhart knelt before King George in Westminster
Hall and received a 'tap on each shoulder with a small dirk', after which
he was shuffled 'down the runway to a room where flunkeys' removed the

collar and star pin placed upon him by his sovereign. Hands were shaken, congratulations muttered and he was then shown the door while a brass band played a celebratory tune. 'From moment of advance to end,' he wrote briskly in his diary, the 'whole ceremony takes about one minute'.[7]

Sir Robert Bruce Lockhart should have been elated as 1943 commenced but, typically, this moment of professional triumph was marred by personal problems. In the process of making PWE his own, Lockhart fell out with Leeper, who stubbornly insisted on keeping a cadre of propagandists at Woburn under his command. The tension between the two was such that Leeper declared he could no longer watch his creation 'slipping from me as the work of PWE becomes more and more centred on London' and so quit Woburn to return to the Foreign Office. He served out the rest of the war as ambassador to the Greek government-in-exile in Cairo. It was a temporary spat – the two were back corresponding and dining together by the end of the year – but the episode left Lockhart with mixed feelings. He recognised the vital role Leeper had played in supporting his mission to Russia and remembered how, years later, he had offered him a path to redeeming its failure by working for Van's network and then for PID. Still, Lockhart couldn't get over his old friend's reluctance to concede that PWE was growing beyond its teething days at Woburn. Torn as always by emotion and pragmatism, Lockhart felt both satisfaction at having steered PWE into the realms of credibility and guilt that this had been achieved at Leeper's expense.[8]

As he entered this contretemps with Leeper, Lockhart's mood was further soured by the fact that decades of unhealthy living and the stress of running an expanding war department were catching up to him. In the autumn of 1942, Lockhart first noted in his diary that he 'felt very ill and "nervy" after a week of hard work by day and of dissipation by night'. This sick feeling of exhaustion was followed by him developing eczema on his hands and face and swelling in his legs, which left him in pain so great that he struggled to walk. He exacerbated this condition by using the bottle to manage the pain. '[My] drink record for the past three months,'

Lockhart noted in the weeks after Torch, 'is shameful, both for the amount of alcohol and excess of expenditure.' Run down and increasingly debilitated, Lockhart tried to restore his health by taking a few weeks' leave to his father's house outside Sandhurst in January 1943 and, when that didn't work, by checking himself into a hospital in Edinburgh that specialised in skin conditions. However, as he wrote to Beaverbrook from his sickbed, 'months of neglect cannot be repaired in a fortnight'. Lockhart's two-week convalescence stretched into May, during which he abandoned the hospital in frustration and retreated to Tomintoul in the hope that clean Highland air and the gentility of village life would alleviate his ills.

Back in London, PWE was preparing to replicate the success of its Torch operation by offering support for Operation Husky, the plan to land Allied troops in Sicily. Having placed control of Husky preparations into Brooks' hands, Lockhart was meant to spend the weeks leading up to the invasion rereading *War and Peace* and staring blankly out of his hospital window at the bitter Scottish rain. He trusted Brooks but, having poured so much of himself into PWE, Lockhart struggled to let go. Bedbound, he still took phone calls at all hours from Bush House and even held meetings with PWE staff who travelled up to Tomintoul to brief their boss in person. Lockhart's inability to unplug himself from work – and, indeed, every facet of the war, which he kept apprised of by always having a radio with him – did little to alleviate the stress that the doctors concluded was fuelling his condition. Such was Lockhart's resolve to return to PWE that he accepted a partial receding of the skin inflammation as cause to take the train down to London, arriving on the evening of 29 June. He was back at his desk the next morning, ready to review Brooks' plans for Husky.[9]

Most of it was cut and dried. PWE would broadcast official announcements of the landings and develop contingencies for how to narrate the invasion to radio listeners across Europe if the progress of the Allied invasion stalled. One idea, however, caught Lockhart's unfavourable attention: a suggestion from the chiefs of staff for the BBC to broadcast a fake news item via Aspidistra after the invasion, which would report that Mussolini had requested an armistice. The idea of sapping Italian resolve to resist via deception was tempting but Lockhart felt that the credibility of Delmer's RUs and other PWE and BBC programming would be undermined in the long term once the truth of the lie was uncovered. On this basis, he scotched the plan. He did, however, approve of Delmer's proposal to use Aspidistra to hijack enemy radio. This meant that when the Germans occupied Italy in September 1943 with the aim of repulsing the Allies, Delmer inserted fake news stories cooked up at Milton Bryan into the broadcasts of National Fascist Radio. These stories suggested that Italian women were being press-ganged into labour battalions by the Nazis and that Hitler had ordered SS commandos to raid the Vatican and kidnap the pope. Like many of PWE's myths, the pope story implanted a scenario into the Second World War's history that some historians later believed was true.[10]

By the time Delmer unleashed these falsehoods Lockhart had relapsed into illness and returned to Edinburgh, the rash on his skin having become so intense that his head had to be shaved and his body covered in silver nitrate-soaked bandages. Bracken advised him to not repeat the same mistake and to wait until he was fully recovered before returning to PWE. A concerned Beaverbrook fired off missives demanding updates on Lockhart's condition and, when he learned he was ensconced in the Edinburgh Royal Infirmary rather than in a private clinic, sent a cheque for £1,000 to cover his former right-hand's medical expenses. Lockhart appreciated the gesture but decided to stay at the infirmary, where his treatment continued until he was finally given something approximating a clean bill of health in February 1944. His discharge came with doctor's orders to stick to regular working hours and avoid unnecessary stress.

Whatever thoughts Lockhart had of following this utopian advice amid the madness of war were dashed when he met his chauffeur at King's Cross Station. His face dour and his voice gloom-stricken, the driver apologetically reported that he would have to take Lockhart to the Savoy, as his rooms at the St James's had been destroyed in an air raid the night before.

Lockhart was meant to have taken the train a day earlier. Had he done so, he would likely have been in bed when the bombs fell.[11]

Despite this rough start to a new, supposedly less stressful existence, Lockhart tried to follow his doctor's orders. He talked with Eden and Bracken about reducing his hours and getting a second deputy in addition to Brooks to help run PWE, the staff of which now numbered in the thousands, comprising propagandists, musicians, radio engineers, field operatives and typists. To periodically escape this sprawling fiefdom, Lockhart rented a cottage in the quiet village of Radlett in Hertfordshire to relax away from London, something that Beaverbrook's personal doctor – who was summoned at the press baron's insistence to examine the patient – concluded was the only means by which he could avoid another relapse. He also tried to cut down on his drinking. When Moura pressed Lockhart for a dinner date upon his return to London, he explained that he had to get lots of rest and keep 'regular hours and meals' which, given that his old flame was in the habit of consuming multiple cocktails, pints of beer and dozens of vodka shots every time she visited a restaurant, 'rules out dinner'.[12]

These attempts at normality were always going to be thwarted by the enormous task that PWE and every other Whitehall department faced in the first months of 1944 – preparing for Operation Overlord. The suggestions floated at Bush House for supporting the D-Day landings aligned with Lockhart's long-stated policy that rebellion in Germany should only be encouraged once the military situation proved favourable. Now, with 150,000 Allied troops preparing to storm Normandy's beaches, the time had come for PWE's insurrection-hungry imaginations to run wild. A plan code-named 'Cuckoo' typified this moment of giddy catharsis. As D-Day unfolded, a Hitler impersonator at Milton Bryan would take to the airwaves, using a German channel hijacked by Aspidistra to deliver a series of unintelligible rants that would convince the Nazi leadership and the *Volk* that their Führer had finally lost the plot. This would precipitate either a palace coup or an uprising from below that would bring the war to a swift conclusion. Not unlike SOE's various schemes for assassinating Hitler, this suggestion floundered on the problem that the Führer's downfall might put someone more competent in his chair. Derided as 'ingeniously amateurish' and 'perhaps, well named' by PWE's own planners, 'Cuckoo' never got beyond the drawing board.[13]

More consideration was given to Operation Braddock, a scheme supported by the ever-energetic Crossman to drop hundreds of thousands of easy-to-operate incendiary weapons – the eponymous 'Braddocks' – across Europe, with leaflets urging those under Nazi rule to use the devices to burn down barracks and bases. Particular attention was paid in this plan to the 7 million forced labourers who were scattered across the Reich. If the Braddocks could be dropped in or near their camps, the Allies could create a massive army of restive souls deep within enemy territory. The fear of the Braddocks would be enhanced by Aspidistra, which would be used to broadcast false reports of Braddock attacks in districts where none had been dropped. The outcome would be 'administrative confusion and panic' among the German authorities and a breakdown of order across the Reich. As the initial idea had come from the mind of Churchill's lauded chief scientific advisor, Professor Frederick Lindemann, the prime minister supported Operation Braddock. So too did the chiefs of staff, who sketched out the plan with input from Crossman and other PWE revolution-seekers. Eisenhower was also a fan and so authorised a drop of 200,000 Braddocks in the weeks after D-Day.

Lockhart acknowledged that the plan had benefits and that, as it had the approval of military planners concerned with the invasion of France, it should go ahead. However, he voiced concerns about Braddock's central premise of targeting the labour camps and felt both angered and sickened when Crossman 'admitted glibly that many foreign workers might be killed'. He was also worried about the image Braddock would give off – how would the Allies' recourse to 'terroristic' tactics look to those in Europe awaiting liberation? Bracken was even more opposed. He bristled at the chiefs of staff's assumption that they could commandeer Aspidistra

– which, as minister of information, he technically controlled – and argued that the operation would reveal PWE's secret radio weapon to the Germans. This was problematic, as Bracken felt that German resistance to the Allied invasion might prove stiffer than assumed, necessitating a grander psychological warfare operation down the line in which the Aspidistra secret would be needed to stir a more comprehensive anti-Nazi uprising. Bracken saw Braddock as 'a small trial operation' that would gratuitously 'inform Germany that we have a means of penetrating their wave-lengths'. Because of these objections, only a handful of Braddock drops were made between August 1944 and the war's final days, none of which achieved the operation's aim of unleashing a pall of panic among the Nazis or insurrections in their labour camps.[14]

In the end, PWE's plans for Overlord comprised a series of targeted operations that reflected how the department had grown from the days of dreaming up pointless sibs to integrating psychological warfare into regular military operations. As had happened in North Africa, PWE agents advanced with the troops, disseminating explanatory leaflets and earmarking captured German soldiers who showed a willingness to broadcast anti-Nazi propaganda. At Ike's request, leaflets and broadcasts encouraged acts of railway sabotage to hinder the German response to the landings. Delmer's *Atlantiksender* and *Soldatensender Calais* were also put to work spreading fake stories about German generals sacrificing entire divisions on the French coast to cover their retreat, and the unfathomable numbers of Allied saboteurs that had infiltrated behind the lines. Additional broadcasts via Aspidistra disseminated false orders from Reich authorities for workers to stay put rather than evacuate themselves to munitions factories away from the Allied advance. Comebacks on this initiative indicated that it had deprived Germany of essential workers at a critical time and created confusion on the roads by countermanding the real orders from Berlin for mass evacuations. Amid these tried-and-true schemes to disrupt Germany's war machine, there was still room for unsavoury innovation. Intelligence gleaned from the chief medical officer of the *Wehrmacht*'s Fourteenth

Army confirmed that PWE's air-dropped 'malingerer' booklets – which contained instructions on how to mutilate oneself with a knife to avoid active duty – were leading to scores of Hitler's troops following PWE's gruesome advice.[15]

Lockhart's key task for D-Day seemed simple in theory but in practice galling. Adhering to PWE's core mission to raise morale in the occupied territories, he had organised for de Gaulle to broadcast a message of liberation and hope to the people of France in the minutes after Allied boots hit Normandy's shores. Too nervous to sleep yet too exhausted to rest, Lockhart stayed up the night before D-Day with his staff at Bush House. After hours spent smoking cigarettes and sharing worries over how the invasion would play out, Lockhart and his people welcomed the dawn by marvelling at the sight and sound of Allied war planes cutting a swathe through London's skies. The cathartic excitement this stirred in Lockhart was swiftly consumed by stress once de Gaulle arrived. Having refused a request that PWE vet his script for anything not in line with key propaganda themes, the notoriously prickly leader of the Free French next caused a scene by acting affronted at the presence of American generals at Bush House. De Gaulle believed that D-Day was France's moment above all others and that he alone should be its herald. Nursing the general through an awkward round of limp handshakes with his American allies, Lockhart managed to calm de Gaulle down and get him to his microphone in time to broadcast. It was a day of great tension but as news that the Normandy beachheads had been secured came through, Lockhart's visage changed from one of hardened fret to softening glee. As night fell over London, Lockhart fell back exhaustedly into his desk chair, grinning at the sight of hands being shaken and embraces being shared by the men and women of Bush House. They, like him, were revelling in the realisation that the war was entering its final phase.[16]

Behind the director-general's smile, however, there lay festering pain. The eczema had not gone away. Indeed, in the weeks leading up to the invasion fresh patches of itching red skin had developed on Lockhart's neck and cheeks. The stress of preparing for D-Day was not the only reason for this latest flare-up. During his various bouts of convalescence, Lockhart had pondered the state of his life and drawn conclusions that depressed him greatly. His elevated status in Whitehall was all well and good, but working for PWE had become exhausting without being interesting. Lockhart despaired at the thought that 'I have not written a word for over five years' and, consumed with developing propaganda policy and managing inter-departmental quarrels, had lost his 'sense of the natural (and proper) curiosity in arts, letters, music, life itself'. Moreover, once the spell of D-Day's success wore off, Lockhart struggled to see these lights of his life returning soon to pierce the war's darkness. On 13 June 1944, Hitler launched his V-weapon campaign, in which long-distance rockets and flying bombs descended from Britain's skies with indiscriminate menace onto the cities and countryside below. Not only was Bush House damaged in the attacks but while Lockhart was trying to enjoy a break from the capital at Eden's country home in West Sussex a V-1 was shot down nearby, the detonation of which blew out his bedroom window just as he was turning in for the evening. Between this renewal of the Blitz and his persistent illness, Lockhart, like so many people, had become literally sick of the war. The news that PWE would be assisting in the denazification of German prisoners once the fighting ended was Lockhart's final straw. On 14 November 1944, he informed Eden that he needed to leave PWE.

Eden accepted that Lockhart was burned out as director-general. However, having become an admirer of his abilities and capacity to work unreasonable hours even while ailing, the foreign secretary was not prepared to let Lockhart abandon government service completely. He suggested that once peace returned to the world Lockhart could take charge of a foreign embassy, preferably one on the periphery of the Soviet Union's sphere of influence. This job would have removed the restless Scot from moribund Britain and provided him with the financial stability and decent pension he needed as he entered his sixties. However, drawing on a grievance he had nursed since first arriving in Whitehall back in 1911, Lockhart implored Eden to realise that the 'people of this country, especially the young people, demand a reformed Foreign Office'. To enact such changes the foreign secretary would need young blood after the war to slay the 'bureaucratic goliaths'. His ill-health aside, Lockhart was simply 'too old to be a David'. In refusing Eden's offer, Lockhart reminded him that he only assumed control of PWE because 'in the war, one has to do one's duty'. Through muddle and exhaustion Lockhart had completed his servitude, managing to 'restrain a band of wild propagandists' while transforming PWE into a bona-fide wartime department. Now, with the Western Allies pushing through France and the Soviets about to launch a decisive push into the Reich from the east, the time had come for Lockhart to return to the life the war had stolen from him. He needed to travel abroad and, when in Britain, he needed the Highland air. He needed his typewriter and the solitude required to summon books from its ink ribbon. Then and only then, Lockhart believed, would his illness abate and his stifling sense of depression fade.[17]

Beyond his personal wishes, Lockhart had also reached a sobering conclusion about the PWE monster he had helped to create. Though he lauded Delmer and Crossman's contributions to fighting Germany, he felt that the ground they had broken in the fields of fake news and radio hijacking had set a foreboding precedent. He feared a future in which governments would bend reality, not to fight external foes but to control their own people's perceptions. A taster of this future emerged in December 1944 when Operation Matchbox – a scheme to deceive the British and American public into believing a faction within Hitler's government was suing for peace – was raised at a PWE meeting. The plan went nowhere, but Lockhart took note that it had gotten far enough to be committed to paper and discussed with the chiefs of staff. This was why he reacted warily to the news that PWE, despite supposedly being a wartime expedient, would continue working into the period of Germany's occupation. What if this wasn't a final phase of operations but a bridge to a new normal, in which PWE's techniques of deception would continue to be practised and improved on? Driven by these concerns, Lockhart spent much of 1945 trying to scale back PWE's work. This involved petitioning Eden and Bracken to narrow the department's range of activities, while ensuring that like-minded cynics would remain in positions of influence in PWE after Lockhart abandoned the helm. The outgoing director-general also suggested that once Germany surrendered, the secrecy surrounding PWE should be lifted, and its name changed to the less nefarious PID from which it had partly sprung.

Ironically, on account of Lockhart's work in expanding PWE's purview, his efforts to shut it down were unsuccessful. Even as the staff – who, no less than their director-general, were eager to find new post-war careers – abandoned Bush House over the course of 1945, the department's brief grew to include both the denazification programme in Germany and the dissemination of propaganda in the Far East, albeit only for a few months before the atomic bombings of Hiroshima and Nagasaki ended that final front of the war. By this time, Lockhart had secured Eden's agreement that he would cease to be PWE's director-general on 31 August 1945. Much as he hoped the department would fade into the night with him, Lockhart was compelled to choose a successor in the form of General Kenneth Strong, a decorated soldier with a background in intelligence. Strong shepherded PWE – which, per Lockhart's request, was now known as PID – through its final operations in occupied Germany until its official dissolution in 1946.[18]

As he packed up his desk at Bush House and prepared to hand the reins over to Strong, Lockhart took stock of the part PWE had played in the second war to end all wars. At a party in January 1945, an inebriated Bracken had asserted to a room of admirals and generals that 'PWE had won the war but were too humble' to crow about it. Embarrassed, Lockhart played down Bracken's boast and gently ushered the minister of information into a side room. The boorish spectacle was amusing, but Bracken's claims compelled Lockhart to think seriously about the comebacks PWE had received. These suggested that many of the RUs had a wide listenership and that some of the leaflets had sown doubt and division in the *Wehrmacht*.

What this amounted to in practice, Lockhart couldn't be sure. He believed that PWE had sapped some of Germany's morale and, within the limits of what he somewhat derisively called 'wordy warfare', his propagandists had worked hard to support Allied military operations.

As to his personal contributions to PWE's campaign, Lockhart was heartened by the plaudits he received from Whitehall officials, the head of SOE, Colin Gubbins, the 'C' of MI6, Stewart Menzies, Beaverbrook, Bracken, Churchill and the denizens of Bush House, who threw him a farewell party at the Dorchester Hotel on his final night as their leader. Laughing through the pain of his inflamed limbs, Lockhart enjoyed the occasion. He bowed in acceptance to toasts and tributes and talked playfully of how his job had been 'to act as a buffer between the enthusiasm' of the propagandists assembled before him and the 'cynical experience' of the Whitehall lifers. It was a job that only a person with a scandalous soul and the temperament of an old hand could pull off. Lockhart's success to this end was evident. It was not enough, however, to sway him from the path he had chosen. The next morning, he rose from his bed in eczema-ridden pain, the edge of which was taken off by a tremendous sense of relief at the thought that his war was finally over. So too was Lockhart's career in service to Britain – this time, seemingly, for good.[19]

CHAPTER 16

BE ALL SINS MISREMEMBERED

'My whole life is a lie.'

– Robert Bruce Lockhart

L ockhart walked into the BBC's studios with tears in his eyes. He held in his hand a script for the evening's edition of *World Affairs*, a programme he had been broadcasting to the people of Czechoslovakia since June 1947. The show was immensely popular. It had an audience that numbered in the millions, making Lockhart a household name in the country to which he was bound by memory and experience in a manner comparable only to his everlasting bond with Russia.

Typically, *World Affairs* featured its presenter interspersing irreverent reminiscences – 'Molotov's wife was intelligent and attractive, but he himself had a sour disposition' – with despairing reflections on the divisions of a post-war, nuclear-armed world. Lockhart also offered his opinion on the state of things in Czechoslovakia which, following the Munich Agreement's repudiation in 1942, had become an independent state again after the German occupation ended in 1945. As he had hoped, Lockhart's old friend Beneš had been appointed president of the restored nation and Masaryk its foreign minister. During an emotional parting of the ways in February 1945, the Czech leaders had spoken to Lockhart of the difficulties they would face in governing the restored country for, in the spirit of national unity, their cabinet would contain communist politicians. Ever the optimist, Beneš assured Lockhart that he would keep the communists in check and ensure that his homeland's politics remained finely balanced. This had not happened.

On 21 February 1948, militiamen and activists affiliated with the Czech Communist Party took over government buildings and instigated street demonstrations in a bid to seize power. As sickly and run down by the war as Lockhart was, Beneš lacked the strength to resist the communist coup and so stood down. Heartbroken, Masaryk committed suicide by defenestrating himself from the second floor of the Czernin Palace. As someone who loved and respected these men and shared their dream of building a democratic Czechoslovakia from the detritus of war, Lockhart was enraged at the communist takeover and struck numb by the death of 'one of my closest friends', whom he had 'known intimately for a quarter of a century'.[1]

For this reason, the *World Affairs* programme that broadcast on 11 March 1948 was different to any that had preceded it. His voice broken by tragedy, Lockhart delivered an emotional performance, lauding Masaryk as a 'jovial, unconventional diplomat' whose 'name will be remembered everywhere free men meet, in his own country or in other lands'. Lockhart was tempted to derail the eulogy by spitting bile at the communists who had destroyed Beneš' government. He could also have joined the chorus of conspiracy theorists who alleged that Masaryk had been murdered by the usurpers – even though Lockhart personally never bought into this idea. At the very least, he could have pointed a verbal finger at the Kremlin, which had backed the coup as a means of bringing Czechoslovakia into the Eastern European empire Stalin had carved out of the Red Army's territorial gains in the war's final months. Instead, Lockhart confined himself to praising his friend's character and speaking vaguely of how Czechoslovakia had been 'violated' by ill-defined forces of 'injustice'. He had borne witness to and involved himself in the genesis of the great war between the capitalist West and the communist East and had navigated the difficult truce both sides brokered to defeat Hitler. Now that the truce had ended and a fresh phase of the ideological conflict had resumed, Lockhart was unwilling to return to the fray. His time as a propagandist, intelligence gatherer and intriguer had passed and he was now a private citizen, committed to living by his pen as he shuffled into retirement.[2]

This was what Lockhart told himself. After leaving PWE in the autumn of 1945, he eagerly rediscovered the world he was forced to abandon that day by the river near Tomintoul six years earlier. This great reset started with his health. The morning after his farewell party at the Dorchester, Lockhart headed north to Edinburgh for medical treatment which, months later, brought his eczema under control. To keep things that way he moved out of London, spurning it as 'the nearest approach to hell, with no accommodation, food and difficulties worse than at any time during the war'. He lived temporarily with his old flame Tommy Rosslyn at her country home in Surrey, before the spark died and their relationship ended. He then bounced between Tomintoul and his brother John's house in Sedbergh for a few months, before renting rooms on the waterfront promenade in Brighton. There, Lockhart embarked on a new phase of his personal life with his secretary Frances Mary Beck – known as Mollie – who, having been there through the worst of his health problems, mood swings, drinking habits and workaholic tendencies during the war, agreed to marry him in 1948. Being twenty-five years older than her, Lockhart recognised that his relationship with Mollie had 'limitations' and that there 'are many things which I cannot give her'. But, unlike his marriage to Jean, this union was devoid of drama and provided Lockhart with a sense of stability that he greatly appreciated.[3]

It was in this settled world by the sea that Lockhart began sorting through his notes and diaries from the war years in preparation for a new memoir covering his work for PWE. At the time of the German surrender, Campbell Stuart had proposed that Lockhart should write the organisation's official history. Instinctively averse to the word 'official', Lockhart passed the duty over to one of his former staffers in favour of penning a more personalised version of events. The final product, *Comes the Reckoning* (1947), sold a healthy 22,000 copies on its initial run and contained typically unvarnished criticisms of Woburn, Whitehall and Britain's psychological warfare campaign. Lockhart's honest account of PWE's ups and downs won him plaudits from reviewers, who were tiring of the triumphal war stories that were starting to clutter Britain's bookshelves. More importantly, *Reckoning* got Lockhart back into the book-writing habit.

In the years that followed, he completed a long-simmering passion project on his love of fishing, *My Rod My Comfort* (1949), and a similarly self-indulgent history of his favourite beverage, *Scotch: The Whisky of Scotland in Fact and Story* (1951). For the more mercenary purposes of a pay-day, the money-hungry writer also produced what he conceded was a 'dull and boring book on the Royal Marines' in the Second World War, *The Marines Were There* (1950). He maintained this prolific output while delivering his weekly *World Affairs* show for the BBC and, for a time, penning the *Sunday Times'* Atticus column, the substance of which was not dissimilar to Londoner's Diary. Lockhart was happy to play the part of the anonymous Atticus. Not only was he paid a decent wage of £2,500 per year, but he felt that the column's relative levity and straight-talking style provided its readers with a necessary counterbalance to the distortions of truth that had been created during the war by the likes of PWE and MOI.[4]

Lockhart had successfully returned to the writer's existence he had briefly enjoyed in the 1930s. However, like the decade that preceded the war, the years after Hitler's defeat were wracked with political crises and ideological quarrels that Lockhart could not ignore. Defeated Germany had been divided into zones of occupation administered by the British, the Americans, the French and the Soviets. It was an arrangement that fed the already growing tensions between Stalin and his erstwhile allies over the question of which of the war's victors was owed the spoils of the Reich. This meant that as Lockhart was starting to withdraw from political life, Stalin was installing puppet governments across Eastern Europe, Churchill was speaking of an 'Iron Curtain' descending across the continent and the American diplomat George Kennan was advising his government that the 'Kremlin's neurotic views of world affairs' meant that a clash between

East and West was near inevitable. As the Soviet Union was central to these dramatic developments of the nascent Cold War, the ex-British Agent was pulled back into the political vortex he had pledged to escape.[5]

During the war, Lockhart had regularly acquired intelligence on the state of the Red Army from the Czech ambassador and military attaché in Moscow. He was also tasked by the Foreign Office with analysing Stalin's speeches, drawing on his intimate knowledge of the Soviet mindset to assess the dictator's true intentions towards his allies. Six months after supposedly leaving government service to become a hermit-like author, Lockhart was still being summoned by Eden – now in opposition following the Labour landslide victory of 1945 – to provide a similar service. He informed his old boss that 'Russia is the ex-Borstal boy who thinks people are not unnaturally holding his past against him (as in fact they are!) . . . suspicion will breed intrigue and secret attempts to injure and, finally, open hostility. We seem to have nearly reached that point now.' Not long after reporting to Eden, Lockhart was invited to deliver a lecture on Anglo-Soviet relations at the Royal College of Defence Studies and was asked to brief the American ambassador, Averell Harriman, on psychological warfare strategies that the West could adopt in its struggle against the Kremlin.[6]

For all that he had talked of wanting 'to retire to a cottage, if I could find one, and write books' after the war, Lockhart embraced his continuing relevancy. He hoped it would portend one final adventure. In 1946, Lockhart ignored the death sentence still hanging over him and made soundings to Maisky about visiting the Soviet Union to take the measure of the country and its leadership. He also enjoined the British ambassador in Moscow, Maurice Peterson, to put the suggestion to Molotov. Lockhart's timing could not have been worse, for a book called *The Great Conspiracy Against Russia* had just been released. Authored by the American Communist Party member Albert E. Kahn and the left-wing Irish poet Michael Sayers, several of the book's chapters recounted the events of 1918, characterising Lockhart as an inveterate conspirator who had been despatched to Russia on a secret mission by the 'British diplomatic Intelligence Service'.

With these skeletons of the past freshly dug up, Peterson asked Lockhart how he could possibly convince Molotov to furnish the ex-British Agent with a visa. Lockhart responded by offering a tweaked version of his long-standing story of innocence. He lamented to Peterson that he hoped the 'myth had died', but clearly the Russians still believed their two-decades-old spin. Contradicting his own memoirs, Lockhart then claimed to Peterson that he had never had dealings with the Latvian Riflemen or Savinkov, and had even warned the British government about working with the known terrorist. Such was Lockhart's desperation to return to Moscow, he was prepared to rewrite his already doctored history.

Even if Peterson was willing to call his hosts liars, the Soviet press's response to *The Great Conspiracy* added fresh layers of accusation to Lockhart's case that would have been impossible to protest without risk-ing Stalin's wrath. *Pravda* attacked Lockhart for his friendship with 'the agent of imperialist reaction – Trotsky – on whom British intelligence long had its eyes' as a potential ally. *Izvestia* picked up this thread, asserting that it was Trotsky and Lockhart who planned the coup against Lenin. This demonising of Trotsky was born of Stalin's loathing for the man. Not con-tent with hounding his rival from the Soviet Union as part of the race to succeed Lenin in the 1920s, Stalin had Trotsky murdered in the supposed refuge of a Mexico City villa in 1940. To be mentioned in the same breath as Trotsky was to be Stalin's enemy. For this reason, when Peterson finally agreed to raise Lockhart's request with Molotov the commissar instantly 'lost his beam' and replied curtly that 'Lockhart is well known in the Soviet Union'. Understanding Molotov's meaning, Peterson ended both the con-versation and Lockhart's hopes of visiting Russia one last time.[7]

Denied this chance to return to the field, Lockhart was left to fight the Cold War from behind his microphone at Bush House, from the lec-tern of British Council-sponsored tours and through articles he penned for publication – often under assumed names – in newspapers and magazines across Europe. Whereas in the 1930s his mission had been to disseminate anti-fascist propaganda, now Lockhart took aim at Soviet expansionism, evoking the story of the Czech coup as a warning to all Europe of the thin thread by which the continent's freedoms now hung. Mindful that the BBC was not an RU broadcasting from Milton Bryan, Lockhart had initially tempered his anti-Soviet remarks. However, after the deaths of Masaryk and Beneš – who deteriorated rapidly in the months after the 1948 coup – Lockhart's broadcasts became more overtly anti-Kremlin and his writing pulled no punches.

In a 1951 article he tore strips off Stalin's claim to be Lenin's heir by recalling how he barely saw the ambitious nonentity in Moscow in 1918, let alone found him sitting under Lenin's learning tree. He was similarly critical of Nikita Khrushchev, who assumed control of the Soviet Union after Stalin died in 1953. Writing off Khrushchev's claims to be a reformer, Lockhart told his readers that 'the new look in Moscow represents a change in tactics. Smiles are now to achieve what years of sourness had failed to accomplish.' The rot of the system remained. It was just that now 'the prison camps are well concealed'. These scathing commentaries on the Soviet regime and his freedom-lauding messages made *World Affairs* a beacon for Czechs aggrieved by the communist takeover. In 1948, an American social scientist researching public attitudes in Czechoslovakia figured that 50 per cent of the Czech population who possessed a radio tuned in weekly to hear Lockhart speak. This included the anti-communist underground, the leaders of which contacted Lockhart via the Czech minister for Ireland, Pavel Růžička, and asked him to relay coded messages to their members via *World Affairs*.[8]

None of this was comparable to the 'black' propaganda operations Lockhart oversaw at PWE, but his efforts to maintain morale in Czechoslovakia and damn the Soviet Union were, to his mind, a final mission – one he was unwilling to tolerate being obstructed from completing. Back in government in 1951, Eden informed Lockhart that funding for the BBC's anti-communist broadcasts to Eastern Europe was being reduced. This prompted Lockhart to angrily question how this could be justified when the Kremlin was increasing both the number of its radio shows and its hours of broadcast time. He complained similarly to his old friend Vansittart about how fluctuations in Anglo-American policy towards the Soviets were confusing his propaganda themes.

Between the griping, Lockhart tried his best to be a good soldier. He travelled to West Germany on a few occasions in the 1950s to tour the facilities of Radio Free Europe – a Central Intelligence Agency-backed initiative that broadcast into the Soviet Union – and reported back favourably to Whitehall on the Americans' progress in the field of strategic propaganda. Still, Lockhart felt ill-suited in the role of psychological warfare's elder statesman, particularly as this exalted position didn't spare him from the same old quarrels he'd been having for decades. His exchanges with the BBC and the Foreign Office over support for anti-Soviet propaganda gave him a depressing feeling of déjà vu, as if the British Council funding problem of the 1930s and the government's uncertain 'good German' policy of the 1940s were coming back in frustrating tandem. After years of spats with Whitehall, Lockhart was too tired to fight any more. His protests over the funding reduction ebbed and his interest in being a Cold Warrior dissipated. By 1961, he was telling anti-communist Czechs who wrote to him in praise of *World Affairs* that 'I am an old man and, although I do my best to help your country, I am out of the official world.'[9]

Discontent with the government was not the only reason for Lockhart's final withdrawal from political life. Despite ongoing treatments, he was still battling perpetual exhaustion and recurring bouts of eczema. He struggled to make it through his chairmanship of a three-day conference at Oxford University in 1951, at which young mandarins were schooled in the art of dealing with Soviet machinations. Similarly, Lockhart's tenure as propaganda policy advisor to the prime minister's cabinet – a post Eden secured for him in 1952 – only lasted a few weeks. He claimed that travelling to London more than his regular once-a-week trip to broadcast *World Affairs* was too much to bear. The fact that Lockhart still managed to drag himself to the capital at this time for lunches at the Carlton Grill with old friends like Moura, Leeper and Nicolson, however, indicates that shifting priorities were also a factor in his stepping away from official duties. He knew he was entering the twilight of his life and that the sickness he had battled since the 1940s would only get worse. Lockhart resolved to exert what little energy he had left on things that mattered.[10]

Friends mattered to Lockhart, particularly as opportunities to toast better days with them were being culled by the march of time. After being left bedridden for months by crippling arthritis, Vansittart died in February 1957. Bracken followed him a year later after a short battle with throat cancer. Leeper and Nicolson lived for a further ten years and the latter corresponded with Lockhart regularly, usually to complain that his hearing was failing and his mobility was decreasing. Having left the marines and become governor of the Australian state of Victoria after the war, Brooks died in 1966. Ransome held on until 1967, albeit while lamenting to Lockhart that his mind was so confused he could no longer trust his memories. Moura remained robust. Now into her sixties, the baroness could still 'drink an amazing quantity, mostly gin, without it showing any apparent slow-up in her mental processes'. Moreover, she kept herself busy in a way that Lockhart was no longer able to by working for MI5 as an informer and pledging to report on 'every person moving in her sphere whom she suspects of being a traitor to this country'. The revelation that her friend Guy Burgess was part of the infamous Cambridge Five spy ring of Soviet agents, however, led to a renewal of the suspicions that she was working for the Kremlin. As always, Lockhart was unbothered by this, seeing Moura only for what she was to him – a cherished companion who was still willing to call him her 'darling baby' and offer words of encouragement and compassion on everything from his illness to his financial difficulties.[11]

Regarding the latter issue, Beaverbrook's death in 1964 was a bitter blow for Lockhart, who had been receiving a personal pension from his benefactor since 1950. Moreover, although the Beaver grumbled about having to reach into his pocket because 'old man' Lockhart 'was starving and unable to live or move into a flat or something', he increased this pension in 1952 and gave Lockhart additional loans in the years that followed. Beaverbrook, however, was more than a cash machine to Lockhart, who 'had known him intimately for over forty years' and, while working on Fleet Street, 'more or less woke him in the morning and put him to bed at night'. During the war, Lockhart had been Beaverbrook's confidant, sharing long discussions on everything from Anglo-Soviet relations to the press baron's prime-ministerial aspirations. Their relationship remained unchanged into the 1950s, during which Lockhart regularly visited Cherkley Court to discuss the shifting dynamics of the Cold War and Britain's decline as a world power. They also exchanged novels and commiserated with one another over the rise of the television set, which Beaverbrook was convinced would spell the end of reading. Theirs was both a business relationship and a friendship, which the two men maintained through marked disagreements and times good and bad. The loss of Beaverbrook was the loss of one of the cherished constants of Lockhart's life.[12]

At least his other constant – writing – remained. On New Year's Eve 1949, Lockhart declared to his diary that he had 'three or four volumes left in me: a personal history of the past four years, a fishing and travel book and two or three volumes of real autobiography, that is, the inner story of my life as distinct from its external excitements and successes'. He had delivered on the fishing book and, deviating slightly from the plan, published reflections on the decades of seismic change he had witnessed on the continent in *My Europe* (1952) and a reflective post-war meditation on the state of Britain, *Your England* (1955). He also penned two books of praise and sorrow about Czechoslovakia: *What Happened to the Czechs?* (1953) and *Jan Masaryk: A Personal Memoir* (1956). Drawing on his countless notebooks, Lockhart next compiled two anthologies of his interactions with the famous and infamous: *Friends, Foes and Foreigners* (1957) and *Giants Cast Long Shadows* (1960). Though these books contained fascinating insights into the minds of Trotsky, Lenin, Kerensky, Eden, Churchill, Vansittart, Savinkov, Crossman and Beaverbrook, neither made Lockhart much money. This was a trend of diminishing returns on his recollections that he first observed when *Your England* sold half the number of copies that *Reckoning* did on its first print. This wound to Lockhart's finances was exacerbated when his *World Affairs* programme, which had been his only consistent source of income since 1947, finally wrapped up in 1964, with Lockhart speaking of his enduring love of the Czech people 'who, in many ways are akin to my own race, the Scots'. Signing off through a voice weakened by age and illness, he declared that 'I am now an old man, but I believe that before my death Czechoslovakia will have opened its arms again to all men and women of goodwill. Long live a free Czechoslovakia in a free Europe.'[13]

By this time, Lockhart had moved to Falmouth in Cornwall and was writing his final book, *The Two Revolutions: An Eye-witness Study of Russia 1917* (1967). This reproduced much of the material from *British Agent*, albeit through the reflective lens of fifty years' distance from the most formative events of Lockhart's life. *Two Revolutions* was criticised by some reviewers for being misleading – Lockhart didn't witness the Bolshevik takeover of 1917 – and containing unnecessary background material on Russian history that made the first half of the book 'the least satisfactory'. Still, its release coincided with a renewed interest in the 'Lockhart Plot'. This was engendered by the revolution's fiftieth anniversary and an interview given by an aged Buikis to Soviet newspapers, in which he stated that Lockhart had ordered him to kill Lenin.

That same year, Robin Bruce Lockhart's *Ace of Spies* (1967) was released. This biography was the culmination of Robin's lifelong fascination with Reilly, which was fuelled by a hazy memory he had as a toddler of the mysterious grifter coming to visit his family's home in Prague. In preparing for the book, Robin talked to his mother, Leeper, Moura, Hill and anyone else he could find still alive with a connection to the plot. This included Lockhart himself, who was more inclined to rue his present than pore over his past. 'I am now 76,' Lockhart wrote to Robin as the latter tried to piece together the jigsaw of Reilly's life story, 'and cannot walk as easily or as quickly as I want to do.' Nor could he comfortably travel to London any more. Even picking up a pen with which to shape a memory was becoming too burdensome a task for the once prolific writer.[14]

After sufficient prodding from Robin, however, Lockhart showed that he could still regale him with the story of Reilly, Moura, Cromie, Savinkov, Dzerzhinsky and the once dashing British Agent whose end was drawing near. Robin never recorded specifics, but Lockhart told him that the tale spun in *British Agent* was not accurate and 'that the Russian version is essentially the true one'. This was an aged father confiding to his son rather than permission to publicise a secret long kept. When the historian Richard Ullman raised the topic of the Russian version of events with Lockhart in 1961, the latter shot it down completely, asserting for good measure that he never discussed subversive activities with counter-revolutionaries and only met Savinkov after he had left Russia in 1918. For his part, Robin explained to the Foreign Office that 'while my father is alive, I feel I cannot, even with his approval, explain that *Memoirs of a British Agent* did not tell the whole truth'. Lockhart's story – the one he had told with only minor alterations for over half a century – was all that mattered.

It was a story he stuck with until the end. When delivering one of his final public lectures in 1960 – 'Last Words on Lenin' at Old College Hall in Edinburgh – Lockhart denied any knowledge of counter-revolutionary plots against the Bolshevik leader and once more shot down the idea that he was anything more than a victim of circumstance in 1918. He also gently chided the historians George Kennan and A. J. P. Taylor for claiming to write the truth about Russia's revolutions, despite having no physical connection to those great events or personal knowledge of the Goliaths of history who shaped them. Smiling in a mischievous way that for a moment turned back the years, Lockhart reminded his audience that he was the only man still living who could claim to have shaken Lenin's hand, seen the Red Army's inception, broken bread with Trotsky and seen the inside of a Cheka jail cell. One gets the sense that Lockhart was enjoying watching his personal recollections of the past become the histories of the future.[15]

Having provided two contradictory versions of what happened in 1918 to his son and to the public, Lockhart entered the final phase of his life. He had never enjoyed living in Cornwall and so moved from Falmouth back to

Brighton in 1967, where first Robin and then staff at a nursing home looked after him for the remainder of his days as he battled cerebral sclerosis. His body and mind were shattered and what little money remained in his bank account was drawn from a small civil service pension he was issued with in 1965 for his services to literature.

Still, Lockhart's passport was cluttered with stamps and his memories were a kaleidoscope of great events, fascinating people and curious adventures. He had few regrets. When asked in 1953 to return to Fettes College and deliver the Founder's Day speech, Lockhart used the opportunity to urge his young audience to 'be adventurous', to 'respond to the appeal of the unknown' and to realise that 'the making of money merely for money's sake is a poor end in itself, and safety first and youth go ill together'. It was an honest reflection of a mantra that had shaped an extraordinary eighty-two-year existence, which came to an end peacefully while Lockhart slept on the night of 27 February 1970. The coda that followed says much about his life and the way he lived it. Staff at the D'Arcy Nursing Home in Brighton opened a letter addressed to Lockhart from the famous writer Paul Einzig, who reminded him that his name had been on the list of those to be executed by the Gestapo in the event of a successful German invasion in 1940. As the thirtieth anniversary of this dire pronouncement was looming, would he be interested in attending a commemorative dinner? Owing to the eternally wandering Lockhart's whereabouts being unknown when Einzig posted the invitation, it arrived at the nursing home on 30 March 1971 – a year and a month after Lockhart had died.[16]

Having received the news she feared was coming, Moura conducted herself in a manner that would have pleased her convention-spurning 'baby boy'. While friends, family and former colleagues descended on St Peter's Church in Hove for a Catholic funeral, Moura remained in London at the Russian Orthodox Church in Ennismore Gardens. There, on 5 March 1970, she convened a private ceremony for the man she had always loved. Incense was lit and the choir sang mournful hymns reminiscent of the gypsy songs she and Lockhart had once listened to together. Robed in a cassock and clutching a cross of gold, the bearded priest said prayers in Russian as Moura stood alone in the nave dressed in black with her head bowed.

Her thoughts burned with memories of the brilliant young charmer who had been derided, disgraced and written off as a man who fell short of his endless potential. Still, Moura would not cry for Lockhart. She knew that for all his troubles he had lived the life he wanted, travelling extensively, loving passionately, making countless friends and outlasting his foes. He had written the history of his life and times. For this he had earned praise and, on occasion, riches, which he spent without a thought to the dangers of overindulgence or the perils of an uncertain future. He was not sensible, but nor was the age of extremism and war through which he lived. Amid these dangerous times, Lockhart became a best-selling author, a respected gatherer of intelligence and one of the most well-connected people of his generation, from whom advice was sought by everyone from revolutionaries to prime ministers to spymasters. As Moura expected, the obituaries in the newspapers spoke ad nauseam of 1918 but she above all others knew the truth – Lockhart was always more than Britain's Agent.[17]

ACKNOWLEDGEMENTS

This biography began with a pencil mark I saw in a book nearly fifteen years ago. The mark had been made next to a footnote about a man named Robert Bruce Lockhart, whom the note's author could not believe had never been the subject of a full biography. My friend and mentor Michael Durey made that pencil mark, and when I asked him about it, he explained to me who Lockhart was and why he was so interesting. It took all of five minutes for me to be convinced that this man did, indeed, need his life story told. In the years since that conversation, Mike has helped guide my research into Lockhart. It is to him I must issue my first and most heartfelt acknowledgement. As always, Chris Vaughan has been very supportive, as has my agent Andrew Lownie. Lorne Forsyth, Robin Harvie and Pippa Crane from Elliott & Thompson showed great interest in Lockhart's story and have been a pleasure to work with in helping me share it. I have benefited from advice and encouragement during the production of this book from Richard Spence, Jonathan Schneer, Alan Philps, Beatriz Lopez, Robert Service, Christopher Andrew, John R. Ferris, Rory Cormac, Jo Fox and Frank McDonough. Dugald and Karen Bruce Lockhart were also very kind and forthcoming in discussing their ancestor with me and allowing me to make use of the papers and letters he left behind. The production of this book was made possible by the Everett Helm Research Fellowship I was awarded by Indiana University and the assistance given me by Penny Ramon at the Lilly Library. I was similarly helped by my colleagues David Clampin and Nick White, who arranged a semester sabbatical from teaching so that I could get this book written. The John Foster Building at Liverpool John Moores is a place where I have always felt supported. Those who roam its halls and from whom I have received advice and encouragement include Gillian O'Brien, Cathy Cole, Tom Beaumont, Matthew Hill, Andre Keil, Susan Grant, Daniel Feather, Lucasz Grzymski, Andrew Galley and Olivia Saunders. Pandora must also be acknowledged for the assistance she provided during the long hours of editing. In her willingness to both be told Lockhart stories and provide me the space to write, my wife Sarah struck a perfect balance between offering loving support and necessary distance. She knows how her husband works and he works better for it. You are my love – by north, south, east and west.

NOTES

Preface

1 'Delightful' from 'Sir Robert Bruce Lockhart obituary', *The Times*, 28 February 1970; 'Dynamic' from *The Second World War Diary of Hugh Dalton, 1940–1945*, ed. Ben Pimlott (London: Jonathan Cape, 1986) – 10 September 1941, quoting Brendan Bracken, p.279; 'Circumspect' from Sefton Delmer, *Black Boomerang* (London: Secker and Warburg, 1962), p.79.

2 'Behaved' from *Diaries of Sir Robert Bruce Lockhart, 1915–1938*, ed. Kenneth Young, vol.1 (New York: St. Martin's Press, 1973), vol.1 – 20 January 1934, p.284; 'Weak' from Office of War Information dossier on Lockhart, cited in Charles Cruickshank, *The Fourth Arm: Psychological Warfare, 1938–1945* (London: Davis-Poynter, 1977), p.184; 'Prima dona' from *Dalton Diaries*, 5 December 1940, p.115; Papers of Sir Robert Bruce Lockhart, *Lilly Library, Indiana University*, hereafter LL:RBL/1 – Lockhart to Keenan, 23 January 1957.

3 'Adventurous' from Jonathan Schneer, *The Lockhart Plot: Love, Betrayal, Assassination and Counter-Revolution in Lenin's Russia* (Oxford: Oxford University Press, 2020), p.8; 'Wild' and 'unbridled' from Gordon Brook-Shepherd, *Iron Maze: The Western Secret Services and the Bolsheviks* (London: Pan, 1999), p.25.

4 *National Archives of the United Kingdom*, hereafter TNA:FCO 12/121 – Graham to Simons, 14 June 1971 and Denning to Child, 23 February 1971; Papers of Sir Robert Bruce Lockhart, *Hoover Institution, Stanford University*, hereafter HI:RBL/10 – D. J. Johnson Diaries overview, December 1985.

5 'My whole' from LL:RBL/1 – Lockhart to Nicolson, 13 June 1932; HI:RBL/12 – Exchanges between Robin and FCO from 1972–1974.

Introduction: A Plot Undone

1 'The Bolshevik' from Robert Bruce Lockhart, *Memoirs of a British Agent* (Barnsley: Frontline, 2011), hereafter *MBA*, p.317.

2 'From among' from p.209; Louis Fischer, *The Life of Lenin* (New York: Harper and Row, 1964), pp.282–284; George Leggett, *The Cheka: Lenin's Political Police* (London: Clarendon, 1981), pp.106–107.

3 The most comprehensive account of the 'Lockhart Plot' is Schneer's *Lockhart Plot*. See also John W. Long, 'Plot and Counterplot in Revolutionary Russia: Chronicling

the Bruce Lockhart Conspiracy, 1918', *Intelligence and National Security*, 10:1 (1995), pp.122–143.

4   *Izvestia* quote in Richard K. Debo, 'Lockhart Plot or Dzerzhinskii Plot?', *Journal of Modern History*, 43:3 (1971), pp.413–429, p.414; Pavel Malkov, *Reminiscences of a Kremlin Commandant* (Moscow: Progress, 1977), pp.272–274; Robert Service, *Spies and Commissars: Bolshevik Russia and the West* (London: Pan Macmillan, 2011), pp.156–157.

5   'From Petrograd's dungeons', *Daily Mail*, 18 October 1918.

Ch1: No Drop of English Blood

1   Robert Bruce Lockhart, *My Scottish Youth* (Edinburgh: B & W, 1993 edition), hereafter *SY*, pp.14–26, 63; 'Frugal' from p.24; 'Small boy' from p.97; HI:RBL/1 – Bertie Letter, 1895.

2   'No drop' from *MBA*, p.3; 'Experimentalists' from HI:RBL/6 – 'Fettes College Founders' Day Speech', 27 June 1953; 'The Englishman' from *SY*, p.134. 42, 104 and 148.

3   HI:RBL/10 – Prof W. Vietor testimonial, undated; *SY*, pp.355–356.

4   LL:RBL/5 – 'Cast Up by the Tide' 1912; Robert Bruce Lockhart, *Return to Malaya* (London: Putnam's Sons, 1936), hereafter *RTM*, p.23; *Singapore Free Press and Mercantile Advertiser*, 1 December 1908.

5   *MBA*, pp.13–14; Tsuyoshi Kato, 'When rubber came: the Negeri Sembilan experience', *Journal of Southeast Asian Studies*, 29:2 (1991), pp.109–157; Margaret Shennan, *Out in the Midday Sun: The British in Malaya, 1880–1960* (London: John Murray, 2000), pp.48–52.

6   *MBA*, pp.18–22. 'Radiant' from p.18. 'At the frail' from p.19; HI:RBL/10 – 'Eastern Love Song'.

7   Poem quotes from HI:RBL/10 – 'Eastern Love Song', 'An Eastern Storm'; *RTM*, pp.201–203. 'The focus' from p.201.

8   *MBA*, pp.23–26. 'Her little' from p.26; Robert Bruce Lockhart, *Retreat from Glory* (Garden City: New York, 1934), hereafter *RFG*, p.155.

9   All quotes from HI:RBL/10 – 'A farewell to GPC' and 'To A' and Box 2, 'I have seen' from 'Eastern Diary', 16 July 1910; *MBA*, pp.32–34.

Ch2: Our Man in Moscow

1   'You're in' and 'passed' from *MBA*, pp.44–45; TNA:CSC 11/166 – Lockhart appointment file, 19 September 1911; LL:RBL/1 – Ian Macgregor reference, 2 April 1911; HI:RBL/1 – Exam results, 24 July 1911.

2   Zara Steiner, *The Foreign Office and Foreign Policy, 1898–1914* (Cambridge: Cambridge University Press, 1969), pp.78–82, 'The long' from p.81; 'A serious' from *MBA*, p.77; pp.49–50; HI:RBL/1 for correspondence with Moura. Box 5 for quotes from *Jean*. Box 10 contains poems about Amai; Robert Bruce Lockhart, *My Europe* (London: Putnam, 1952), hereafter *ME*, pp.4–5; T. G. Otte, *The Foreign Office Mind: The Making*

of British Foreign Policy, 1865–1914 (Cambridge: Cambridge University Press, 2011), pp.315–322.

3   *MBA*, pp.53–55, 60. 'Steaming' from p.53; 'Cheerful and 'good mixer' from Arthur Ransome, *The Autobiography of Arthur Ransome*, ed. Rupert Hart-Davis (London: Jonathan Cape, 1976), p.231; 'Happiest' from Robert Bruce Lockhart, *The Two Revolutions: An Eyewitness Study of Russia 1917* (London: Bodley Head, 1967), hereafter *TR*, p.46; LL:RBL/5 – 'This I Believe' (undated post-war essay); Sheila Fitzpatrick, *The Russian Revolution* (Oxford, Oxford University Press, 2008), pp.21–23.

4   *ME*, pp.16–18; Claudia Verhoeven, 'The Making of Russian Revolutionary Terrorism' in *Enemies of Humanity: The Nineteenth Century War on Terrorism*, ed. Isaac Land (Basingstoke: Palgrave, 2008), pp.99–116.

5   'Poking' from *TR*, p.46; Nevile Henderson, *Water Under the Bridges* (London: Hodder and Stoughton, 1945), pp.29–31.

6   Michael Hughes, *Inside the Enigma: British Officials in Russia, 1900–1939* (London: Hambledon, 1997), pp.32–33; LL:RBL/5 – Vice-consul appointment, 1 January 1912.

7   HI:RBL/6 – 'The way of the English: How Hugh Weston kept the flag flying', May 1914; 'Russian extravagance', *Nottingham Evening Post*, 14 March 1913; HI:RBL/5 – 'Some Contemporary Russian Writers', *Everyman*, 22 May 1914; The full collection of Jean D'Auvergne articles is in LL:RBL/5.

8   'A liberal' from *The Secret Letters of the Last Tsar: Being the Confidential Correspondence between Nicholas II and his mother, Dowager Empress Maria Feodorovna*, ed. Edward J. Bing (New York: Longmans, Green and Co., 1938), pp.9–10; *The Confessions of Aleister Crowley: An Autohagiography*, eds John Symonds and Kenneth Grant (London: Penguin, 1989), pp.711–715; William F. Ryan, 'The "Great Beast" in Russia: Aleister Crowley's theatrical tour to Moscow in 1913 and his beastly writings on Russia' in *Symbolism and After: Essays on Russian Poetry in Honour of Georgette Donchin*, ed. Arnold McMillin (London: Bristol Classical, 1992), pp.137–145; *MBA*, pp.74–78.

9   LL:RBL/5 – 'Two Declarations', July 1940; Michael Hughes, '"Revolution was in the air": British officials in Russia during the First World War', *Journal of Contemporary History*, 31:1 (1996), pp.75–97.

10 RBL Diaries (unpublished), *Houses of Parliament Archives*, hereafter HPA:LOC/1 – Jan–March 1915. All quotes from 4 June, 6, 23, 25 August 1915.

11 'To observe' from Robert Bruce Lockhart, *Guns or Butter* (London: Putnam, 1938), hereafter, *GOB*, p.124; Other quotes from TNA:FO 371/2454 – Lockhart to Buchanan, 21 July 1915; TNA:FO 498/o – Lockhart to Buchanan, 22 January 1916 and 30 October 1916; *ME*, p.22; LL:RBL/1 – Grove to Balfour, 29 September 1915.

12 'Excellent work' from George Buchanan, *My Mission to Russia and Other Diplomatic Memoirs*, vol.2 (London: Cassell and Company, 1923), p.244; 'Masterful' and 'interesting' from TNA:FO 371/2254 – FO Minute Sheet, 25 July 1915; 'Mr Lockhart' from TNA:FO 371/2255 – FO Minute Sheet and Buchanan to FO, 15 October 1915; TNA:FO 498/9 – Buchanan to Grey, 28 January 1916; HPA:LOC/1 – 18 March 1916.

13 'The most' from FO to Lockhart, 15 May 1916; 'Pessimistic' from HI:RBL/10 – Last Words on Lenin, 1960; LL:RBL/1 – FO to Lockhart, 11 October 1916.

Ch3: Implosion

1 'Rioting' from *RBL Diaries*, vol.1, 11 March 1917, p.28; 'The peasantry' from Buchanan, *Mission*, vol.2, p.27; 'Situation' from William Henry Chamberlain, 'The First Russian Revolution', *Russian Review*, 26:1 (1967), pp.4–12; Meriel Buchanan, *Petrograd: The City of Trouble, 1914–1918* (London: Collins, 1919), pp.92–102, quotes from p.102; Anthony D'Agostino, *The Russian Revolution, 1917–1945* (Santa Barbara: Praeger, 2011), pp.37–39.

2 Neil Faulkner, *A People's History of the Russian Revolution* (London: Pluto, 2017), pp.134–137, 'provisional Government' from p.137; 'On the question of the dual power', *Izvestia*, 2 and 29 March 1917 in *The Russian Provisional Government, Documents*, eds Robert Paul Browder and Alexander F. Kerensky, vol.3 (Stanford: Stanford University Press, 1916), pp.1210–1211 and 1218–1219; David Stevenson, *1917: War, Peace and Revolution* (Oxford: Oxford University Press, 2017), pp.167–168.

3 'Great scenes', 'workmen' and 'impossible' from *RBL Diaries*, vol.1, 13 and 23 March, pp.28–29; *MBA*, pp.170–171.

4 'Dismiss' from Robert Bruce Lockhart, 'The Unanimous Revolution – Russia, February 1917', *Foreign Affairs*, 35:2 (1957), pp.320–333; 'Russia' from TNA:FO 438/10 – Memorandum on the Moscow Revolution, 23 March 1917; *RBL Diaries*, vol.1, 16 September 1915, pp.24–25.

5 Quotes from 'Order Number 1 of the Petrograd Soviet', 14 March 1917 – *Project Avalon Digital Archive*, https://avalon.law.yale.edu/20th_century/soviet_001.asp; 'Russia has' from TNA:FO 438/10 – Lockhart to Buchanan, 10 May 1917; John Boyd, 'The origins of Order No. 1', *Soviet Studies*, 19:3 (1968), pp.359–372; Orlando Figes, *A People's Tragedy: The Russian Revolution*, 1891–1924 (London: Pimlico, 1997), pp.407–409.

6 'Voices' from TNA:FO 438/10 – Lockhart to Buchanan, 30 April 1917 and 2 May 1917; 'Kerensky' from Robert Bruce Lockhart, *Comes the Reckoning* (London: Putnam, 1947), hereafter *CTR*, p.93; Hughes, *Inside the Enigma*, pp.90–96.

7 'Paid' from 'What Bolshevism is', *Daily Telegraph*, 15 January 1919; Hughes, *Inside the Enigma*, pp.97–99.

8 Quotes on Kerensky from George Alexander Hill, *Go Spy the Land: Being the Adventures of IK8 of the British Secret Service* (London: Biteback, 2014 edition), p.83; LL:RBL/5 – 'The Forgotten Revolution', 1957; Richard Pipes, *The Russian Revolution* (New York: Vintage, 1991), pp.302–303.

9 'Undertaken' from Buchanan, *Mission*, vol.2, p.108; Nicolas Werth, 'Russia 1917: The soldiers' revolution', *South Central Review*, 34:3 (2017), pp.48–57; David Mandel, *The Petrograd Workers in the Russian Revolution, February 1917–June 1918* (Leiden: Brill, 2017), pp.197–200.

10 'Knew' from Hill, *Go Spy*, p.177; 'Most' and 'details' from Sir Samuel Hoare, *The Fourth Seal: The End of a Russian Chapter* (London: William Heinemann, 1930), pp.252–253.

11 All quotes from *MBA*, pp.91–92; HPA:LOC/1 – 1–10 October 1915.

12 'Nerves' from HPA:LOC/1 – 28 February 1915; Schneer, *Lockhart Plot*, p.15; According to Young in *Diaries*, vol.1, Jean claimed it was Hugh Walpole who reported the affair to Buchanan, p.15; The Maksimovna story was given to me by Professor Richard Spence, who was told it by the Soviet journalist Lev Bezymensky based on information he copied from KGB files. Though it isn't hard evidence, the story aligns with Grove's warnings to Lockhart about Okhrana surveillance.

13 'Installed' from Louis de Robien, *The Diary of a Diplomat in Russia 1917–1918*, trans. Camilla Sykes (London: Michael Joseph, 1969) – 31 July 1917, p.91; Pipes, *Russian Revolution*, pp.436–437.

14 'Mental' from *MBA*, p.195.

Ch4: Agent of Britain

1 Quotes from 'One who knows him', *Daily Mail*, 13 September 1917; *MBA*, pp.195–196.

2 'All through' from M. Buchanan, *Petrograd*, pp.192–193; 'A few' and 'Shell hole' from Morgan Philips Price, *Dispatches from the Revolution: Russia, 1916–1918*, ed. Tania Rose (London: Pluto, 1997), p.93; Alexander Rabinowitch, *The Bolsheviks Come to Power: The Revolution of 1917 in Petrograd* (New York: Pluto, 2017), pp.273–278. Lenin quote on p.274; Ian D. Thatcher, *Trotsky* (London: Routledge, 2002), pp.85–92.

3 Robert D. Warth, *The Allies and the Russian Revolution: From the Fall of the Monarchy to the Peace of Brest-Litovsk* (Durham: Duke University Press, 1954), pp.174–179; Pipes, *Russian Revolution*, pp.188–189; *MBA*, pp.198–200.

4 'Abandon' from 'Russia's economic future', *The Times*, 13 December 1917; *MBA*, p.198.

5 HPA:LOC/3 – 1–3 January 1918; 'A perfect' and 'not a' from Buchanan, *Mission to Russia*, pp.239–240.

6 'Vague' and 'British government' from Evelyn Baring (Lord Cromer), *Modern Egypt*, vol.1 (London: Macmillan, 1916), p.345 and 323. Milner worked with Cromer in Egypt and would have been familiar with the concept of a British Agent – Roger Owen, *Lord Cromer: Victorian Imperialist, Edwardian Proconsul* (Oxford: Oxford University Press, 2005), pp.247–249; For the French Agent in Ukraine see TNA:FO 371/3283 – Bertie to FO, 5 January 1918.

7 'Do as' from *MBA*, p.206, p.220; 'If any' from Brook-Shepherd, *Iron Maze*, p.37; For meetings see HPA:LOC/3 – 2–8 January 1918 and 2–4 February 1918.

8 'Lean' from Malkov, *Reminiscences*, p.270; HPA:LOC/3 – 7–9 January 1918. 'Hickie' from 4 March 1918; 12 February 1918; Hugh Walpole, 'Denis Garstin and the Russian Revolution: A Brief Word in Memory', *Slavonic and East European Review*, 17:51 (1939), pp.587–605.

9   'Was drunk' from *MBA*, p.205, pp.215–217; 'Imperial' from Robien, *Diary of a Diplomat*, 13 January 1918, p.190 and 9 January 1918, p.187; 'Shrieking' and 'these men' from M. Buchanan, *City of Trouble*, p.245 and 228; HPA:LOC/3 – 14 January–3 February 1918. 'Everyone' from 30 January; LL:RBL/1 – Phelan to Lockhart, 17 November 1932.

10 'Assertive' from Hugh Walpole, 'Memoirs of a British Agent Review', *The Book Society News*, 4:11, November 1932; TNA:CAB 24/41/59 – Lindley to Lockhart, undated, February 1918; TNA:FO 371/3283 – Lindley cable, 15 Feb. 1918; Wardrop letter from Brook-Shepherd, *Iron Maze*, pp.37–38; 'Evacuation of Petrograd', *The Times*, 7 March 1918; *Hansard*, 'British representative in Petrograd', vol.104, 18 March 1918.

11 'That the Germans', 'burning papers' and 'have shown' from Robien, *Diary of a Diplomat*, 19, 26 and 28 February 1918, p.227; 'His nails', 'impending', 'pro-Boche' and 'our number' from HPA:LOC/3 – 15, 18, 20 and 21 February 1918.

12 All quotes from Papers of Lord Milner, *Bodleian Library, Oxford*, hereafter OBL:MS DEP/364B – Lockhart cable, 16 February 1918; Warth, *Allies and Russian Revolution*, pp.193–195.

13 Cecil quotes from TNA:CAB 24/5/32 – War Cabinet minutes, 7 February 1918; 'Young Lockhart' from Alfred Knox, *With the Russian Army, 1914–1917*, vol.2 (London: Hutchinson, 1921), p.591 and 618; Lockhart agreed with Kerensky's accusation, see LL:RBL/1 – Kerensky to Lockhart, 7 July 1956 and Lockhart to Beaverbrook, 23 July 1956.

14 Knox quotes from OBL:MS DEP/364B – General Staff to War Office, 18 March 1918; 'Greatest Jew' from *RBL Diaries*, vol.1, 12 February 1918, p.33; Lloyd George quotes from TNA: CAB 24/5/32 – War Cabinet minutes 7 February 1918; David S. Foglesong, *America's Secret War Against Bolshevism: U.S. Intervention in the Russian Civil War, 1917–1920* (Chapel Hill: University of North Carolina, 1995), pp.108–110.

15 Lenin quote from Pipes, *Russian Revolution*, p.591; John W. Wheeler-Bennett, *Brest-Litovsk: The Forgotten Peace, March 1918* (London: Macmillan, 1963), pp.265–269.

16 OBL:MS DEP/364B – Lockhart cable, 2 March 1918 and H. W. to War Office, 18 March 1918; Diary entries from *RBL Diaries*, vol.1, 12 and 14 March, p.34.

Ch5: Crossroads

1   'Little, simple' from Ransome, *Autobiography*, p.240; *MBA*, pp.236–237; HPA:LOC/3 – 27–28 February 1918; Albert Rhys Williams, *Journey into Revolution, Petrograd 1917–1918* (Chicago: Quadrangle, 1969), pp.250–252.

2   'My position' from OBL:MP/MS Dep 364/B – Lockhart cable, 10 March 1918; TNA:FO 371/3285 – FO Minute, 27 March 1918.

3   HPA:LOC/3 – 15–16 March 1918; Pipes, *Russian Revolution*, pp.594–595; *MBA*, p.245.

4   'We do' from *MBA*, p.262. p.247.

5   'Rarely' from HI:RBL/10 – Last Words on Lenin, 1960; David Francis, *Russia from the American Embassy, April 1916–November 1918* (London: Scribner and Sons, 1921), pp.237–238; Alan Philps, *The Red Hotel: The Untold Story of Stalin's Disinformation War* (London: Headline, 2023), pp.48–50; Brook-Shepherd, *Iron Maze*, p.64.

6   'A game' from TNA:FO 371/3283 – Lockhart cable, 3 March 1918; 'Holy war' from TNA:FO 371/3285 – Lockhart cable, 5 March 1918; Clifford Kinvig, *Churchill's Crusade: The British Invasion of Russia, 1918–1920* (London: Continuum, 2006), pp.5–9; David Stevenson, *With Our Backs to the Wall: Victory and Defeat in 1918* (London: Penguin, 2012), pp.91–93.

7   OBL:MP/MS Dep 141 – Lockhart cable, 13 April 1918; Evan Mawdsley, *The Russian Civil War* (Edinburgh: Birlinn, 2008), pp.72–75; Ian Moffat, *The Allied Intervention in Russia, 1918– 1920: The Diplomacy of Chaos* (Basingstoke: Palgrave, 2015), ch.3; William Hard, *Raymond Robins' Own Story* (New York: Harper, 1920), pp.161–168.

8   'Proposed' from Brook-Shepherd, *Iron Maze*, p.58; Lockhart quotes from TNA:FO 371/3285 – Lockhart cables, 1, 2 and 8 March 1918 and OBL:MP/MS Dep 364/B – Lockhart cable, 5 March 1918; Paul E. Dunscomb, *Japan's Siberian Intervention, 1918–1922* (Lanthan: Lexington Books, 2011), pp.32–40; Warth, *Allies and Russian Revolution*, pp.190–193.

9   For criticisms of Lockhart see minute sheets in TNA:FO 371/3285 between March and April 1918; Balfour quotes from TNA:FO 371/3285 – 13 March 1918 and OBL:MP/MS Dep 364/B – Balfour to Lockhart, 6 March 1918.

10 'Splendid' from Hill, *Go Spy*, pp.190–191; Richard Spence, 'The tragic fate of Kalamatiano: America's Man in Moscow', *International Journal of Intelligence and Counterintelligence*, 12:3 (1999), pp.346–374; DeWitt Poole, *An American Diplomat in Bolshevik Russia* (Madison: University of Wisconsin Press, 2014 edition), pp.142–144; Foglesong, *America's Secret War*, pp.92–116; For Allied support to the Whites see generally TNA:FO 371/3283.

11 'Close touch' from Papers of Major General Frederick Poole, *Liddell Hart Military Archives*, King's College London, hereafter, KCL:POOLE – Hill's Report on Work Done in Russia, 26 November 1918; Ward, *Robins' Own Story*, p.76; *Papers Relating to the Foreign Relations of the United States*, hereafter *FRUS*, Russia 1918, vol.1 – Francis to Secretary of State 11 May 1918; Moffat, *Allied Intervention*, pp.36–38.

12 Neil V. Salzman, *Reform and Revolution: The Life and Times of Raymond Robins* (Kent, OH: Kent State Press, 1991), pp.270–275, 'The tide' from p.270; 'Colonel Robins' from TNA:FO 371/3319 – Wiseman to Drummond, 15 June 1918; HPA:LOC/3 – 30 April 1918.

13 'To escape' from *MBA* p.284; 'Lockhart strongly' from *FRUS*, Russia 1918, vol.1 – Francis to Secretary of State 11 May 1918; An attempt was made to recall both Lockhart and Hicks in early June, but the former resisted it strongly by pointing out that after the flight of the Allied ambassadors, he had been left alone to hold down the British fort in Russia – TNA:FO 371/3313 – FO to Lockhart and reply, 1 June 1918. FO Memo 3 June 1918.

Ch6: Double Game

1   Quotes from HI:RBL/6 – 'Baroness Budberg', 1958; Deborah McDonald and Jeremy Dronfield, *A Very Dangerous Woman: The Lives, Loves and Lies of Russia's most Seductive Spy* (London: Oneworld, 2016), p.13; Schneer, *Lockhart Plot*, p.51.

2   'Drank' from Meriel Buchanan, *Ambassador's Daughter* (London: Cassell, 1958), pp.143–144; Nina Berberova, *Moura: The Dangerous Life of the Baroness Budberg*, trans. Marian Schwartz and Richard D. Sylvester (New York: New York Review of Books, 2005), pp.6–12; Roy Bainton, *Honoured by Strangers: The Life of Captain Francis Cromie CB DSO RN, 1882–1918* (Shrewsbury: Airlife, 2002), pp.137–138; McDonald and Dronfield, *Dangerous Woman*, pp.6–16.

3   See generally TNA:KV 2/979 and 2/980; 'A flair' from TNA:KV 2/980 – 'Ernest' memo, 28 June 1940; Other quotes from Hill, *Go Spy*, pp.84–85; 'Baroness Marie Ignatievna Budberg', 6 August 1937; TNA:KV 2/979 – Letter from Air Attaché, 15 December 1936.

4   'Nice, happy' from HI:RBL/1 – Moura to Lockhart, 10 March 1919; 'Reports' from HPA:LOC/3 – 18 March 1918; LL:RBL/1 – Clerk to Jean, 17 May 1918; See also Lockhart to Jean, 18 and 22 January, 28 February and 4 April 1918, Leeper to Lockhart, 28 Feb 1918 and Leeper to Jean, 21 April 1918 and May (undated) 1918; Moura initially called him 'Lockhart' in her letters but by March was using the term 'babykins' – Box 2, Moura to Lockhart, undated March 1918.

5   'Remain' from Hill, *Go Spy*, p.169; Roland Chambers, *The Last Englishman: The Double Life of Arthur Ransome* (London: Faber, 2010), pp.204, 210 and 245–250; McDonald and Dronfield, *Dangerous Woman*, pp.70–76; Service, *Spies and Commissars*, pp.221–224; Information on Hill in HI:RBL/11 – Robin's notes on Sidney Reilly; For Moura's intel see LL:RBL/2 – letters from May 1918.

6   'Military' from OBL:MP/MS Dep 364/B – Lockhart cable, 10 March 1918; Brise later worked for the Ministry of Information feeding propaganda into Russia – TNA:FO 395/184 – Hall cable, 4 August 1918 and Cypher to HM Consuls, 29 July 1918.

7   'In touch' from TNA:FO 371/3313 – Lockhart to FO, 23 May 1918; 'Too gay' from Schneer, *Lockhart Plot*, p.63; 'A red cloth' from Ransome, *Autobiography*, p.231; 'The mission' from HI:RBL/1 – Moura to Lockhart, 10 March 1918 and undated letter, probably May 1918; 'Reliable source' from TNA:FO 371/3332 – Lockhart cable, 18 May 1918; 'Mata Hari' from LL:RBL/1 Moura to Lockhart, 18 June 1932; *FRUS*, Russia 1918, vol.3 – Lindley to Secretary of State, 16 May 1918; For Moura's work in Ukraine see McDonald and Dronfield, *Dangerous Woman*, pp.88–90; TNA:KV 2/979 – Captain Liddell's Report on 'Moura Budberg', 22 Feb 1935 and Profile Summary, 1932.

8   'You should' from TNA:FO 371/3332 – War Cabinet circular 23 May 1918. Lockhart to War Cabinet, 16 May 1918 and 26 May 1918; Jonathan D. Smele, '"Mania Grandiosa" and the "turning point in world history": Kerensky in London in 1918', *Revolutionary Russia*, 20:1 (2007), pp.1–34; *MBA*, p.277.

9 *FRUS* – Russia 1918, vol.2, Caldwell to Secretary of State, 5 April 1918; HPA:LOC/3 – 26–27 April 1918; J. F. N. Bradely, 'The Allies and the Czech Revolt against the Bolsheviks in 1918', *Slavonic and East European Review*, 43:101 (1965), pp.275–292.

10 'Group of' from *Bolshevik Propaganda: Hearings before a Subcommittee of a Committee of the United States Senate, 65th Congress, 11 February 1919–10 March 1919* (Washington: Government Printing, 1919) – Raymond Robins' testimony, pp.822–823; TNA:FO 371/3333 – Wardrop cable, 9 June 1918; Lars T. Lih, *Bread and Authority in Russia, 1914–1921* (Berkeley: University of California Press, 1990), pp.128–132; Paul Avrich, *The Russian Anarchists* (New Jersey: Princeton University Press, 1967), pp.183–189.

11 'Black pope' from 'The Red Terror', *The Times*, 16 January 1920; 'Anarchist' and 'innumerable' from Malkov, *Reminiscences*, pp.226–229; Donald Rumbelow, *The Houndsditch Murders and the Siege of Sidney Street* (Stroud: History Press, 2009); Schneer, *Lockhart Plot*, pp.94–95.

12 'Learn if' from OBL:MP/MS Dep 364/B, Lockhart cable, 6 March 1918; HI:RBL/11 – Robin's interview with George Hill; OBL:MP/MS Dep 141, Lockhart cable 29 May 1918; *RBL Diaries*, vol.1 – 31 May and 2 June 1918, p.37; Richard B. Spence, *Boris Savinkov: Renegade on the Left* (New York: Columbia University Press, 1991), pp.193–199.

13 'Murder all' and 'military dictatorship' from TNA:FO 371/3332 – Lockhart cables, 17 and 26 May 1918; 'I approve' from FO to Lockhart 27 May 1918; 'Methods' from FO Minute sheet, 30 May 1918, Notes on Lockhart file, 25 May 1918.

Ch7: Enter ST1

1 'Madman' from HPA:LOC/3 – 8 May 1918; 'A dark' from Hill, *Go Spy*, p.189; LL:RBL/2 – Moura to Lockhart, undated March 1918; Christopher Andrew, *Secret Service: The Making of the British Intelligence Community* (London: Heinemann, 1985), p.213; Andrew Cook, *Ace of Spies: The True Story of Sidney Reilly* (Stroud: History Press, 2004), pp.155–160.

2 'Clever' from Richard B. Spence, *Trust No One: The Secret World of Sidney Reilly* (Los Angeles: Feral House, 2002), pp.153–159; 'Great abilities' from TNA:KV 2/827 – Letter from T. H. Owen Thurston, 19 January 1918; '£500' from Alan Judd, *The Quest for 'C': Mansfield Cumming and the Founding of the Secret Service* (London: Harper, 2000), pp.429–430; 'Pass equally' from Norman Thwaites, *Velvet and Vinegar* (London: Grayson & Grayson, 1932), p.183; 'Jewish-Jap' from Cook, *Ace of Spies*, p.155.

3 'Sending bad' from TNA:KV 2/827 – GHQ Report on Reilly, 8 April 1919 and Report on Reilly's movements, 7 March 1918; 'With patriotism' and 'untrustworthy' from Benny Morris, *Sidney Reilly: Master Spy* (New Haven: Yale University Press, 2022), pp.52–53; 'Very doubtful' and 'great gamble' from Keith Jeffery, *MI6: The History of the Secret Intelligence Service, 1909–1949* (London: Bloomsbury, 2010), pp.135–136; Keith Neilson, '"Joy rides?", British intelligence and propaganda in Russia, 1914–1917',

Historical Journal, 24:4 (1981), pp.885–906; For a mythologised retelling of Reilly's origins see Michael Kettle, *Sidney Reilly: The True Story of the World's Greatest Spy* (New York: St Martin's, 1983), pp.11–19. For a debunking of the Reilly myth see Cook, *Ace of Spies*, pp.27–50, 115–122 and Andrew, *Secret Service*, pp.83–85.

4   All quotes cited in Sidney Reilly, *Adventures of a British Master Spy: The Memoirs of Sidney Reilly* (London: Biteback, 2014 edition), pp.9–11 and Reilly's report to 'C' reproduced in Cook, *Ace of Spies*, p.157; HI:RBL/2 – Alley to Robin, 13 May 1966; Spence, *Trust No One*, pp.189–190.

5   'Dressed' from *MBA*, p.277; 'It was' from Robin Bruce Lockhart, *Reilly: Ace of Spies* (London: Penguin, 1964), pp.82–84; John W. Long, 'Searching for Sidney Reilly: The Lockhart Plot in Revolutionary Russia, 1918', *Europe-Asia Studies*, 47:7 (1995), pp.1225–1241; Reilly, *Adventures*, p.20.

6   OBL:MP/MS Dep 365, Box C – Lockhart cable, 1 June 1918; 'Tone' from TNA:FO 371/3333 – FO Minute Sheet, 26 June 1918; Richard B. Spence, 'The Terrorist and the Master Spy: The Political "partnership" of Boris Savinkov and Sidney Reilly, 1918–1925', *Revolutionary Russia*, 4:1 (1991), pp.111–131; A photograph of the cigar case is in HI:RBL/9.

7   'Had independent' from George Alexander Hill, *Dreaded Hour* (London: Cassell, 1936), p.9; 'Took two' from HI:RBL/10 – Some notes on Sidney Reilly (undated); 'Agitation' from ADM 137/1731 – Cromie to Admiralty, 8 May 1918 and 23 May 1918; 'Several' from TNA:FO 371/3333 – Woodhouse cable no.265, 17 June 1918; TNA:FO 371/3332 – Lockhart cable, 26 May 1918; Cook, *Ace of Spies*, pp.157–158.

8   TNA:FO 371/3348 – Secret and Confidential Memorandum on Alleged Allied Conspiracy, 5 November 1918; *MBA*, p.300; TNA:FO 371/3287 – Lockhart cable, 8 August 1918; Alfred Erich Senn and Harold J. Goldberg, 'The Assassination of Count Mirbach', *Canadian Slavonic Papers*, 21:4, vol.21 (1979), pp.438–445; For Lockhart's possible connection to the French/SR Plot see Schneer, *Lockhart Plot*, pp.140–141.

9   'To strengthen' from TNA:FO 371/3348 – Lockhart's Report on 'Internal Situation in Russia', 7 November 1918; 'Been' from TNA:FO 371/3287 – Lockhart cable, 14 July 1918; 'Can successfully' from Lockhart cable, 25 July. Details of money requests are in Lockhart cable, 16 July 1918.

10 HPA:LOC/3 – 18 July 1918; TNA:FO 371/3286 – Lockhart to FO, 1 June 1918; *FRUS* – Francis to Secretary of State, 4 August 1918; Helen Rappaport, *Ekaterinburg: The Last Days of the Romanovs* (London: Windmill, 2009), pp.184–196.

11 'Made in' from TNA:FO 371/3287 – Lockhart cable, 6 July 1918; Robert Bruce Lockhart, *Friends, Foes and Foreigners* (London: Putnam, 1962), hereafter *FFF*, p.111; HI:RBL/11 – Some notes on Sidney Reilly (undated); Kinvig, *Churchill's Crusade*, pp.33–36; Spence, *Renegade on the Left*, pp.211–216.

12 'After capturing' from Denis Garstin, *The Shilling Soldiers* (London: Hodder and Stoughton, 1918), p.vi; 'Converting' from TNA:FO 371/3335 – Howard cable of Wardrop's report, 19 August 1918; *RBL Diaries*, vol.1, 5 August 1918, pp.39–40;

KCL:POOLE – Hill's Report, 26 November 1918; Michael Occleshaw, *Dances in Deep Shadows: The Clandestine War in Russia, 1917–1920* (New York: Carroll and Graf, 2006), pp.211–214; Hill, *Go Spy*, pp.216–220; Lockhart's passes are in LL:RBL/6.

13 'I cannot' from TNA:FO 371/3287 – Lockhart cable, 18 July 1918; 'Was unwilling' from *MBA*, p.288; McDonald and Dronfield, *Dangerous Woman*, p.93, pp.101–102 and 104–108.

Ch8: The Great Gamble

1 Geoffrey Swain, '"An interesting and plausible proposal": Bruce Lockhart, Sidney Reilly and the Latvian Riflemen, Russia, 1918', *Intelligence and National Security*, 14:3 (1999), pp.81–102; Andrew Ezergailis, *The Latvian Impact on the Bolshevik Revolution, The First Phase, September 1917 to April 1918* (Boulder: East European Monographs, 1983), pp.150–156.

2 'Reports' from TNA:FO 371/3333 – Lockhart cable, 6 June 1918; 'Foreign' from Reilly, *Memoirs*, pp.18–19; 'Conviction' from Thwaites, *Velvet and Vinegar*, p.184; TNA:ADM 137/1731 – Cromie to Admiralty, 5 July 1918; Hill, *Go Spy*, pp.89–90; Bainton, *Honoured by Strangers*, pp.238–239.

3 TNA:FO 371/3335 – Cromie cable (via Findley), 19 August 1918; *RBL Diaries*, vol.1, 6 August 1918, p.40; Pipes, *Russian Revolution*, pp.660–666.

4 'Organise' from TNA:FO 371/3348 – Secret Memorandum, 5 November 1918; *MBA*, pp.314–316; Lockhart claimed he first met the Latvians on 14 August and that it was Schmidkhen and Berzin who gave him Cromie's letter. Russian sources claim that Lockhart initially met with Schmidkhen and Bredis in the first week of August before the Hotel Elite was raided – see Cook, *Ace of Spies*, pp.165–166, Long, 'Searching for Sidney Reilly', p.1230; Kettle, *Sidney Reilly*, p.35, *ME*, p.32; TNA:FO 371/3332 – Lockhart cable, 4 June 1918 and FO to Browne, 28 May 1918.

5 'Extremely able' from TNA:FO 371/3348 – Secret Memorandum, 5 November 1918; 'She sang' from *MBA*, p.316.

6 'Would be' from KCL:POOLE – Hill's Report, 26 November 1918; TNA:FO 371/3335 – Findley cable, 21 August 1918; OBL:MP/MS Dep 365/C – Derby cable, 15 July 1918.

7 This report had limited circulation in Whitehall but was still 'on the record' enough for Lockhart to make amendments to the final version – 'Smoothly' from TNA:FO 371/3348 – Secret Memorandum, 5 November 1918. 'One or two' from draft version; 'Desirous' from TNA:FO 371/3287 – Rumbold cable, 6 August 1918; 'Opportunity' from TNA:FO 371/3336 – Clive cable, 7 September 1918; TNA:FO 371/3287 – Lockhart cable, 21 July 2018; McDonald and Dronfield, *Dangerous Woman*, pp.127–128.

8 Long, 'Plot and counter-plot'; For a discussion of American involvement in the plot see Barnes Carr, *The Lenin Plot: The Unknown Story of America's War Against Russia* (Stroud: Amberley, 2020). A focus on Reilly's contributions is made in Robin Bruce Lockhart's *Ace of Spies* and Spence's *Trust No One*.

9   'The proposed' from KCL:POOLE – Hill's Report, 26 November 1918; 'A movement' from TNA:FO 371/3348 – Secret Memorandum, 5 November 1918; 'Although' from Hill, *Dreaded Hour*, p.9.

10 'Do away' from Christopher Andrew and Oleg Gordievsky, *KGB: The Inside Story* (New York: HarperCollins, 1990), p.51; KCL:POOLE – Hill's Report, 26 November 1918; Schneer, *Lockhart Plot*, pp.196–197; Long, 'Searching for Sidney Reilly', pp.1233 and n.66, p.1240.

11 'Categorically' from *MBA*, p.316; Other quotes from TNA:FO 371/3348 – Secret Memorandum, 5 November 1918.

12 'Close my' from OBL:MP/MS 365/C – Lockhart cable (via Findlay), 3 September 1918; KCL:POOLE – Hill's Report, 26 November 1918; Schneer, *Lockhart Plot*, pp.198–199; Reilly, *Memoirs*, pp.26–27.

13 All quotes from René Marchand, *Allied Agents in Soviet Russia* (London: People's Russian Information Bureau, 1918), p.4; LL:RBL/6 – René Marchand's letter to French president, 22 August 1918; 'Uneasy' and 'the room' from Reilly, *Memoirs*, pp.26–27; Harry Thayer Mahoney, 'The saga of Xenophon Dmitrivich Kalamatiano', *International Journal of Intelligence and Counterintelligence*, 8:2 (1995), pp.179–201; Schneer, *Lockhart Plot*, pp.198–200.

14 'An intriguer' and 'unconcerned' from Malkov, *Reminiscences*, pp.268–270; *ME*, p.33; Debo, 'Lockhart Plot'; Swain, 'An interesting and plausible proposal'; Leggett, *Cheka*, pp.280–281.

15 'Certain' from TNA:FO 371/3337 – Lockhart cable (via Clive), 11 October 1918; 'Counter-revolutionary' from Malkov, *Reminiscences*, p.280; James Ryan, *Lenin's Terror: The Ideological Origins of the Early Soviet State* (London: Routledge, 2012), pp.106–109; Alexander Orlov, *The March of Time: Reminiscences* (London, St. Ermin's, 2004), pp.133–135; Spence, 'The tragic fate of Kalamatiano'; Hill, *Go Spy the Land*, pp.227–228.

16 'Our whole' from TNA:FO 371/3287 – Lockhart cable, 14 July 1918; 'Terrifying' from *MBA*, p.309; Malkov, *Reminiscences*, p.229.

17 'Secretary' from Malkov, *Reminiscences*, pp.273–275; 'Do you' from TNA:FO 371/3348 – Secret Memorandum, 5 November 1918; TNA:FO 371/3319 – Findlay cable, 30 September 1918; David Stafford, *Churchill and Intelligence* (London: John Murray, 1997), pp.120–122. Cook, *Ace of Spies*, pp.171–174, 228.

Ch9: Mission's End

1   'Arrested' from TNA:FO 371/3336 – Paget cable, 9 September 1918; 'In prison' from David R. Francis, *Russia from the American Embassy, April 1916–November 1918* (New York: Charles Scribner's Sons, 1921), p.283; *FRUS* – 'Report of the Netherlands Minister relating to conditions in Petrograd', 5 October 1918.

2   'Un-checked' from 'Russian Anarchy', *Daily Telegraph*, 13 September 1918; 'Up to' from 'Russian orgies of murder', *Aberdeen Journal*, 12 September 1918; 'Gallant' from

'British Attaché murdered', *The Times*, 5 September 1918; *FRUS* – 'Report of the Netherlands Minister', 5 October 1918; TNA:FO 371/3335 – Paget cable, 5 September 1918; Poole, *An American Diplomat*, pp.310–311.

3   'That if' from *Daily Mail*, 4 October 1918; 'The Moscow Terror', *The Times*, 10 September 1918; TNA:FO 371/3336 – FO circular, 11 September 1918.

4   'The connexion' from 'Bolshevik story of attack', *The Times*, 5 September 1918; 'Disclose' from TNA:FO 371/3335 – Paget cable, 20 September 1918; TNA:FO 371/3339 – Clive cable, 19 September 1919; TNA:FO 371/3336 – Lindley cable, 6 September 1918.

5   'You saved' from *MBA*, p.325; HPA:LOC/2 – 1–4 September 1918; TNA:FO 371/3348 – Secret Memorandum, 5 November 1918; Semion Lyandres, 'The 1918 attempt on the life of Lenin: a new look at the evidence', *Slavic Review*, 48:3 (1989), pp.432–448.

6   'Troops' from TNA:FO 371/3335 – 'News translated through the wireless stations of the Russian government', 3 September 1918; 'Some foundation' from *FRUS* – Poole to Secretary of State, 26 September 1918 and 'Report of the Netherlands Minister', 5 October 1918; HI:RBL/7 – 'Allied invasion of Russia to Suppress Workmen's Revolution and Re-establish Tsarism'. Lockhart pushed the Cromie obfuscation theory in the press after his release – 'Mr Lockhart's captivity', *Manchester Guardian*, 18 October 1918; TNA:FO 371/3336 – Clive cables, 9 and 12 September 1918; TNA:FO 371/3348 – Secret Memorandum, 5 November 1918; Leggett, *Cheka*, pp.282–283.

7   'Given' from TNA:FO 371/3666 – Clive cable, 20 September 1918; HPA:LOC/2 – 7–10 September 1918; *MBA*, pp.327–328.

8   McDonald and Dronfield, *Dangerous Woman*, pp.143–144; HPA:LOC/2–8 September 1918; LL:RBL/2 – Moura to Lockhart, undated September 1918.

9   'I am' from HPA:LOC/2 – 23 September 1918; *MBA*, p.337; See generally September 1918 letters in LL:RBL/2.

10   'Necessary' from TNA:FO 371/3336 – Hicks cable (via Findlay), 22 September 1918; TNA:FO 371/3348 – Secret Memorandum, 5 November 1918; TNA:FO 371/3336 – Clive cable, 12 September 1918 and Findlay cable, 14 September 1918.

11   *MBA*, pp.343–344. 'Capitalism' from p.340; 'Heroine of' from *ME*, p.48; *RBL Diaries*, vol.1 – 1 October 1918, p.46; TNA:FO 371/3336 – FO Circular, 20 September 1918.

12   'Cash box' and 'doomed' from HI:RBL/12 – Moura to Robin, undated, probably 1960s; 'Various' from TNA:KV 2/980 – Note on Baroness Budberg, undated; On Moura's knowledge of the plot see McDonald and Dronfield, *Dangerous Woman*, p.128; Schneer, *Lockhart Plot*, pp.178–179; Carr, *Lenin Plot*, pp.258–259.

13   'Incredible' from TNA:FO 371/3337 – Lindley cable, 3 October 1918; 'The Bolsheviks' from TNA:FO 371/3348 – Secret Memorandum, 5 November 1918; 'You are' from *MBA*, p.340; 'All the letters' from Schneer, *Lockhart Plot*, p.247. The original coded diary entry can be found in HPA:LOC/2 – 16 September 1918.

14   'Remember' from LL:RBL/2 – Moura to Lockhart, 3 October 1918; KCL:POOLE – Hill's Report, 26 November 1918; *MBA*, pp.345–347.

Ch10 – A Night Without Dawn

1 'Socialist' from 'Red Bolshevism', *Daily Mail*, 12 November 1918; 'All over' from 'Kaiserism and after', *The Times*, 11 November 1918; Robert Gerwarth, *November 1918: The German Revolution* (Oxford: Oxford University Press, 2020), pp.90–105; John Paul Newman, 'Revolution and counterrevolution in Europe, 1917–1923' in *The Cambridge History of Communism*, eds Silvio Pons and Stephen A. Smith (Cambridge: Cambridge University Press, 2017), pp.96–120; Figes, *People's Tragedy*, pp.508–516.

2 HPA:LOC/3 – 19–29 October 1918; 'Card up the sleeve of the Hun', *Daily Express*, 11 October 1918; 'No bargaining with the Kaiser', *Daily Mirror*, 8 October 1918; 'Mr. Bruce Lockhart', *Daily Telegraph*, 21 October 1918; LL:RBL/1– United Russia Societies Association to Lockhart, 21 October 1918 and Lockhart memo to Balfour on Bolshevik leaders, 25 November 1918; Discussing Robin's *Ace of Spies*, Leeper told Jean that 'you and I are the only people who know the background of all this and, knowing the background as we do, it is most important that none of this past should be raked up', as it would 'play straight into the hands of the Soviet Government' for propaganda purposes – HI:RBL/11 – Leeper to Jean, 16 March 1966.

3 'A surprising' from HPA:LOC/3 – 23–29 October 1918. 'Enemies' from 22 October 1918. 'Perfectly' from 25 October 1918, p.47.

4 'HI:RBL/11 – 'The salvation' from Reilly to Lockhart, 24 November 1918. 'Serve under' from Reilly to Lockhart, 25 November 1918.

5 'Been exalted' from Robert Bruce Lockhart, *Your England* (London: Putnam, 1955), hereafter *YE*, p.80; 'Give me' from HI:RBL/1 – Moura to Lockhart, 27 February 1919. 'The thought' from 14 December 1919, 'Baby' from 19 April 1919; 'Always' from LL:RBL/2 – Moura to Lockhart 3 October 1918; 'It is' from 26 November 1918; 'Do you' from 13 February 1919; See in general letters from October 1918 to February 1919 in this collection.

6 'My thoughts' from *MBA*, p.348; *RFG*, pp.24–25.

7 'Secret service' from 'What Bolshevism is', *Daily Telegraph*, 15 January 1919; 'Scene at a lecture', *Daily Mail*, 15 January 1919; HPA:LOC/4 – 14 January 1919.

8 LL:RBL/1 – Milner to Lockhart, 15 March 1919. Steel-Maitland to Lockhart, 15 May 1919 and Gregory to Lockhart, 25 May 1919; HPA:LOC/4 – 24 October 1919; LL:RBL/5 – Memorandum on the Internal Situation in Russia, 31 October 1918; 'Drifting into Another War', *New Statesman*, 18 December 1918; For the fear of Bolshevism in Britain after the war see Simon Webb, *1919: Britain's Year of Revolution* (Barnsley: Pen & Sword, 2016).

9 The menu for the 'Liquidation Lunch' signed by attendees is in HI:RBL/11; 'For those' from LL:RBL/5 – 'An Angler in Bohemia', undated.

10 Mary Heimann, *Czechoslovakia: The State that Failed* (New Haven: Yale, 2009), pp.38–42; The legation received a budget increase just prior to Lockhart's arrival, see TNA:T 1/2432 – Prague folio.

11   *RFG*, pp.45–47. 'Pleaded' from p.46; Gerald Protheroe, 'Sir George Clerk and the
     struggle for British influence in central Europe, 1919–26', *Diplomacy & Statecraft*,
     12:3 (2001), pp.39–64; TNA:FO 371/5830 – Annual Report on Czechoslovakia, 1920;
     LL:RBL/1 – Report on Antonin Švehla 6 Dec. 1922; TNA:FO 418/171 – Clerk to
     Curzon, 26 January 1921 and 24 August 1921.

12   *RFG*, pp.73–75 and 94; TNA:FO 608/8 – Gosling to Balfour 31 March 1919.

13   Spence, *Savinkov*, pp.307–308; Spence, *Trust No One*, pp.241–244 and 280–282; Cook,
     Ace of Spies, pp.215–216; TNA:FO 371/5831 – Memorandum on Radium Corporation,
     15 September 1921; HI:RBL/11 – Robin to Hill, undated, 1966.

14   Papers of Major General Edward Spears, *Churchill College Archives*, hereaf-
     ter CHURCH: Spears Papers – Spears to Robin, 2 January 1967; HPA:LOC/3
     – 19 October–30 November 1918; TNA:FO 418/171 – Clerk to Curzon, 26 January
     1921; TNA:FO 371/4024 – Hill to Curzon, 22 June 1919 and Knothe to Leeper,
     14 August 1919.

15   *RFG*, pp.110–111, 135–136, 140, 228 and 266–267. 'Taught' from p.84.

16   'Very ill' and 'nervous' from HPA:LOC/5 – 30 July 1923 and LOC/7 – 16 September
     1926; *RFG*, pp.149–150 and 168. 'Humdrum' from p.161.

17   LL:RBL/1 – Offer letter to Lockhart, 1 June 1922; *Archives of the Bank of England*,
     hereafter BOE:C40/118 – Commercial Secretary's Memorandum, 30 August 1922.

18   'Critical' from *RBL Diaries*, vol.1 – 20 March 1928, p.69; 'Two cocktails' 30 August 1926,
     p.65 and 30 November 1924, pp.59–60; 'A peasant state: the crisis in Yugoslavia', *The
     Times*, 26 April 1927; 'England and Russia', *The Times*, 14 April 1924; 'Czechoslovak
     problems and personalities', *Financial Times*, 22 March 1923; Lockhart's reports for
     the bank are in BOE:OV109/1 and 112/1.

19   'Unable' from HI:RBL/1 – Moura to Lockhart, 24 June 1921; Andrea Lynn, *Shadow
     Lovers: The Last Affairs of H. G. Wells* (Boulder: Westview Press, 2001), pp.104–109;
     McDonald and Dronfield, *Dangerous Woman*, pp.192–194, 207–211.

20   'The change' from *RFG*, pp.220–223; *RBL Diaries*, vol.1 – 3–4 August, pp.58–59.

Ch11 – Hell on Fleet Street

1   'Strange' from *RFG*, p.307; 'one of' from *RBL Diaries*, vol.1 – 23 May 1928, p.70; D.
     George Boyce, 'William Maxwell Aitken, First Lord Beaverbrook' – *Oxford Dictionary
     of National Biography*, Online Edition (23 September 2004); Anne Chisholm and
     Michael Davie, *Lord Beaverbrook: A Life* (New York: Alfred A. Knopf, 1993), pp.176–
     177, 186–187, 200 and 247.

2   *YE*, p.108; Houses of Parliament Archives, *Papers of Lord Beaverbrook*, hereafter,
     HPA:BBK/C/221 – Lockhart to Beaverbrook, 28 and 29 February 1928 and 10 April
     1928; Geoffrey Jones, 'Public policy and the British multinational banks, 1914–1982',
     Business and Economic History, 21 (1992), pp.209–218; LL:RBL, Box 5 – Agreement
     to become Honorary Consul for the Republic of Austria, 1927.

3   'Did my exercises' was a common refrain of his diary in this period – HPA:LOC/10
    – 10 June–24 August 1928.
4   'International morality' from 'Treaty of Versailles', art. 227, 29 June 1919 – *Project
    Avalon Digital Archive*, https://avalon.law.yale.edu/imt/partvii.asp; 'A fine' from *RBL
    Diaries*, vol.1 – 22 November 1928, p.73, 23–26 November 1928, pp.73–77; 'His per-
    sonal' and other quotes from 'Exiled Emperor's love of the sea', *Evening Standard*,
    20 December 1929; *Evening Standard,* 12 February 1929; Christopher Clark, *Kaiser
    Wilhelm II: A Life in Power* (London: Penguin, 2009), pp.346–348.
5   'More genuine' from *YE*, p.123; LL:RBL/3 – *End of an Epoch* (unfinished book, 1939),
    hereafter *EOAE*, p.13; See entries for 1928–1929 in *RBL Diaries*, vol.1; 'Feeling' from
    24 September 1929, p.107. 'This life!' from 28 June 1929, p.94. 'Ill, depressed' from
    26 April 1930; Martin Pugh, *We Danced All Night: A Social History of Britain Between
    the Wars* (London: Vintage, 2009), pp.218–221.
6   LL:RBL/3 – *EOAE*, p.32; 'Although Bolshevist' from Londoner's Diary, *Evening
    Standard* – 4 May 1929; 'Talkies' from 1 May 1929; Sacré Cœur from 18 March 1929;
    Rugby from 28 December 1928; 'The cure' from 8 July 1929; Stamps and coin machine
    from 13 May 1929; *RFG*, p.331.
7   'Something immoral' from *RBL Diaries*, vol.1 – 15 May 1931, p.166; LL:RBL/3 –
    EOAE, pp.83–84; 'The United Empire Party', *Evening Standard*, 18 February 1930;
    Jerry M. Calton, 'Beaverbrook's split imperial personality: Canada, Britain, and the
    Empire Free Trade movement of 1929–1931, *The Historian*, 37:1 (1974), pp.26–45;
    Ruth Henig, 'Britain, France and the League of Nations in the 1920s' in *Anglo-French
    Relations in the Twentieth Century*, eds Alan Sharp and Glyn Stone (London: Routledge,
    2000), ch.8; LL:RBL/1 – Nicolson to Lockhart, 22 July 1929.
8   *RBL Diaries*, vol.1 – 26 April 1930, p.119; HPA:BBK/C/221 – correspondence with
    Beaverbrook, June–August 1930; *RFG*, pp.308–309.
9   'But for' from *RBL Diaries*, vol.2 – 22 June 1941, p.106; 'Very egocentric' from
    RBL Diaries, vol.1 – 13 April 1930, p.117–118; For Tommy's social circles see
    28 August–15 September 1926, pp.64–65. For Lockhart's conversion to Catholicism
    see p.57.
10 'Politically' from TNA:KV 2/279 – Baroness Budberg memo, 8 June 1933; LL:RBL/2
    – Moura to Lockhart 18 January 1929. Also see 30 July 1932 and undated letters
    from April 1933; *RBL Diaries* 30 July 1923, p.56, 16 September 1926, p.65,
    13 November 1930, p.134, 1–3 January 1931, p.143; For Boyce accusations see Edward
    P. Gazur, *Secret Assignment: The FBI's KGB General* (London: St Ermin's, 2001),
    pp.519–520.
11 'She was' from *RBL Diaries*, vol.1 – 16–18 December 1930, pp.138–391; 'I am' and
    'love and adore' from 19 December 1930, p.141; 'I cannot' and 'whole outlook' from
    22 December 1930, p.141; 3–10 January 1931, p.144–146; LL:RBL/1 – Beaverbrook
    to Lockhart, 23 December 1930.
12 'Bore no' from *FFF*, p.175; LL:RBL/2 – Moura to Lockhart, 18 June 1932; This
    calculation is based on Lockhart's record of words put in his diary, which ranged

from 189,000 to 279,000 per year in the 1950s – HI: RBL/5 – Notes on diary entries; The rights fees for *British Agent* and the advance paid by Putnam's for a sequel earned Lockhart £2,560.11, approximately £153,000 today (2023) – HI:RBL/10 – Putnam's memo, 8 September 1933; McDonald and Dronfield, *Dangerous Woman*, pp.258–259.

13 Quotes from 'Russia's red dawn', *Daily Telegraph*, 5 December 1932; 'Book Society's Choice for November' – *The Times*, 4 November 1932; 'Russia Agonistes', *Illustrated London News*, 31 December 1932; 'An adventure in diplomacy', *New York Times Book Review,* 5 February 1933; 'The truth' from *Daily Express*, 17 March 1933 headline; 'Memories from Moscow', *Times Literary Supplement*, 10 November 1932.

14 Quotes from 'Retreat from Glory', *Times Literary Supplement*, 18 October 1934; 'The confessions of Mr. Lockhart', *Sunday Times*, 21 October 1934; 'British Agent in Jugoslavia', *Daily Telegraph*, 16 October 1934; LL:RBL/1 – Lockhart to Clerk, 31 August 1934. Nicolson to Lockhart, 26 August 1934; *RBL Diaries*, Vol.1 – 23 and 24 October 1934, pp.309–310, 27 October 1934, p.311, 9 December 1934, p.312.

15 'Fatter' from *RBL Diaries*, vol.1 – 31 December 1934, p.314; 'Search' from LL:RBL/1 – Beaverbrook to Lockhart, 11 December 1934; Lockhart had considered writing a book on his Malaysian experience years earlier but hadn't been able to secure a publisher – LL:RBL/1 – Herbert Jenkins to Lockhart, 24 Jan 1919.

16 *RTM*, pp.12–17, 67–69. 202–209. 'Singapore as' from p.84; 'The living' from 'Malaya revisited', *Times Literary Supplement*, 28 November 1936; 'Full book' from 'Malaya revisited', *The Times*, 20 December 1936; 'Anecdotes' from 'Scottish Youth', *Times Literary Supplement*, 4 December 1937.

17 'An unsavoury' from *RBL Diaries*, vol.1 – 11 March 1937, p.368. 15 February 1927, p.365; TNA:J/77/3757/4445 – 'Petition of Robert Hamilton Bruce Lockhart', 26 April 1937.

18 'Leave' from *RBL Diaries*, vol.1, 4–7 June 1937, p.373 and 6 June 1935, p.322; LL:RBL/1 – from Lockhart to Beaverbrook, 8 June 1937. Lockhart to Moray McClaren, 21 April 1936. Beaverbrook to Lockhart, 15 June 1937 and McLaren to Lockhart, 14 February 1936 and 19 October 1936.

19 'Fascist' from *RFG*, p.298; 'Quite pro' from *RBL Diaries*, vol.1 – 13 July 1933, pp.262–263; LL:RBL/1 – Précis of *Nationalsozialisticshe Monatshefte*. Box 5 – 'Memorandum on visit to Occupied Territories in Germany, July–August 1923'; *RTM*, pp.84–85.

Ch12 – Whither Europe?

1 'Hitlerist' from *RBL Diaries*, vol.1 – 13 May 1933, p.253 and 21 August 1931, p.181; 'Little' from *RFG*, p.129.

2 *RBL Diaries* – 8 February 1933, p.243. 28 April 1933, p.253. 1 May 1931, p.164. 13 May 1933, p.253; 'Hitler thanks his Fascist army', *Evening Standard*, 23 April 1932.

3 *RBL Diaries*, vol.1 – 24 March 1933, pp.250–251. 'Rot' from 13 May 1933, p.253; 'Imitate' from Londoner's Diary, *Evening Standard*, 29 September 1932; Thost story in

Londoner's Diary, *Evening Standard*, 5 December 1931; Professor story in Londoner's Diary, *Evening Standard*, 24 February 1932; LL:RBL/2 – Moura to Lockhart, undated (probably April) 1932; Chisholm and Davie, *Beaverbrook*, pp.322–323.

4   Dan Stone, *Responses to Nazism in Britain, 1933–1939* (Basingstoke: Palgrave, 2009); Tony Kushner, 'Beyond the pale? British reactions to Nazi anti-Semitism, 1933–39', *Historical Studies of Ethnicity, Migration and Diaspora*, 8:1–2 (1989), pp.143–160.

5   Reilly and Savinkov were lured into Russia as part of the OGPU's 'Operation Trust', see Christopher Andrew and Vasili Mitrokhin, *The Mitrokhin Archive: The KGB in Europe and the West* (London: Allen Lane, 1999), pp.43–46; Moura doubted that Reilly had been killed and, writing for the *Standard* in 1926, Lockhart suggested he might still be alive. Hill confirmed Reilly's fate to Lockhart in February 1931, see *RBL Diaries*, vol.1 – 5 February 1931, p.151; 'Mystery of a "spy"', *Evening Standard*, 27 September 1927.

6   Matthew Worley, 'What was the New Party? Sir Oswald Mosley and the associated responses to the "crisis" of 1931–1932', *History*, 92:305 (2007), pp.39–63; Richard Thurlow, *Fascism in Britain: From Oswald Mosley's Blackshirts to the National Front* (London: I.B. Tauris, 1998), pp.1–30; 'Red terrorism' from p.63.

7   'Political' from HI:RBL/3 – 1930s Notebook; 'Intends' from *RBL Diaries*, vol.1 – 9 July 1929, p.95. 25 September 1930, p.125; For manifesto see 4 December 1930, pp.135–136; 'Sir O. Mosley's bombshell', *Evening Standard*, 4 December 1930; Harold Nicolson, *Diaries and Letters, 1930–1939*, ed. Nigel Nicolson (London: Collins, 1966) – Letter to Mosley, 4 March 1931.

8   Shock troops' from *Nicolson Diaries* – 6 January 1932, p.106; 'At one' from TNA:KV 2/2494 – 'Communist Party' report 16 April 1936; 'Financial' from TNA:KV 2/1546 – Report on Cockburn, 19 June 1934.

9   'Fascism is' from HPA:LOC/16 – 29 September 1932. For accusations of pro-fascism see 18 January 1932; 'Obviously' from LOC/19 – 16 June 1934; 'Very divided' from 9 June 1934; See also LOC/18 – 5 June 1933.

10   'Quite brainless' from *RBL Diaries*, vol.1 – 5 September 1935, p.327; For Nieland see 16 January 1932, p.200; For Thost's rant see 1 September 1933, pp.270–271; LL:RBL/1 – Lockhart to Hanfstaengl, 8 January 1934; Hanfstaengl to Lockhart, 15 January 1934; Lockhart also missed a chance to interview Hitler in 1932 – LL:RBL/3 – *EOAE*, p.49.

11   All quotes from LL:RBL/1 – Bernstorff to Lockhart, 23 June, 16, 25, 22 and 27 August 1935; *FFF*, pp.140–150.

12   'Nothing' from *RBL Diaries*, vol.1 – 5 January 1937; 'We could' from 15 November 1938, pp.409–410. For Britain's defences see 26 April 1934, p.290, 14 February 1932, p.204, 16 October 1938, p.402; 'Far too' from LL:RBL/1 – Nicolson to Lockhart, 4 May 1937.

13   'Flat' from Delmer, *Black Boomerang*, p.62; 'Early prophet' credited to Anthony Eden in Derek Drinkwater, 'Reginald Wildig Allen (Rex) Leeper' – *Oxford Dictionary of National Biography* (2004); LL:RBL/3 – *EOAE*, p.37; TNA:BW 69/3 – Memorandum

on Central European Countries, Jan 1937; TNA:BW 82/5 – Meredith to Lord Derby, 27 August 1935; Ronald Seth, *The Truth Benders: Psychological Warfare in the Second World War* (London: Leslie Frewin, 1969), pp.26–27.

14 'A tireless' from HI:RBL/6 – Moura Budberg Essay; John R. Ferris, 'Indulged in all too little: Vansittart, intelligence and appeasement', *Diplomacy and Statecraft*, 6:1 (1995), pp.122–175; Robert Vansittart, *The Mist Procession* (London: Hutchinson, 1958), p.543; Kevin Quinlan and Calder Walton, 'Missed Opportunities? Intelligence and the British Road to War' in *The Origins of the Second World War: An International Perspective*, ed. Frank McDonough (London: Continuum, 2011), pp.205–222; McDonald and Dronfield, *Dangerous Woman*, p.293; *GOB*, pp.10–11.

15 LL:RBL/ 5 – 'An Englishman Looks at the World'; 'Urbane' from 'Bruce Lockhart: famed British Agent sails', *Evening Star*, 21 March 1939; 'The effect' from LL:RBL/5 – Notes on Central European Tour, Winter 1937; 'Mysticism' from *RBL Diaries*, vol.1, 18 February 1937, p.366. 17 March 1938, p.386; *GOB*, pp.226–227, 250–253.

16 'Little demagogic' and 'greatest master' from *GOB*, pp.346–347; See also pp.169–170; LL:RBL/5 – Notes on Central European Tour, Winter 1937.

17 LL:RBL/5 – 'Communists and a Free Press' (undated, probably 1950s); *GOB*, p.170; *RBL Diaries* vol.1 – 6 December 1938, p.412.

18 'It is' from LL:RBL/1 – Leeper to Lockhart, 23 October 1935; 'An informed' from 'Bruce Lockhart's travels in darkest Europe', *New York Times*, 13 November 1938; 'Your people' from *RBL Diaries*, vol.1 – 4 October 1938, p.399. *GOB* sales figure from 17 October 1938, pp.402–403; 'Are these' from 'A still bigger jigsaw', *Evening Standard*, 16 September 1938.

19 All quotes from HI:RBL/7 – Some reflections on the state of American opinion, 15 April 1939; Michael L. Roi, *Alternatives to Appeasement: Sir Robert Vansittart and Alliance Diplomacy, 1934–1937* (Westport: Praeger, 1997), pp.153–154; Robert Bruce Lockhart, *Giants Cast Long Shadows* (London: Putnam, 1960), hereafter, *GCLS*, pp.15–19; Cruickshank, *Fourth Arm*, p.11.

20 *RBL Diaries*, vol.1 – 3 November 1938, p.407, 27 September 1938, p.397; TNA:FO 800/868 – Leeper to Lockhart, 31 Oct 1938; The British Council was absorbed into MOI shortly after the invasion of Czechoslovakia in 1939 – TNA:BW 82/7 – Leeper to Lloyd, 20 March 1939; Michael Balfour, *Propaganda in War, 1939–1945: Organisations, Policies and Publics in Britain and Germany* (London: Faber and Faber, 1979), p.53; Ian McLaine, *Ministry of Morale: Home Front Morale and the Ministry of Information in World War II* (London: Allen and Unwin, 1979), pp.12–13.

21 All quotes from *CTR*, pp.47–48; LL:RBL/5 – Two Declarations, 1940.

Ch13: Fighting 'Phoney'

1 *CTR*, pp.53–55; HI:RBL/10 – MOI to Lockhart, 5 September 1939 and Leeper to Lockhart 4 September 1939; LL:RBL, Box 1 – Vansittart to Lockhart 18 December 1936; For PID setup see TNA:FO 371/24054 – Leeper to Stevenson, 11 October 1939.

2   'Freaks' from *Diaries of Sir Robert Bruce Lockhart, 1939–1965*, ed. Kenneth Young (London: Macmillan, 1980), vol.2 – 29 December 1940, p.87; TNA:FO 371/23759 – Leeper to Nichols, p.10, November 1939.

3   'Genteel' from Ellic Howe, *The Black Game: British Subversive Operations Against the Germans During the Second World War* (London: Queen Ann Press, 1982), p.42; 'Leeper's sleepers' and 'Atmosphere' from Dalton, *Fateful Years: Memoirs, 1931–1945* (London: Frederick Mueller, 1957), p.378; 'Den of' from *RBL Diaries*, vol.2 – 19 and 25 March 1942, pp.152–154.

4   'Facile' from TNA:FO 371/24054 – Donnelly to Kirkpatrick, 11 November 1939. See file generally for criticism of PID; Campbell Stuart, *The Secrets of Crewe House: The Story of a Famous Campaign* (London: Hodder and Stoughton, 1921); Philip M. Taylor, 'The Foreign Office and British propaganda during the First World War', *Historical Journal*, 23:4 (1980), pp.875–898; Howe, *Black Game*, p.41.

5   Other quotes from TNA:FO 1093/131 – Publicity in Enemy Territories, 26 October 1939; TNA:FO 898/462 – Extracts for reports on leaflets, 29 November 1939; Cruickshank, *Fourth Arm*, p.44; Seth, *Truth Benders*, p.38–39; *CTR*, p.55.

6   'I insist' from *RBL Diaries*, vol.2 – 1 July 1940, p.64. See also 25 May 1940, p.58 and 13 June 1940, p.62. For Lockhart's musings on the 'Agent' title see 5 August 1940; HI:RBL/12 – Strang to Leeper, 24 October 1939; Michael Dockrill, 'The Foreign Office, Dr Edouard Beneš and the Czechoslovak government-in-exile, 1939– 1941', *Diplomacy and Statecraft*, 6:3 (1995), pp.701–718; TNA:FO 371/242287 – Minutes, 11 and 22 March 1940; *CTR*, p.95.

7   'Some private' from *RBL Diaries*, vol.2 – 7 Nov 1939, p.44; 'The atmosphere' from 17–18 March 1940, pp.48–49; *Nicolson Diaries*, 29 September 1938, pp.371–372; *The Diaries of Sir Alexander Cadogan*, ed. David Dilks (New York: Putnam's, 1972) – 27–30 August, pp.202–204, 9–21 October, pp.223–225, 28 December 1939, p.241 and *Documents of German Foreign Policy* (Washington: Government Printing Office, 1954), Series D, Vol.8 – Memo on conversation between Dahlerus, Göring and Hitler, 26 September 1939, pp.140–141; Lynne Olson, *Troublesome Young Men: The Churchill Conspiracy of 1940* (London: Bloomsbury, 2007), pp.233–239.

8   'Much grimmer' from *Express*, 10 January 1940 and 'New Threat of Invasion' 31 January 1940; 'The whole' from 'What is the Damage?', *Daily Express*, 5 May 1940; '*RBL Diaries*, vol.2 – 1 May 1940. 'Cut down' from 10 and 15 May 1940; Chilsom and Davie, *Beaverbrook*, pp.350–355, 370–373.

9   'Through Franco' from *RBL Diaries*, vol.2 – 29 May and 28 June 1940. 14 October 1940; Olson, *Troublesome Young Men*, pp.227–238; *Die Sonderfahndungsliste*, GB (1940) – www.iwm.org.uk/collections.

10 'Military' from TNA:FO 371/24288 – Summary of conversation with Czech Maffia, 30 March 1940.

11 'Prospects' from *RBL Diaries* – vol.2, 6 June 1940, p.62; TNA:FO 371/24288 – Lockhart memorandum, 30 March 1940; Vojtěch Mastný, *The Czechs Under Nazi Rule: The Failure of National Resistance, 1939-1942* (New York: Columbia University Press, 1971).

12 'My Czechs' from *RBL Diaries*, vol.2 – 25 May 1940, p.58; See TNA:FO 898/8 generally for Lockhart's critique of Britain's Czech policy; TNA:FO 371/2488 – FO Minutes,
4 and 7 June 1940 and Memorandum on Hodža's finances, 9 June 1940.

13 'Bore the' from Bickham Sweet-Escott, *Baker Street Irregular* (London: Methuen,
1965), p.98; John Baker White, *The Big Lie* (London: Thomas Cromwell, 1973),
pp.18–19; Cruickshank, *Fourth Arm*, pp.108–109; TNA:FO 898/69 – Examples
of Sibs, August–September 1941; TNA:FO 898/9 – Weekend decisions, 19/20 July
1941.

14 LL:RBL/1 – Wells to Lockhart, 27 June 1940 and Lockhart to Beaverbrook, 18 October
1940. Box 5 'Croatian Broadcast', 3 March 1940; *RBL Diaries*, vol.2 – 13 January 1940;
TNA:KV 2/980 'Other work' from Baroness Budberg memo, 28 June 1940; McDonald
and Dronfield, *Dangerous Woman*, pp.293–295; Berberova, *Moura*, pp.279–282.

15 All quotes from LL:RBL/1 – Lockhart to Beaverbrook, 2 June 1940; M. R. D; David
Garnett, *The Secret History of PWE, the Political Warfare Executive, 1939–1945* (London:
St. Ermin's, 2002), pp.34–36.

16 'Offensive' from *Cadogan Diaries* – 5 June 1940, p.294. See also 25 July 1940, p.315
and 384; 'Dalton show' from *RBL Diaries*, vol.2 – 1 August 1940. 'Windbag' from
25 August 1940. 'Little Czech' from 13 September 1940; M. R. D. Foot, *SOE: The
Special Operations Executive, 1940–1946* (London: Pimlico, 1999), pp.27–30, 35–41.

17 'Political' from TNA:FO 800/868 – Lockhart to Dalton, 19 December 1940, Dalton
to Lockhart, 22 December 1940; 'Most well' from Dalton, *Fateful Years*, p.379;
TNA:FO 371/26394 – FO Minutes, 24 April 1941 and Lockhart to Strang, 20 April
1941; *RBL Diaries*, vol.2 – August–November 1940.

18 'Nothing' from *RBL Diaries*, vol.2 – 5 February 1941; See also 28 April, 30 May and
23 June 1941; Nigel West, *The Secret History of British Intelligence in the Americas,
1940–45* (New York: Fromm International, 1999), ch.2.

19 All quotes from TNA:FO 898/9 – Lockhart's report, 14 July 1941; See also
TNA:FO 898/10 – Eden to Lockhart, 22 August 1941; The story of Lockhart's journey
from Chair of the Executive Committee to Director-General of PWE is complicated
and tedious. Details can be found in Balfour, *Propaganda in War*, pp.90–92; Garnett,
PWE, pp.76–79, 123–24. The term 'political warfare' was generally used in Britain,
while 'psychological warfare' was adopted in the USA. The latter has since become
more entrenched in the lexicon as a means of describing strategic propaganda and
subversion directed against an enemy.

20 'Week' from *RBL Diaries*, vol.2 – 5 and 26 October 1941. For Whitehall's drink-
ing culture see 4 December 1941, p.130; *CTR*, p.75; The two books were *End of an
Epoch* and *Ordeal by Oratory*, the latter intended to be co-written with Alexander
Kerensky. Much of the material from *Epoch* was later amalgamated into *Comes the
Reckoning*. The draft, unfinished forms of these books can be found in LL:RBL/3 and
4; HI:RBL/10 – Butler to Lockhart, 22 January 1940.

21 'Produced' and 'metaphorically' from *CTR*, p.117; On Lockhart's negotiations to take
over PWE see generally TNA:FO 898/10.

Ch14 – Cancel the Revolution

1   All quotes from TNA:FO 898/3 – Voigt memo, 2 May 1941.

2   'Better to' from HI:RBL/12, Moura Budberg Essay; *CTR*, pp.162–163.

3   'Inner pigdog' from Delmer, *Black Boomerang*, p.41; 'Think like' from Baker White, *The Big Lie*, p.62; TNA:FO 898/67 – Secret Paper, 8 March 1942; 898/69 – Examples of Sibs, August–September 1941; TNA:FO 898/3 – Suggestions for the 'Long War' theme, September 1940.

4   *RBL Diaries*, vol.2 – 8 December 1942, p.211; Lockhart first met Delmer in 1933 and was impressed by his knowledge of the Nazi mindset – *RBL Diaries*, vol.1 – 28 April 1933, p.253; Delmer, *Black Boomerang*, pp.42–51.

5   'Fantastically' from *RBL Diaries*, vol.2 – 25 March 1942, p.153; The *Widerstand* (conservative German resistance) spoke grandly but falsely. It wasn't until the war was all but lost that they moved against the regime via Claus von Stauffenberg's botched attempted to assassinate Hitler in 1944 – Klemens von Klemperer, *German Resistance Against Hitler: The Search for Allies Abroad, 1938–1945* (Oxford: Clarendon Press, 1992); For the 'Good Germans/Bad Germans' debate see McClaine, *Ministry of Morale*, pp.137–170; Cruickshank, *Fourth Arm*, pp.74–77.

6   'Handmaid' from TNA:FO 800/868 – Lockhart to Bracken, 3 May 1944; 'We should' from Lockhart's report to Chiefs of Staff, reproduced in *RBL Diaries*, vol.2 – 29 May 1942, pp.169–171; 'Undermine' from LL:RBL/5 – Address to Royal Institute of International Affairs, 25 July 1946. 'The Chances of Revolt in the Oppressed Countries', undated 1941.

7   'A notorious' from Willie Gallacher MP, *Hansard*, vol.372, 3 July 1941, column 1537, vol.378, 18 March 1942; Other quotes from HI:RBL/6 – New British Broadcast Station: Bruce Lockhart's Secret Mission to Russia, 19 May 1942 and *RBL Diaries*, vol.2 – 10–20 May 1942, pp.163–165; 'Bruce Lockhart', *Hakenkreuzbanner*, 15 September 1941; 'Famous bedfellows', *Kölnische Zeitung*, 12 July 1941.

8   LL:RBL/1 – Report on meeting with Maisky, 25 September 1941; Invitation to celebration, 10 February 1942, Maisky to Lockhart, 16 December 1942.

9   'Frightful' from *Dalton Diaries*, 16 September 1941, p.283; 'Was bounded', from *CTR*, p.164, p.97; Kirk Robert Graham, 'Germany on the couch: psychology and the development of British subversive propaganda to Nazi Germany', *Journal of Contemporary History*, 54:3 (2018), pp.487–507.

10 'Not by' from TNA:FO 898/3 – F. A. Voigt memo, 2 May 1941; Religion and propaganda memo, 30 July 1940; 'One of' and 'always' from *RBL Diaries*, vol.2, 29 December 1940 and 6 Feb. 1942; 'With hurt' from *GCLS*, p.92; Franklin Reid Gannon, *The British Press and Germany, 1933–1939* (London: Clarendon, 1971), pp.81–84.

11 'Glorious' from Howe, *Black Game*, p.84; 'Often' from Baker White, *The Big Lie*, p.63; LL:RBL/1 – Lockhart to McClure, 3 April 1947; TNA:FO 898/189 – The Fundamental Plan, 26 March 1941; *GCLS*, pp.94–96; *RBL Diaries*, vol.2 – 6 August

1942, pp.184–185; Allan Merson, *Communist Resistance in Nazi Germany* (London: Lawrence & Wishart, 1986).

12   TNA:FO 898/12 – The Peasants' Revolt, 4 February 1942; TNA:FO 898/11 – Operational Propaganda outline, 22 April 1942.

13   All quotes from 'V' programme schedules for 19 December 1941 and 2 January 1942 – TNA:FO 898/342-343; Balfour, *Propaganda in War*, pp.214–216.

14   'Potential' from TNA:FO 898/342 – Lockhart to Ritchie, 8 May 1942; 'Britons' from TNA:FO 898/11 – Incitement to violence in occupied territories, 19 January 1942; Cruickshank, *Fourth Arm*, pp.51–52, 183–184.

15   Balfour, *Propaganda in War*, p.215; TNA:FO 898/11 – Incitement to violence in occupied territories, 19 January 1942.

16   See generally TNA:HS 3/69; Robert Gerwarth, *Hitler's Hangman: The Life of Heydrich* (New Haven: Yale University Press, 2011), chs 1 and 9.

17   TNA:FO 898/13 – PWE Directive, 24 September 1942; *RBL Diaries*, vol.2 – 16 October 1942, p.197.

Ch15 – Wordy Warfare

1   Delmer, *Black Boomerang*, p.79–80; *RBL Diaries*, vol.2 – 19 October 1942, p.198; For an overview of the RUs and their methods see Garnet, *PWE*, pp.193–211.

2   'Religious' from *RBL Diaries*, vol.2 – 23 June 1942, p.178; TNA:FO 898/60 – Lockhart to Eden, 20 June 1942; Cruickshank, *Fourth Arm*, pp.81–82.

3   'An alacrity' from Delmer, *Black Boomerang*, p.79; 'More radio' from TNA:FO 898/61 – Lockhart to Kirkpatrick, 29 October 1941 and Delmer to Kirkpatrick, 20 September 1941.

4   Howe, *Black Game*, pp.156–164, Lockhart and Churchill quotes from p.163; Cruickshank, *Fourth Arm*, p.139; There was a ministerial-level spat over whether the BBC or PWE would control the transmitter, see *RBL Diaries*, vol.2 – 3 February 1942, pp.137–138.

5   'With our' from TNA:FO 898/131 – Report of Colonel K. Johnstone, 15 November 1942; 'A brawl' from TNA:FO 898/13 – North Africa: For All Members of the United States Expeditionary Force and Lockhart to Eden 4 December 1942; 'A better' from *RBL Diaries*, vol.2 – 10 November 1942, p.205; TNA:FO 898/133 – Johnston Memo, 9 January 1943; Garnett, *PWE*, p.255.

6   Howe, *Black Game*, pp.174–175, 'The best' from p.175; 'For the' from Delmer, *Black Boomerang*, p.81. For details of *Atlantiksender* see pp.81–89; Seth, *Truth Benders*, pp.72–74.

7   'Dubbing' from *RBL Diaries*, vol.2 – 2 February 1943, p.225; LL:RBL/5 – Europe's Greatest Prime Minister, 1955.

8   *CTR*, pp.226–227; 'Slipping' from LL:RBL/1– Leeper to Lockhart, 10 December 1942.

9   'Felt very' from *RBL Diaries*, vol.2 – 21 October 1942, p.199. 'Drink record' from 27 November 1942, p.209; See generally entries for May–June 1943, pp.237–243;

'Month of' from PA:BBK/C/222 – Lockhart to Beaverbrook, 7 May 1943; LL:RBL/1
– Lockhart to Beaverbrook, 25 September 1943.

10   TNA:FO 898/349 – Husky outline, 27 June 1943 and Annex II of Air Ministry to
     Mediterranean Air Command, 3 July 1943; Owen Chadwick, *Britain and the Vatican
     during the Second World War* (Cambridge: Cambridge University Press, 1988),
     pp.274–276.

11   *CTR*, pp.287–288; LL:RBL/1 – Bracken to Lockhart, 11 November 1943;
     PA:BBK/C/222 – Beaverbrook to Lockhart, 6 July 1943 and Lockhart to Beaverbrook,
     14 December 1943; HI:RBL/1 – Lockhart to Moura, 28 November 1943.

12   Quotes from HI:RBL/1 – Lockhart to Moura, 23 February 1944; *RBL Diaries*, vol.2
     – 22 March 1944, pp.290–291.

13   'Ingeniously' from TNA:FO 898/24 – Wheeler-Bennett to Brooks, 9 June 1944 and
     Plan 'Cuckoo' outline, 7 June 1944; Denis Rigden, *Kill the Fuhrer: Section X and
     Operation Foxley* (Stroud: Sutton, 1999).

14   'Administrative' from TNA:FO 898/397 – Chiefs of Staff meeting, 17 August 1944;
     'Aspidistra' from Bracken to Ismay, 18 August 1944; 'Admitted' from *RBL Diaries*,
     vol.2 – 16 August 1944; Cruickshank, *Fourth Arm*, pp.128–133.

15   TNA:FO 898/374 – SHAEF Directive, 1 May 1944; TNA:FO 898/25 – Brooks to
     Delmer, 4 July 1944; TNA:FO 898/348 – PWE/OWI Special Directive, 14 June 1944;
     Garnett, *PWE*, pp.410–411; Cruickshank, *Fourth Arm*, p.155.

16   *RBL Diaries*, vol.2 – 6 June 1944, pp.319–320.

17   'Wild propagandists' from LL:RBL/1 – Lockhart to Beaverbrook, 7 March 1945.
     Other quotes from Lockhart to Eden, 14 November 1944. See generally *RBL Diaries*,
     vol.1 – 12–17 August 1944, pp.338–341.

18   LL:RBL, Box 1 – Lockhart to Velacott, 22 August 1944. Lockhart to Peterson, 7 March
     and 22 May 1945; TNA:FO 898/102 – Lockhart to McClure, 8 December 1944;
     TNA:PREM 3/193/3 – Chiefs of Staff to Eisenhower, 23 February 1945.

19   'PWE had' from *RBL Diaries*, vol.2 – 6 June 1945, p.444. 'To act' from 31 August 1945,
     p.501. See also 16 August and 1 September 1945, p.492 and pp.501–502; LL:RBL/1 –
     Lockhart to Beaverbrook, 28 August 1945; Garnett, *PWE*, p.431.

Ch16 – Be All Sins Misremembered

1   'Molotov's wife' from LL:RBL/5 – World Affairs script, 2 February 1962. 'One of'
     from World Affairs script, 12 March 1948; Lockhart to Whitmore, 20 March 1948;
     RBL Diaries, vol.2 – 17 February 1945, pp.400–402.

2   All quotes from LL:RBL/5 – World Affairs script, 12 March 1948; The latest research
     confirms Masaryk's death was by suicide – Jan Špička and Martin Čermák, 'Forensic
     analysis and the new investigation into the death of the Czechoslovak Minister of
     Foreign Affairs in 1948', *Journal of Forensic Identification*, 72:3 (2022), pp.245–286.

3   'The nearest' from LL:RBL/1 – Lockhart to Peterson, 2 February 1946; 'Limitations' from
     RBL Diaries, vol.2 – 2 September 1952, p.742. 24–27 June 1945, pp.454–458; 'Marriages',

The Times, 11 November 1948; Lockhart told Robin his marriage to Mollie was about companionship rather than romance – HI:RBL/12 – Robin to Kathy Bedford, 6 February 1996.

4   'Political warfare secrets', *Sunday Times*, 16 November 1947; LL:RBL/1 – Stuart to Lockhart, 4 May 1945 and Lockhart to Stuart, 8 May 1945; Lockhart to Beaverbrook, 11 January 1948. Lockhart to Wheeler-Bennett, 22 January 1946; The official PWE history was written by David Garnett but buried in the cabinet office archives until 1952 – Garnett, PWE, pp.xiv.

5   'Kremlin's neurotic' from Telegram to Secretary of State, 22 February 1946 – *Wilson Centre Digital Archive*, www.digitalarchive.wilsoncentre.org/document/george-keegans-long-telegram; Thomas G. Paterson, *Soviet-American Confrontation: Postwar Reconstruction and the Origins of the Cold* War (Baltimore: Johns Hopkins, 1975).

6   'Russia is' from LL:RBL/1 – Lockhart to Eden, 18 February 1946; 'Russian psychology' from TNA:FO 800/877 – Sargent minute, 14 March 1942; Lockhart memorandum, 23 February 1942. Cadogan Minute, 14 March 1942; *RBL Diaries*, vol.2 – 10 April 1946, p.542 and 18 September 1946, pp.567–568; TNA:FO 800/878 – Lockhart memorandum, 12 October 1942; TNA:FO 800/874 – Intelligence reports from Fierlinger and Pika, 1942–1943.

7   'To retire' from *RBL Diaries*, vol.2 – 31 July 1945, p.476; 'British diplomatic' from Michael Sayers and Albert E. Kahn, *The Great Conspiracy Against Russia* (New York: Boni and Gaer, 1946), p.7; LL:RBL/1 – 'That myth' from Lockhart to Peterson, 25 June 1946; 'Lost his' from Peterson to Lockhart, 19 July 1946. Peterson to Lockhart, 15 July 1947.

8   'The new' from LL:RBL/5 – The Kremlin and the Satellites, 1956. Stalin and the Bolshevik Revolution, 1951. World Affairs script 15 October 1954. Lockhart to Seton-Watson, 13 September 1948; Růžička to Lockhart, 1 April 1949. Rodnick to Czech Section, 4 December 1948; HI:RBL/12 – Robin to Lyn Smith, 12 February 1997.

9   LL:RBL, Box 1 – 'Russian broadcasts' from Lockhart to Eden, 1 April 1951. 'Vacillations' from Lockhart to Vansittart, 22 December 1955. 'I am' from Lockhart to L. Ploskal, 25 March 1961; TNA:FO 1110/743 – Lockhart's reports on visit to Radio Free Europe, Munich, 24 June 1955.

10 LL:RBL, Box 1 – Lockhart to G. H. Middleton, 20 August 1950. Foreign Office to Lockhart, 17 September 1952 and Lockhart to Eden, 5 November 1952; *RBL Diaries*, vol.2 – 16 November 1951, p.739; 10 March 1954, p.743.

11 'Drink' from TNA:KV 2/981 – Budberg report, 23 November 1951. 'Every person' from Budberg report, 25 October 1951; For terms of affection see LL:RBL/5 – Moura to Lockhart, undated letters 1948 and 1959; LL:RBL/1 – Ransome to Lockhart, 17 March 1961. Vansittart 19 January 1957. Nicolson to Lockhart, 14 December 1960.

12 'Was starving' from PA:BBK/C/222 – Beaverbrook memo, 29 September 1952; 'Old man' from PA:BBK/C/223 – Beaverbrook memo, 27 December 1955; Millar to Lockhart, 28 December 1955; 'More or' from LL:RBL/1 – Lockhart to Terkelsen, 8 April 1963; *RBL Diaries*, vol.2 – 8 July 1951, pp.737–738.

13 'I have' from *RBL Diaries*, vol.2 – 31 December 1949, p.712; 'Who in' from TNA:FO 1110/1851 – Broadcast script, 28 March 1964; PA:BBK/C/223 – Lockhart to Beaverbrook, 10 September 1950 and 29 December 1955.

14 'I am' from HI:RBL/2 – Lockhart to Robin Lockhart, 16 January and 21 March 1964; LL:RBL, Box 1 – Lockhart to Robin, 26 October 1956; 'Russian agent planted on Sir R. Bruce Lockhart', *The Times*, 14 March 1966; Robin Bruce Lockhart, 'Engineering a plot', *Sunday Times*, 20 March 1966; 'The least' from 'Our man in Moscow', *The Economist*, 1 March 1967.

15 'That the' and 'while my' from HI:RBL/11 – Robin to Wright, 9 February 1967; LL:RBL/1 – Lockhart to David Harcus, 27 June 1960; from Lockhart to Ullman, 28 January 1961.

16 Quotes from LL:RBL/5 – Fettes Founder's Day Speech, 27 June 1953; HI:RBL/1 – Einzig to Lockhart, 30 March 1971; TNA:PREM 5/513 – Robin to John Hewitt, 12 January 1969 and Hewitt to Lockhart, 5 March 1965.

17 'Today's engagements', *The Times*, 5 March 1970; 'Deaths', *The Times*, 28 February 1970; HI:RBL/12 – Robin to Kathy Bedford, 6 February 1996.

BIBLIOGRAPHY

ARCHIVES

Archives of the Bank of England, London
  Anglo-International Bank Records
Bodleian Library Archives, Oxford
  Papers of Lord Milner
Churchill College Archives, Cambridge
  Papers of Major General Edward Spears
Hoover Institution Archives, Stanford University, Palo Alto
  Robert Bruce Lockhart Collection
Liddell Hart Archives, King's College, London
  Papers of Major General Frederick Poole
Lilly Library Special Collections, Indiana University, Bloomington
  Robert Bruce Lockhart Collection
National Archives of the United Kingdom, London
  Robert Bruce Lockhart Series
  War Office, Foreign Office, Secret Service, Cabinet and Treasury Files
Parliamentary Archives, London
  Diaries of Robert Bruce Lockhart
  Papers of Lord Beaverbrook

NEWSPAPERS

Daily Express, Daily Mail, Daily Mirror, The Economist, Evening Standard, Evening Star, Financial Times, Hakenkreuzbanner, Illustrated London News, Kölnische Zeitgung, New Statesman, New York Times, New York Times Book Review, Nottingham Evening Post, Telegraph, The Times, Times Literary Supplement, Singapore Free Press and Mercantile Advertiser, Sunday Times

WEBSITES

Historic Hansard
  www.hansard.parliament.uk

Imperial War Museum Digital Archive
  www.iwm.org.uk/collections
Oxford Dictionary of National Bibliography
  www.oxforddnb.com
Papers Relating to the Foreign Relations of the United States
  www.history.state.gov
Project Avalon Digital Archive
  www.avalon.law.yale.edu
Wilson Centre Digital Archive
  www.digitalarchive.wilsoncentre.org

MEMOIRS, DIARIES AND PUBLISHED PRIMARY SOURCES

Baring, Evelyn, *Modern Egypt*, vol.1 (London: Macmillan, 1916)
Bing, Edward, J., ed., *The Secret Letters of the Last Tsar: Being the Bolshevik Propaganda: Hearings before a Subcommittee of a Committee of the United States Senate, 65th Congress, 11 February 1919–10 March 1919* (Washington: Government Printing, 1919)
Browder, Robert Paul and Kerensky, Alexander F., eds, *The Russian Provisional Government, Documents*, vol.3 (Stanford: Stanford University Press, 1916)
Buchanan, George, *My Mission to Russia and Other Diplomatic Memoirs*, vol.2 (London: Cassell and Company, 1923)
Buchanan, Meriel, *Petrograd: The City of Trouble, 1914–1918* (London: Collins, 1919)
—— *Ambassador's Daughter* (London: Cassell, 1958)
Confidential Correspondence between Nicholas II and his mother, Dowager Empress Maria Feodorovna (New York: Longmans, Green and Co., 1938)
Dalton, Hugh, *The Fateful Years: Memoirs, 1931–1945* (London: Frederick Mueller, 1957)
Delmer, Sefton, *Black Boomerang* (London: Secker and Warburg, 1962)
Dilks, David, ed., *The Diaries of Sir Alexander Cadogan* (New York: Putnam's, 1972)
Documents on German Foreign Policy (Washington: Government Printing Office, 1954), Series D, Vol.8
Francis, David, *Russia from the American Embassy, April 1916–November 1918* (London: Scribner and Sons, 1921)
Garstin, Denis, *The Shilling Soldiers* (London: Hodder and Stoughton, 1918)
Hard, William, *Raymond Robins' Own Story* (New York: Harper, 1920)
Henderson, Nevile, *Water Under the Bridges* (London: Hodder and Stoughton, 1945)

Hill, George Alexander, *Dreaded Hour* (London: Cassell, 1936)

—— *Go Spy the Land: Being the Adventures of IK8 of the British Secret Service* (London: Biteback, 2014 edition)

Hoare, Samuel, *The Fourth Seal: The End of a Russian Chapter* (London: William Heinemann, 1930)

Knox, Alfred, *With the Russian Army, 1914–1917*, vol.2 (London: Hutchinson, 1921)

Lockhart, Robert Bruce, *Retreat from Glory* (Garden City: New York, 1934)

—— *Return to Malaya* (London: Putnam, 1936)

—— *Guns or Butter* (London: Putnam, 1938)

—— *Comes the Reckoning* (London: Putnam, 1947)

—— *My Europe* (London: Putnam, 1952)

—— *Your England* (London: Putnam, 1955)

—— *Giants Cast Long Shadows* (London: Putnam, 1960)

—— *Friends, Foes and Foreigners* (London: Putnam, 1962)

—— *The Two Revolutions: An Eye-witness Study of Russia 1917* (London: Bodley Head, 1967)

—— *My Scottish Youth* (Edinburgh, B & W, 1993 edition)

—— *Memoirs of a British Agent* (Barnsley: Frontline, 2011 edition)

Malkov, Pavel, *Reminiscences of a Kremlin Commandant* (Moscow: Progress, 1977)

Marchand, René, *Allied Agents in Soviet Russia* (London: People's Russian Information Bureau, 1918)

Nicolson, Harold, *Diaries and Letters, 1930–1939*, ed. Nigel Nicolson (London: Collins, 1966)

Orlov, Alexander, *The March of Time: Reminiscences* (London: St. Ermin's 2004)

Philips Price, Morgan, *Dispatches from the Revolution: Russia, 1916–1918*, ed. Tania Rose (London: Pluto, 1997)

Pimlott, Ben, ed., *The Second World War Diary of Hugh Dalton, 1940–1945* (London: Jonathan Cape, 1986)

Poole, DeWitt, *An American Diplomat in Bolshevik Russia* (Madison: University of Wisconsin Press, 2014 edition)

Ransome, Arthur, *The Autobiography of Arthur Ransome*, ed. Rupert Hart-Davis (London: Jonathan Cape, 1976)

Reilly, Sidney, *Adventures of a British Master Spy: The Memoirs of Sidney Reilly* (London: Biteback, 2014 edition)

Robien, Louis de, *The Diary of a Diplomat in Russia 1917–1918*, trans. Camilla Sykes (London: Michael Joseph, 1969)

Stuart, Campbell, *The Secrets of Crewe House: The Story of a Famous Campaign* (London: Hodder and Stoughton, 1921)

Sweet-Escott, Bickham, *Baker Street Irregular* (London: Methuen, 1965)

Symonds, John and Grant, Kenneth. eds, *The Confessions of Aleister Crowley: An Autohagiography* (London: Penguin, 1989)

Thwaites, Norman, *Velvet and Vinegar* (London: Grayson & Grayson, 1932)

Vansittart, Robert, *The Mist Procession* (London: Hutchinson, 1958)

Young, Kenneth, ed. *Diaries of Sir Robert Bruce Lockhart, 1915–1938*, vol.1 (New York: St. Martin's Press, 1973)

—— *Diaries of Sir Robert Bruce Lockhart, 1939–1965*, vol.2 (London: Macmillan, 1980).

BOOKS AND JOURNAL ARTICLES

Andrew, Christopher, *Secret Service: The Making of the British Intelligence Community* (London: Heinemann, 1985)

Andrew, Christopher and Gordievsky, Oleg, *KGB: The Inside Story* (New York: Harper Collins, 1990)

Andrew, Christopher and Mitrokhin, Vasili, *The Mitrokhin Archive: The KGB in Europe and the West* (London: Allen Lane, 1999)

Avrich, Paul, *The Russian Anarchists* (New Jersey: Princeton University Press, 1967)

Bainton, Roy, *Honoured by Strangers: The Life of Captain Francis Cromie CB DSO RN, 1882–1918* (Shrewsbury: Airlife, 2002)

Baker White, John, *The Big Lie* (London: Thomas Cromwell, 1973)

Balfour, Michael, *Propaganda in War, 1939–1945: Organisations, Policies and Publics in Britain and Germany* (London: Faber and Faber, 1979)

Berberova, Nina, *Moura: The Dangerous Life of the Baroness Budberg*, trans. Marian Schwartz and Richard D. Sylvester (New York: New York Review of Books, 2005)

Boyd, John, 'The origins of Order No. 1', *Soviet Studies*, 19:3 (1968), pp.359-72

Brook-Shepherd, Gordon, *Iron Maze: The Western Secret Services and the Bolsheviks* (London: Pan, 1999)

Bruce Lockhart, Robert, 'The Unanimous Revolution – Russia, February 1917', *Foreign Affairs*, 35:2 (1957), pp.320-333

Bruce Lockhart, Robin, *Reilly: Ace of Spies* (London: Penguin, 1964)

Calton, Jerry M., 'Beaverbrook's split imperial personality: Canada, Britain, and the Empire Free Trade movement of 1929–1931, *The Historian*, 37:1 (1974), pp.26–45

Carr, Barnes, *The Lenin Plot: The Unknown Story of America's War Against Russia* (Stroud: Amberley, 2020)

Chadwick, Owen, *Britain and the Vatican during the Second World War* (Cambridge: Cambridge University Press, 1988)

Chamberlain, William Henry, 'The First Russian Revolution', *Russian Review*, 26:1 (1967), pp.4-12

Chambers, Roland, *The Last Englishman: The Double Life of Arthur Ransome* (London: Faber, 2010)

Chisholm, Anne and Davie, Michael, *Lord Beaverbrook: A Life* (New York: Alfred A. Knopf, 1993)

Clark, Christopher, *Kaiser Wilhelm II: A Life in Power* (London: Penguin, 2009)

Cook, Andrew, *Ace of Spies: The True Story of Sidney Reilly* (Stroud: History Press, 2004)

Cruickshank, Charles, *The Fourth Arm: Psychological Warfare, 1938–1945* (London: Davis-Poynter, 1977)

D'Agostino, Anthony, *The Russian Revolution, 1917–1945* (Santa Barbara: Praeger, 2011)

Debo, Richard K., 'Lockhart Plot or Dzerzhinskii Plot?', *Journal of Modern History*, 43:3 (1971), pp.413–429

Dockrill, Michael, 'The Foreign Office, Dr Edouard Beneš and the Czechoslovak government-in-exile, 1939–1941', *Diplomacy and Statecraft*, 6:3 (1995), pp.701–718

Dunscomb, Paul E., *Japan's Siberian Intervention, 1918–1922* (Lanthan: Lexington Books, 2011)

Ezergailis, Andrew, *The Latvian Impact on the Bolshevik Revolution, The First Phase, September 1917 to April 1918* (Boulder: East European Monographs, 1983)

Faulkner, Neil, *A People's History of the Russian Revolution* (London: Pluto, 2017)

Ferris, John R., 'Indulged in all too little: Vansittart, intelligence and appeasement', *Diplomacy and Statecraft*, 6:1 (1995), pp.122–175

Figes, Orlando, *A People's Tragedy: The Russian Revolution*, 1891–1924 (London: Pimlico, 1997)

Fischer, Louis, *The Life of Lenin* (New York: Harper and Row, 1964)

Fitzpatrick, Sheila, *The Russian Revolution* (Oxford: Oxford University Press, 2008)

Foglesong, David S., *America's Secret War Against Bolshevism: U.S. Intervention in the Russian Civil War, 1917–1920* (Chapel Hill: University of North Carolina, 1995)

Foot, M. R. D., *SOE: The Special Operations Executive, 1940–1946* (London: Pimlico, 1999)

Gannon, Franklin Reid, *The British Press and Germany, 1933–1939* (London: Clarendon, 1971)

Garnett, David, *The Secret History of PWE, the Political Warfare Executive, 1939–1945* (London: St. Ermin's, 2002)

Gazur, Edward P., *Secret Assignment: The FBI's KGB General* (London: St Ermin's, 2001)

Gerwarth, Robert, *November 1918: The German Revolution* (Oxford: Oxford University Press, 2020)

—— *Hitler's Hangman: The Life of Heydrich* (New Haven: Yale University Press, 2011)

Graham, Kirk Robert, 'Germany on the couch: psychology and the development of British subversive propaganda to Nazi Germany', *Journal of Contemporary History*, 54:3 (2018), pp.487–507

Heimann, Mary, *Czechoslovakia: The State that Failed* (New Haven: Yale, 2009)

Henig, Ruth, 'Britain, France and the League of Nations in the 1920s' in *Anglo-French Relations in the Twentieth Century*, eds Alan Sharp and Glyn Stone (London: Routledge, 2000)

Howe, Ellic, *The Black Game: British Subversive Operations Against the Germans During the Second World War* (London: Queen Anne Press, 1982)

Hughes, Michael, *Inside the Enigma: British Officials in Russia, 1900–1939* (London: Hambledon, 1997)

—— '"Revolution was in the air": British officials in Russia during the First World War', *Journal of Contemporary History*, 31:1 (1996), pp.75–97

Jeffery, Keith, *MI6: The History of the Secret Intelligence Service, 1909–1949* (London: Bloomsbury, 2010)

Jones, Geoffrey, 'Public policy and the British multinational banks, 1914–1982', *Business and Economic History*, 21 (1992), pp.209–218

Judd, Alan, *The Quest for 'C': Mansfield Cumming and the Founding of the Secret Service* (London: Harper, 2000)

Kato, Tsuyoshi, 'When rubber came: the Negeri Sembilan experience', *Journal of Southeast Asian Studies*, 29:2 (1991), pp.109–157

Kettle, Michael, *Sidney Reilly: The True Story of the World's Greatest Spy* (New York: St Martin's, 1983)

Kinvig, Clifford, *Churchill's Crusade: The British Invasion of Russia, 1918–1920* (London: Continuum, 2006)

Klemperer, Klemens von, *German Resistance Against Hitler: The Search for Allies Abroad, 1938–1945* (Oxford: Clarendon Press, 1992)

Kushner, Tony, 'Beyond the pale? British reactions to Nazi anti-Semitism, 1933–39', *Historical Studies of Ethnicity, Migration and Diaspora*, 8:1–2 (1989), pp.143–160

Leggett, George, *The Cheka: Lenin's Political Police* (London: Clarendon, 1981)

Lih, Lars T., *Bread and Authority in Russia, 1914–1921* (Berkeley: University of California Press, 1990)

Long, John W., 'Plot and Counterplot in Revolutionary Russia: Chronicling the Bruce Lockhart Conspiracy, 1918', *Intelligence and National Security*, 10:1 (1995), pp.122–143

—— 'Searching for Sidney Reilly, The Lockhart Plot in Revolutionary Russia, 1918', *Europe-Asia Studies*, 47:7 (1995), pp.1225–1241

Lynn, Andrea, *Shadow Lovers: The Last Affairs of H. G. Wells* (Boulder: Westview Press, 2001)

McDonald, Deborah and Dronfield, Jeremy, *A Very Dangerous Woman: The Lives, Loves and Lies of Russia's most Seductive Spy* (London: Oneworld, 2016)

McLaine, Ian, *Ministry of Morale: Home Front Morale and the Ministry of Information in World War II* (London: Allen and Unwin, 1979)

Mahoney, Harry Thayer, 'The saga of Xenophon Dmitrivich Kalamatiano', *International Journal of Intelligence and Counterintelligence*, 8:2 (1995), pp.179–201

Mandel, David, *The Petrograd Workers in the Russian Revolution, February 1917– June 1918* (Leiden: Brill, 2017)

Mastný, Vojtěch, *The Czechs Under Nazi Rule: The Failure of National Resistance, 1939–1942* (New York: Columbia University Press, 1971)

Mawdsley, Evan, *The Russian Civil War* (Edinburgh: Birlinn, 2008)

Merson, Allan, *Communist Resistance in Nazi Germany* (London: Lawrence & Wishart, 1986)

Moffat, Ian, *The Allied Intervention in Russia, 1918–1920: The Diplomacy of Chaos* (Basingstoke: Palgrave, 2015)

Morris, Benny, *Sidney Reilly: Master Spy* (New Haven: Yale University Press, 2022)

Neilson, Keith, '"Joy rides?", British intelligence and propaganda in Russia, 1914–1917', *Historical Journal*, 24:4 (1981), pp.885–906

Newman, John Paul, 'Revolution and counterrevolution in Europe, 1917–1923' in *The Cambridge History of Communism*, eds Silvio Pons and Stephen A. Smith (Cambridge: Cambridge University Press, 2017)

Occleshaw, Michael, *Dances in Deep Shadows: The Clandestine War in Russia, 1917–1920* (New York: Carroll and Graf, 2006)

Olson, Lynne, *Troublesome Young Men: The Churchill Conspiracy of 1940* (London: Bloomsbury, 2007)

Otte, T. G., *The Foreign Office Mind: The Making of British Foreign Policy, 1865–1914* (Cambridge: Cambridge University Press, 2011)

Owen, Roger, *Lord Cromer: Victorian Imperialist, Edwardian Proconsul* (Oxford: Oxford University Press, 2005)

Paterson, Thomas G., *Soviet-American Confrontation: Postwar Reconstruction and the Origins of the Cold War* (Baltimore: Johns Hopkins, 1975)

Philps, Alan, *The Red Hotel: The Untold Story of Stalin's Disinformation War* (London: Headline, 2023)

Pipes, Richard, *The Russian Revolution* (New York: Vintage, 1991)

Protheroe, Gerald, 'Sir George Clerk and the struggle for British influence in central Europe, 1919–26', *Diplomacy & Statecraft*, 12:3 (2001), pp.39–64

Pugh, Martin, *We Danced All Night: A Social History of Britain Between the Wars* (London: Vintage, 2009)

Quinlan, Kevin and Walton, Calder, 'Missed Opportunities? Intelligence and the British Road to War' in *The Origins of the Second World War: An International Perspective*, ed. Frank McDonough (London: Continuum, 2011), pp.205–222

Rabinowitch, Alexander, *The Bolsheviks Come to Power: The Revolution of 1917 in Petrograd* (New York: Pluto, 2017)

Rappaport, Helen, *Ekaterinburg: The Last Days of the Romanovs* (London: Windmill, 2009)

Rigden, Denis, *Kill the Fuhrer: Section X and Operation Foxley* (Stroud: Sutton, 1999)

Roi, Michael L., *Alternatives to Appeasement: Sir Robert Vansittart and Alliance Diplomacy, 1934–1937* (Westport: Praeger, 1997)

Rumbelow, Donald, *The Houndsditch Murders and the Siege of Sidney Street* (Stroud: History Press, 2009)

Ryan, James, *Lenin's Terror: The Ideological Origins of the Early Soviet State* (London: Routledge, 2012)

Ryan, William F., 'The "Great Beast" in Russia: Aleister Crowley's theatrical tour to Moscow in 1913 and his beastly writings on Russia' in *Symbolism and After: Essays on Russian Poetry in Honour of Georgette Donchin*, ed. Arnold McMillin (London: Bristol Classical, 1992), pp.137–145

Salzman, Neil V., *Reform and Revolution: The Life and Times of Raymond Robins* (Kent, OH: Kent State Press, 1991)

Sayers, Michael and Kahn, Albert E., *The Great Conspiracy Against Russia* (New York: Boni and Gaer, 1946)

Schneer, Jonathan, *The Lockhart Plot: Love, Betrayal, Assassination and Counter-Revolution in Lenin's Russia* (Oxford: Oxford University Press, 2020)

Senn, Alfred Erich and Goldberg, Harold J., 'The Assassination of Count Mirbach', *Canadian Slavonic Papers*, 21:4, vol.21 (1979), pp.438–445

Service, Robert, *Spies and Commissars: Bolshevik Russia and the West* (London: Pan Macmillan, 2011)

Seth, Ronald, *The Truth Benders: Psychological Warfare in the Second World War* (London: Leslie Frewin, 1969)

Shennan, Margaret, *Out in the Midday Sun: The British in Malaya, 1880–1960* (London: John Murray, 2000)

Spence, Richard B., *Boris Savinkov: Renegade on the Left* (New York: Columbia University Press, 1991), pp.193–199.

—— 'The Terrorist and the Master Spy: The Political "partnership" of Boris Savinkov and Sidney Reilly, 1918–1925', *Revolutionary Russia*, 4:1 (1991), pp.111–131.

—— 'The tragic fate of Kalamatiano: America's Man in Moscow', *International Journal of Intelligence and Counterintelligence*, 12:3 (1999), pp.346–374

—— *Trust No One: The Secret World of Sidney Reilly* (Los Angeles: Feral House, 2002)

Špička, Jan and Čermák, Martin, 'Forensic analysis and the new investigation into the death of the Czechoslovak Minister of Foreign Affairs in 1948', *Journal of Forensic Identification*, 72:3 (2022), pp.245–286

Stafford, David, *Churchill and Intelligence* (London: John Murray, 1997)

Steiner, Zara, *The Foreign Office and Foreign Policy, 1898–1914* (Cambridge: Cambridge University Press, 1969)

Stevenson, David, *With Our Backs to the Wall: Victory and Defeat in 1918* (London: Penguin, 2012)

—— *1917: War, Peace and Revolution* (Oxford: Oxford University Press, 2017)

Stone, Dan, *Responses to Nazism in Britain, 1933–1939* (Basingstoke: Palgrave, 2009)

Swain, Geoffrey, '"An interesting and plausible proposal": Bruce Lockhart, Sidney Reilly and the Latvian Riflemen, Russia, 1918', *Intelligence and National Security*, 14:3 (1999), pp.81–102

Taylor, Philip M., 'The Foreign Office and British propaganda during the First World War', *Historical Journal*, 23:4 (1980), pp.875–898

Thatcher, Ian D., *Trotsky* (London: Routledge, 2002)

Thurlow, Richard, *Fascism in Britain: From Oswald Mosley's Blackshirts to the National Front* (London: I.B. Tauris, 1998)

Verhoeven, Claudia, 'The Making of Russian Revolutionary Terrorism' in *Enemies of Humanity: The Nineteenth Century War on Terrorism*, ed. Isaac Land (Basingstoke: Palgrave, 2008)

Walpole, Hugh, 'Denis Garstin and the Russian Revolution: A Brief Word in Memory', *Slavonic and East European Review*, 17:51 (1939), pp.587–605.

Warth, Robert D., *The Allies and the Russian Revolution: From the Fall of the Monarchy to the Peace of Brest-Litovsk* (Durham: Duke University Press, 1954)

Webb, Simon, *1919: Britain's Year of Revolution* (Barnsley: Pen & Sword, 2016)

Werth, Nicolas, 'Russia 1917: the soldiers' revolution', *South Central Review*, 34:3 (2017), pp.48–57

West, Nigel, *The Secret History of British Intelligence in the Americas, 1940–45* (New York: Fromm International, 1999)

Wheeler-Bennett, John W., *Brest-Litovsk: The Forgotten Peace, March 1918* (London: Macmillan, 1963)

Williams, Albert Rhys, *Journey into Revolution, Petrograd 1917–1918* (Chicago: Quadrangle, 1969)

Worley, Matthew, 'What was the New Party? Sir Oswald Mosley and the associated responses to the "crisis" of 1931–1932', *History*, 92:305 (2007), pp.39–63

INDEX